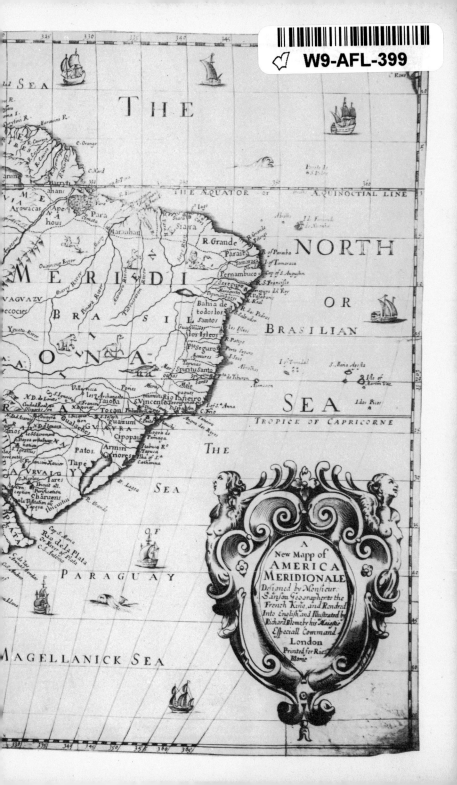

W9-AFL-399

A
New Mapp of
AMERICA
MERIDIONALE
Designed by Monsieur
Sanson Geographer to the
French King, and Rendred
Into English and Illustrated by
Richard Blome by his Majestie
Especiall Command
London
Printed for Ric.
Blome

THE ROSE AND THE LILY

THE ROSE AND THE LILY

THE LIVES AND TIMES OF
TWO SOUTH AMERICAN SAINTS

BY

Frances Parkinson Keyes

HAWTHORN BOOKS, INC.   *Publishers*   *New York*

Copyright © *1961 by Frances Parkinson Keyes.*
Copyright under International and Pan-American Copyright Conventions. All rights reserved, including the right to reproduce this book, or portions thereof, in any form, except for the inclusion of brief quotations in a review. All inquiries should be addressed to Hawthorn Books, Inc., 70 Fifth Avenue, New York 11, N. Y. This book was manufactured in the United States of America and published simultaneously in Canada by McClelland & Stewart, Ltd., 25 Hollinger Road, Toronto 16. Library of Congress Catalogue Card Number: 61-6704. Suggested Dewey Decimal Classification: 922.228.

First Edition
November, 1961

NIHIL OBSTAT
    Edward J. Montano, S.T.D.
    CENSOR LIBRORUM

IMPRIMATUR
    ✠ FRANCIS CARDINAL SPELLMAN
    ARCHBISHOP OF NEW YORK

July 26, 1961

The nihil obstat and the imprimatur are official declarations that a book or pamphlet is free of doctrinal or moral error. No implication is contained therein that those who have granted the nihil obstat and imprimatur agree with the contents, opinions or statements expressed.

TO THE OFFICERS
AND CREWS
OF ALL THE SANTA SHIPS
IN THE GRACE LINE
WHO, FROM 1930 TO THE PRESENT TIME,
HAVE DONE SO MUCH TO
MAKE MY VOYAGES
TO LATIN AMERICA
PLEASANT AND PROFITABLE.

TABLE OF CONTENTS

LIST OF ILLUSTRATIONS

APOLOGIA PRO LIBRO SUO

The first time an article of mine was accepted by a national magazine,* it created considerable excitement in my immediate circle. One friend, conspicuous for insatiable curiosity as to detail, asked me how long it had taken me to write it.

"In first draft, about five hours," I answered after brief reflection. Another member of the group shook his head.

"You're wrong," he said, "it's taken you all your life to draft that article and you're a little over thirty years old. You never could have written it if you hadn't been and done almost everything you have been and done in all that time."

I have since decided that he was probably right. If he was, it has certainly taken me another thirty years to write *The Rose and The Lily*. Since most of my readers (though practically none of my reviewers) seem to enjoy finding out how a book happened to come into being, I have begun this one by giving its background, in a section that I have called exactly that. Any reader who does not consider this really germane to the subject can skip it in its entirety and begin his reading with the Prologue to *The Rose*, confident that no part of either saint's history will be lost by so doing.

—FPK.

* This was "The Satisfied Reflections of a Semi-Bostonian" in *The Atlantic Monthly*, December, 1918.

BACKGROUND OF A BOOK

"I<small>MAGINE</small>——

"Showers of confetti sprinkling the sidewalks; strands of paper ribbon strewn from street to street; gay-colored streamers tossed from one passer-by to another; pompoms perched upon slender sticks swishing and rustling in the hands that shake them; painted plaques, simulating gigantic clowns' heads, pilloried on the palm trees; chains of infinitesimal glass globes—crimson, green, orange, azure—strung along the avenues and looped about the plazas; laden automobiles circulating incessantly about, their tops folded back, and five or six boys and girls perched precariously upon these, in addition to five or six more in the body of the car, and two or three beside the imperturbable driver; young and old, rich and poor, high and low, pouring out in a ceaseless human stream from the doorways of their homes, and merging with the multitudes upon the pavements; all in holiday mood, all wearing costumes, all wielding *chisguetes*—the small siphons filled with a mixture of ether and perfume, which sting and startle and stimulate—all, in short, celebrating carnival time in Lima.

"It began on a Saturday. The shopkeepers pulled down their shutters with an air of finality; the cafés began to fill and then to overflow; the first fluttering streamers were laughingly cast out; the first buffoons and bullfighters, the first colonial ladies and *contadinas*, the first poke-bonnets, laced bodices, tulle skirts, embroidered *mantas* [shawls], high combs, white wigs, and artificial flowers made their appearance. The Queen of the Carnival of Lima—'Her Majesty Aida I'—had already been chosen and had begun her reign, escorted by the auxiliary 'queens,' each selected by popular vote in the movie houses of the different districts—for, though even the most aristocratic forget their exclusiveness during the carnival, it is essentially a festival of the people, for the people, by the people. 'Celeste Aida,' and these exquisite ladies-in-waiting of hers—Irma, Graciela, Rosa, Olga, María, Matilda, Carmen, Edelmina, Raquel—held the center of the stage at every gala gathering

—at the races, at the fancy dress balls, in the preliminary parades which preceded the great procession of Tuesday. There was only one other person who seemed to be as omnipresent, as outstanding, as zestful, as merry, as these pretty, popular queens; and that was Señor Don Augusto Leguía, President of the Republic of Peru. Slim, suave, smiling, he shared the spotlight with them. For a few days at least the cares of the office which he had held for so long were forgotten or laid aside, and if he had any premonitions of the revolution in which, six months later, he was driven out of office, he did not betray them, though here and there we heard a whispered hint that he knew his days of power were numbered, that there was a feverish element in his superabundant vivacity. . . .

"After four days of merry-making so incessant that the average sturdy Anglo-Saxon who had participated in it, even moderately and intermittently, had begun to show signs of strain, and the average Latin, on the contrary, had become more and more blithe and buoyant, the climax came. The sidewalks of the great *Paseo* Colón were packed with an expectant populace; the official pavilion at one end of it, facing its fine length, was hardly less crowded; but the wide avenue itself had been completely cleared. In the midst of the turmoil there was an expectant hush, succeeded by roaring waves of applause; and beating across this sounded the even clatter of horses' feet. There was a flash of brilliant colors, a flutter of pennants, a glitter of metal shining in the streaming sunshine, a gleam of helmets; for one gorgeous, amazing moment it seemed as if a band of victorious Conquistadores were sweeping down again upon their 'City of the Three Kings,' the illusion of past pomp and circumstance was so complete and glowing. For this troop of cavalry, superbly caparisoned, which acted as a vanguard to the open landau, drawn by four horses, in which the President rode, was a splendid sight. The crimson of its livery appeared to be a veritable red badge of courage, the immobility of its fixed lances symbolized the steadfast strength of steel. With swiftness and stateliness, with majesty and might, it advanced, approached, passed; and behind it, its power and significance concentrated in one person, came that slim, suave, smiling man, Señor Don Augusto Leguía, President of Peru.

"Bowing in every direction, alert, erect, animated, he sprang up the steps of the pavilion. His costume was flawless and formal; he carried a silk hat in one hand; but in the other was a *chisguete* with which he sprayed his guests as he greeted them. In an instant he became enmeshed in a tangle of streamers, and sprinkled with a shower of confetti. A band was playing, vociferously, jubilantly; and as it blared forth its clamorous music, the carnival floats began their progress up the Avenue, pausing in their triumphant march, before the pavilion to receive and return the salute of the President. There was a battleship, and a pirate ship, and many other ships; and there was a whole menagerie of animals! In front of one of the floats the immense figure of a snowy-white, winged horse—a veritable Pegasus—plunged and reared; another was dominated by an elephant so solid and substantial that it caused a loyal Republican to covet it, and long to carry it home and save it for the next National Convention! But it was the King of Beasts himself that the 'Queens' had chosen to honor. Their 'throne' towered above his tawny, crouching, powerful form; rainbow-colored ribbons of paper, used in such profusion that they formed a solid, billowing blanket, fell from the seat of 'Celeste Aida,' and sweeping across the lion's mane, flickered down to the very pavement. Threading their way through these fragile, clinging strands, as nymphs might flutter through a waterfall, the 'Queens' descended from their chariot and ascended the pavilion. President Leguía gave his arm to Aida and led her to a seat beside him. She looked like a mediaeval bride, in her white satin gown with its full skirt and tight bodice, and her headdress of pearls; and certainly her attendants, in their raiment of Nile green, of peach color, of silvery blue, would all have found their appointed places in a troubadour's 'Court of Love.' The party, which was merry already, became merrier still with the arrival of these young and lovely visitors. The air was filled with that sweet, stinging spray from the *chisguetes*; and it was permeated with something stronger and subtler still; the stimulating, sparkling spirit of the Carnival of Lima." [1]

Those are some of the aspects of Lima as I first saw it thirty years ago—a gay, carefree city, which celebrated Mardi Gras with such spontaneity that its spirit of abandonment to pleasure was contagious. But its festivities were not confined, by any means, to the Carnival Season; its people were hospitable, its society sophisticated, its Diplomatic Corps distinguished. And, at that period, the raucous cocktail party and the haphazard buffet supper, both so inimical to sustained conversation on any serious subject, had not superseded the quiet, cosy tea and the elegantly appointed dinner in popularity. At the Club Nacional and the Country Club, at the leading embassies and legations and at many beautiful private homes, entertaining was characterized by urbanity and taste; literature, the fine arts and world affairs were all current topics of discussion; and kindred spirits were quickly discovered among the pleasant acquaintances made in such agreeable surroundings.

Two such acquaintances, as far as I was concerned, developed into lasting friendships. One of these was with Maggie Conroy, a very charming and most remarkable woman. Indeed, during the troubled days when feelings over the boundary line between Chile and Peru were most bitter, the Peruvian press coupled the name of Santa Rosa with that of Maggie Conroy, the Peruvian 'Joan of Arc.' Maggie Conroy, in everyday life, was a teacher of languages, with the gift of tongues, partly the legacy of a roving Irish grandfather who finally settled in Lima, married into a distinguished family, and became a Peruvian citizen; and partly a God-given talent which she developed and expanded by unremitting study and constant practice. Miss Conroy was sent by her government as a delegate to the Pan-American Conference in Baltimore—that wonderful gathering, organized and directed by the League of Women Voters, which gave the women of the United States their first general opportunity to meet face to face the Latin leaders in the various fields of feminine endeavor; and the brilliancy and buoyancy which make her so outstanding a figure in Peru immediately won her a host of friends in every one of our cities which she visited. She was next chosen to accompany the *Comisión Plebiscitania* for the Tacna-Arica Controversy, in the capacity of official interpreter, and she remained with it for an entire year on the ship anchored off the disputed territory. Her task was an extremely difficult one; she had no opportunity for diversion, for relaxation, or for exercise, and only a modicum of the elementary comforts of life; and the errand upon which the mission had been sent appeared for so long to be futile and fruitless that there was constantly an atmosphere of depression and hopelessness with which to contend. The tact and skill with which she met the situation, the spirit of cheerfulness which she not only showed herself, but spread about her; and her persistent refusal to admit that the dispute would end not in war but in peace—all these qualities and many others which she displayed, were extremely far-reaching in their influence; and that these have received the wide-spread recognition which they deserve, is a credit to her country as well as to herself.

"Immediately after my arrival in Lima, I presented the letter of introduction which commended me to Miss Conroy's attention, and asked her to accept me as a pupil. She called upon me promptly, looking extremely smart in an ensemble of blue and yellow crepe; and upon being pressed, consented to try and 'wedge in' a little time for me. . . .

And it was due, in no slight measure, to her delightful, vivacious personality that I continued to think of Lima as a carnival city." [1]

The second friendship which was to prove a lasting one was with Dr. Albert A. Giesecke, a person no less remarkable than Maggie Conroy, though in a different way. At that time he had already been in Peru about twenty years. He had come there as a young teacher, with an imposing number of university degrees and a fine record as an instructor in commercial geography and economics, to organize commercial courses in the schools of Peru, at the request of that country's Ambassador to the United States. His success had been so immediate and outstanding that President Leguía had asked him to assume the directorship of the moribund University at Cuzco, ancient capital of the Inca Empire. In this position, also, he had achieved wonders. "Giesecke found himself in a city of dark massive walls and red tile roofs. Set in a stern wilderness, its only ties with other parts of Peru were a train that ran twice a week and a lone and unreliable telegraph wire. About one third of its 33,000 inhabitants were of Spanish descent; two thirds were Indians of Inca ancestry, now Cuzco's laboring class. On either side of its unpaved streets ran open drains.

"The university was one low rambling structure built around a large patio where grass sprouted between flagstones. The entrance was unclean and unpaved. The library was a dark, disordered, ill-furnished room. A musty cell served as the chemical laboratory. Water had to be brought, pail by pail, from a fountain in the city square.

"From the first, Giesecke saw the future of this remote, uncherished place. . . . [He] envisioned the university, rising from this dust, to be the alma mater of the future leaders of Peru, men more proud than ever of their Spanish and Inca past. . . . He even started night classes, so that everyone in Cuzco would come and learn. The people of Cuzco took him to their hearts. . . . The university had been too dignified for sports. The Yankee put two tennis courts in the patio, supervised the building of a swimming pool and gymnasium, revived the ancient footraces of Inca festivals, constructed playing fields where he taught Cuzco the strange games of basketball and baseball. He was both coach and relief pitcher. Many people prophesied students would neglect their studies. It did not happen. The boys liked sports. The university pace stepped up. . . .

"Few travelers had come to Cuzco. Only a handful of its people had ever gone beyond that brazen ring of mountains. Giesecke again broke precedent by establishing scholarships so that students could take

post-graduate courses abroad. He encouraged his faculty to spend their
vacations in other countries and, through his influence, professors from
the United States lectured at Cuzco.

"Giesecke studied constantly to make himself an authority on Peru's
pre-Inca and Inca past. He rode alone in the mountains, broke trail
to the steaming jungle, with its malaria, its savage tribes, its rushing
rivers. He talked with the Indians, with the men who cut mahogany
and tapped rubber. . . .

"Early in his work a committee of civic-minded citizens of Cuzco
called at Dr. Giesecke's home to draft him into the local government.
From 1912 to 1923 he was continuously a councilman and three times
mayor, despite the fact that around election time he always saddled his
horse and went exploring, and did not come back till the voting was
over. . . . Not many people could oppose, for long, the improvements
suggested by a man who was university president all day and mayor
all night, and who never said, 'I'm too busy.' Today Cuzco is a city
with every modern facility, including an airfield, hospital, museums,
libraries. Its beauty is the pride of Peru.

"In 1923, Dr. Giesecke believed his work was done. The university
was on its feet. Devoted as he was to Peru, 14 years was long enough
to stay in a land that was not his own. . . . He took his family to Lima,
engaged passage on the next boat northbound. His trunks had gone to
the pier when he was summoned again to the presidential palace.

" 'Peru will never forget what you have accomplished,' the President
said. 'But you can do still more for my land—and yours. I want you to
take another tough job at another small salary. I'm appointing you
Director General of Education for all Peru.' . . . Giesecke spent the
next six years traveling over Peru. He more than doubled the number
of schools, modernized the buildings, equipment and teaching methods, established courses in North American history and the English
language, introduced vocational studies. Often he clambered up the
last rocky miles to some Andean village to found a school where young
minds had had no chance to learn to read or write. He put education
out of the reach of favoritism." [2]

It was as Director General of Education for all Peru that I first knew
Dr. Giesecke. It was through him that I saw in action the system he
had helped to create and that I came to have great respect for the present day educational opportunities in Peru, not only for Peruvians, but
for outsiders. It was also largely due to him that my stay in Cuzco,
where his personality is still a power, proved far more illuminating and

far more delightful than if I had gone there merely as a casual tourist.

Not that I disdained sightseeing as such. "Here—to paraphrase a famous quotation—is spread before our eyes the glory that was Cuzco, and the grandeur that was Spain. Nowhere are the Conquistadores revealed more relentlessly as destructionists before they were builders; and the civilization which they demolished was one of the most remarkable which ever flowered on the earth. . . . If instead of slaughtering the Incas, the Spaniards had helped them to develop their domain, what a nation might have sprung from a union of the two empires! But the Conquistadores destroyed, where they might have created, and later reaped as they had sown. However, before the day of reckoning came, they superimposed, literally and at the point of the sword, their own faith, their own culture, and their own sovereignty upon the faith, the culture, and the sovereignty which they had destroyed. . . . Yet the monuments which the Spanish left behind them are compellingly splendid. The Cathedral is a superb building; its central choir is exquisitely carved, its high altar is of solid silver; while the pictures and the woodwork with which it is adorned, and the jewelled monstrance which it guards have the beauty of true art as well as great antiquity. The stone facades of the Compañía Church and the adjacent University—founded in 1692—the pulpit of San Blas—a miracle of wood carving—the majestic doorways surmounted by coats-of-arms; the wonderful paintings, fabrics, silver, and furniture, treasured in private homes as well as in public buildings . . . all these surpass anything of the sort we saw in South America and bear comparison with anything we saw in Spain itself. It is startling to find them in a city which, even today, is remote and secluded, and which long was accessible only after weeks and weeks of journeying; and outlasting the era of Colonial Spain, they still serve as manifestations of the luxury of living and worship which was carried to the most distant parts of that far-flung empire." [1]

Sightseeing in Lima at first seems less rewarding. "Many of the magnificent old buildings have been mutilated or completely destroyed; and it seems strange that the Limenians, who take enormous pride—as well they may—in the glorious past of their city, should have permitted these desecrations to occur. But in spite of such artistic sacrileges, there are still many lingering evidences of the fact that 'Lima was long the first city in South America, through which the silver mines poured fabulous wealth,' as Lord Bryce reminds us in his 'Impressions and Observations.' . . . 'Its Viceroy was the greatest man on the continent,'

he continues, 'a potentate whose distant master could seldom interfere with him, for there were no telegraphs or steam vessels in those
days. Nobody but the Archbishop could oppose him; nor need he fear
anybody but the head of the Inquisition and the head of the Jesuits.
The pomp that surrounded him, the pageants with which his entrance
was celebrated were like those of a Mogul Emperor . . . Lima's Viceregal Court was long the center of the best society on the continent.
Its Archbishop was the greatest ecclesiastical potentate on the Southern Hemisphere. It had a closer connection with Spain through its
leading families, as well as through official channels, than any other
place. Loyalty to the Spanish monarch was strongest here. It was the
last great city that held out for the Catholic King, long after all the
other countries, both to the north and south, had followed the examples
of revolt set by Mexico and Argentina. . . . Few riches of antiquity are
left anywhere in Lima. Yet . . . out of the many fine old mansions of
former days, one has been preserved intact, with a beautiful gallery
running along its four sides, a spacious patio, and in front a long-
windowed, richly decorated balcony, a gem of the domestic architecture
of the seventeenth century, perhaps the most perfect that earthquakes,
fire and war have permitted to survive in South America.'

"The building to which Lord Bryce refers with such unqualified
enthusiasm is the Torre-Tagle Palace, for centuries the home of the
family by that name, and a center of the most elegant and cultured
social life of the city, and now the Ministry of Foreign Affairs. It owes
its exquisite state of preservation to Dr. Alberto Salomon, who during
his incumbency as Minister caused it to be skilfully restored to its
original state of magnificence without impairing in the slightest degree its air of antiquity. Nowhere else in the city do those shuttered,
rectangular balconies of dark carved wood, so typically and uniquely
Limenian, and so tastefully reproduced in many of the more modern
dwellings, disclose such delicate craftsmanship; nowhere else are the
sculptured ceilings, the tiled floors, the broad staircases and galleries,
the superb suites of apartments, so imposing and stately. During office
hours, the inevitable bustle and stir of business detracts a little from
Torre-Tagle's air of romance. But if it is possible to go later in the day,
when everything is quiet, the empty house seems peopled from the
past. The lovely Limenian ladies—the *tapadas* (covered ones) as they
were called—who draped their black *mantas* about their heads in such
a way as to leave only one eye exposed, and held these half-concealing,
half-revealing draperies against their breasts with a bejewelled hand;

the Archbishop in his scarlet and purple; the Viceroy in his velvet and lace; the courtiers and Conquistadores, the Jesuits, the ladies-in-waiting —across the patio, up the tiled steps, through the galleries, in and out of the balconies, they seem to pass, filling them with the vibrant life, the vivid color of the carnival city, as it must have been two centuries ago." [1]

And then, of course, there was the *santuario* (sanctuary) of Santa Rosa.

This seemed strangely unrelated to the great churches with their carved choirstalls, their altars all glittering gold and glossy ebony, and their statues robed in velvet and brocade. To be sure, it was flanked on one side by a church and this, as well as the monastery on its other side, formed an integral part of the premises. But it was the garden where you lingered longest and where you felt the strongest tie with the past, the greatest consciousness of the enduring spirit of that gentle and dedicated girl who had once tended its flowers and sold them for the support of her family and the succor of the poor. In its general character it had apparently not changed much in over three hundred years; if there had been no definite effort to keep it exactly as it was when it belonged to the family of Flores y Oliva, neither was there any evidence of a definite effort to change it. It had that undefinable quality which is the result of affectionate and devoted tending rather than of professional pruning. It was not untidy, but neither did it have that clipped, almost shorn look, of many formal gardens whose care has been entrusted wholly or largely to hirelings. Flowers, like children, require love if they are really to flourish. The roses in this one were top heavy with bloom and bright with color; they were warm, fragrant and altogether beautiful. Some lesser flowers and some tall grasses grew among them; these did not detract from the radiance of the roses; they intensified this. It was easy to visualize the garden as having been nurtured by a saint.

At one end of the garden a great door led into the *patio de entrada* or *zaguán* as it was sometimes called. At the right of this was a large room which, we were told, Rosa had once set aside for the care of the sick in her own home. At the rear of this room was a pleasant arcade. At the left of the *zaguán* were two rooms, one small and bare which had once been the bedroom of the saint; the other, larger and lighter, the room where she was born. This was all that was left of a spacious colonial house; the rest had failed to withstand the ravages of time. Nevertheless, in what remained, especially in the little bedroom, you could still feel her presence. It must have been almost as bare, when in use by her, as when we saw it; and it then contained a chair she had used, a letter she had written, framed fragments of crosses she had owned and two portraits which are considered authentic. In the larger room were two windows, at one of which, according to tradition, the saint used to sit with her sewing and pass food to the poor. If you stayed close to this window, you could visualize her industry and her charity; it was harder to do so as far as the rest of the room was concerned, for it had been transformed into a chapel and ornamented with modern paintings and statues. The Stations of the Cross, made of delicately tinted *huamanga* (the smooth white stone, allegedly harder than any marble, which is one of Peru's unique products) were, indeed, beautiful and appropriate; but I had the sensation then, as I have had many times since, that the birthplace of a saint should be left, as nearly as possible, in its original state, that we need to see the saints as human beings, in human surroundings, if we are to come close to them and that one of the best ways to bring this about is to begin our acquaintance with them in the setting of their infancy. However, since the place was otherwise so permeated with the presence of Isabel de Flores y Oliva, who has come down to us in history as Santa Rosa de Lima, it seemed captious to complain that this was lacking in the chapel.

Having seen the remains of the house, we went again into the garden, still conscious of its flowery fragrance, but with our attention focused, this time, on the tiny "hermitage" which the saint had built for herself, with the help of her brother Hernándo, and where she had loved to retire for prayer and meditation. We went to the well where she had drawn water and into which she had thrown the key to the metal girdle she wore, so that she might never give way to the possible temptation of unlocking it. Gentle as she was with all other creatures, not only human beings of every degree, but animals, birds and even insects, she was harsh with herself. To her, mortification was the inevitable attribute of righteousness, the imitation of Christ not only a question of trying to follow His teaching, but of experiencing as many sufferings as it was possible to endure, patterned on His. This was not an isolated viewpoint or a morbid one. It was an essential part of the spirit of the times, one we must accept even if we cannot understand it, and we must try to understand it. I realized that from the first, even if the realization did not lead to success for a long time.

However, it did lead, very definitely, to a yearning for more knowledge of the girl whose home and garden I had seen. Up to then, I had heard very little about her: only the basic facts of a life which did not seem, at first glance, to have been very remarkable, though she was the first inhabitant of this hemisphere to achieve canonization and had been declared the Patron Saint of the Americas—*all* the Americas—the Philippines, and the Indies and, as such, has been the inspiration of many historians, painters and sculptors. I began to collect books about her and, after I left Lima, I was fortunate enough to acquire, in Quito, a polychrome figure, the work of the famous Indian carver, Caspicara, which, by special permission from a high authority, I was graciously allowed to take out of the country (although it came within the category of those works of art whose export is forbidden). This statuette, which shows the saint with roses scattered over her robe instead of circling her head in a crown (the usual representation), is one of the most beautiful, in every respect, that I have ever seen; and for thirty years now it has been not only one of my proudest possessions, but a constant reminder of the saint who had come to seem so real to me in her garden.

As soon as I reached home, the statuette was given a place of honor in my drawing room and I began to read the books I had collected in Quito as well as in Lima (for the veneration in which Santa Rosa is held is equally great in both places). The more I read, the more strongly I felt that I wanted to return to South America—primarily to revisit the *santuario*. This feeling grew deeper with the years and after I had written biographies of Thérèse of Lisieux and Bernadette of Lourdes and both had been cordially received, I began to wonder if I could not also write one of Santa Rosa de Lima. This had not, at first, occurred to me, because it had not then entered my head that hagiography could logically be included in my field of endeavor. Now I began to see such a biography as a joyous possibility. But though my work took me over and over again to Europe, it did not take me back to South America and there seemed to be no prospect that it would.

Finally, however, a cogent reason for making such a journey presented itself, though—and this is very rare—it was a personal and not a professional one: a little granddaughter was born in Chile and her parents asked me to be her godmother. As I put the ancestral christening dress, which is one of our family treasures, into my dispatch case, so that it would never be out of my safekeeping during my travels, I was struck with a new idea: Lima was on my direct route to Santiago, so why should I not make stopovers there on my way both southbound and northbound?

I consulted my publisher and entered into an agreement with her for a book about Santa Rosa and the stopovers gave me two more chances to visit her sanctuary, which in the light of the reading and studying I had done, I found even more spiritually rewarding than I had before. I confided my project to both my old friends, Maggie Conroy and Albert Giesecke. The former, as prominent a figure as ever in the social life of the city, had now entirely given up private tutoring and was teaching English at the important government school with the significant name of Rosa de Santa María. The latter had resigned as Director General of Education for all Peru and had become the Special Assistant to the American Ambassador, a position for which his knowledge of his adopted country and the high esteem in which he is held there quickly made him indispensable.

Both these friends highly approved my project and it gained further impetus when my circle of acquaintance was enlarged to include another remarkable man, Don Pedro de Osma, and his gentle and kindly sister, Doña Angelica, who is most appropriately named! As members of a family distinguished for many generations, their heirlooms include priceless paintings, magnificent furniture and innumerable objets d'art of every description. With the zeal, taste and knowledge of a collector who is also a connoisseur, Don Pedro added to these inherited treasures with such prodigality that the ancestral mansion eventually achieved the status of a private museum, while he and Doña Angelica transformed the charming pavilion at the rear of the garden into their actual dwelling. Needless to say, pictures of Santa Rosa are among the most valued paintings in the museum, which rivals any of its size that I have ever seen in variety, value and splendor. Outstanding among these representations is one of the Cuzco school, which, like the Quitenian school, is patterned on a glorious Spanish tradition, but succeeds in achieving a style uniquely its own. This shows the saint with a golden veil, as well as a crown of roses, to which twin cherubs are adding the finishing touches; whereas a modern interpretation, by Ignacio Merino—no less appealing in an entirely different way—shows her very simply dressed, seated alone with a book in her lap and an expression of great intensity in her eyes. Don Pedro —urbane, witty, genuinely cordial—himself guides his amazed and admiring guests through one crowded room in the museum after another; and at the end of their tour they add refreshment of body to refreshment of spirit as they drink the tea that Doña Angelica pours for them or the *pisco* sours which Don Pedro mixes with a master hand.

I had hardly reached home after my third visit to Lima when I began to receive books and clippings from Dr. Giesecke. Every time he found a new biography of Santa Rosa, an article about her cult, or a news item which referred to her directly or indirectly, he sent it to me. Presently, an entire shelf in my study was devoted to her. But meantime, my publisher's interest had waned. She wanted novels and more novels. She would, of course, stand by her financial agreement with me as far as her share of the expenses for the South American trip was concerned; in return, she hoped I would be willing to forego royalties.

It was a disappointment. With the increased awareness of Latin America's scenic, architectural and archeological treasures and the greater facilities for becoming acquainted with these through better plane service and ship service, it seemed to me a pity that there was not also an increased awareness of its spiritual and historical contribution to civilization. After all, the story of Peru's conquest by the Spaniards was one of the world's greatest epics; and that country had given to this hemisphere not only its first canonized saint, but several additional holy figures of lesser, but important stature, among them the Blessed Martín Porres. I felt sure that other countries must have made similar contributions. Mexico had certainly done so with the Virgin of Guadalupe and my book about her had been well received. With the hope of helping a little to reduce the lack of spiritual and historical awareness to which I have just referred, I longed to do another of like character.

But though my publisher's decision was a disappointment, it was not really a blow. I worried, occasionally, as more and more books and clippings came in from Dr. Giesecke, for fear he would begin to think he was sending them in vain; but I never lost the hope, amounting almost to a conviction, that sooner or later some other publisher would be more interested in hagiography than in fiction, as far as I was concerned. The hope was realized, the conviction justified. In fact, it was more than justified. In the autumn of 1960—thirty years after I had first visited the *santuario* of Santa Rosa—I was back in South America on an assignment to write not only her biography, but also that of Santa Mariana of Quito!

This double mission was due to one of those occurrences to which we are apt to refer as "happy accidents," but which I sincerely believe are nothing of the kind. I believe they are part of a Divine pattern. Seated beside the then Ambassador of Ecuador to the United States, Dr. José Chiriboga, at a Washington dinner party, I mentioned, in the course of casual conversation, how greatly I had enjoyed two visits in his country some years earlier; perhaps, if I ever realized my hope of returning to Peru, in order to write about Santa Rosa de Lima, I might stop briefly in Quito, as it would be on my way. He interrupted me.

"But why should you stop briefly? Why shouldn't you stay long enough to write about our special saint, too?"

"Why, I didn't know you had a special saint!" I confessed.

"Of course we do—a saint born just a year after Rosa de Lima had died. Her name is Mariana and she is often called the Lily of Quito, partly because of the purity which distinguished her life and partly because of the miracle in which lilies are closely associated with her. The Jesuits call her their daughter—*hija de Jesuitas*. She is buried beneath the high altar of their church in Quito, generally known as the Compañia. Even before her death, the people of Ecuador acclaimed her as their saviour from the plague and they have attributed miracles to her ever since. She is our patron saint and our national heroine in the same sense that Joan of Arc and Thérèse of Lisieux are the patron saints and the national heroines of France. One of the most important decorations our government gives is the Order of Mariana de Jesús Paredes y Flores, *heroina nacional*. Stamps are issued in her honor, colleges and communities named for her—and also villas, wards, small shops and buses!"

"But what did this young girl do that qualified her for such regard from the Jesuits—probably the most critical and analytical in their viewpoint of any Order?"

"Why you must understand, Señora, it was not so much what she did as what she was that commended her to the Jesuits. As a matter of fact, I suppose you would say that she did very little. But if you will go to my country, I am sure you will understand both the reasons for the great popular devotion to her and her position in regard to the Jesuits—not to mention the basis for her canonization. I know of several priests, belonging to different Orders, and several historians who will offer to help you and thus you will have the benefit of various viewpoints. But it is not only from clerics and scholars that you will find assistance. Almost everyone you meet will be happy to talk with you about Mariana de Jesús and many of these persons will speak with factual authority. Others will base their statements only on treasured tradition, but that also has its proper place in any story. Some of these persons will gladly accompany you to the places most intimately connected with Mariana's life and death and thus help you to visualize the conditions and circumstances surrounding both; still others will be glad to trace the steps that led to her canonization. And there are many books about her which are easy to obtain. Most of the biographies are in Spanish, though there are several in French and at least one very fine life in Italian, as well as several other languages.[3] And there is no lack of material about the Spanish Colonial Period, of which Mariana was so integral a part, written in English. This, certainly, you can absorb without difficulty. You do not read French or Spanish or Italian?"

"French, yes, with the greatest of ease. Spanish without too much trouble—especially with a dictionary at hand! Italian hardly at all."

"Then you must have help. But I assure you this will be forthcoming. Just go to Ecuador and find out!"

As is inevitable at dinner parties, the conversation switched to other channels; but I was already intrigued. And it was only a few days after this that the publisher I had hopefully, though vaguely, visualized—the one more interested in hagiography than in fiction— actually materialized, came from New York to see me in Washington, and asked if I would care to write something for him and, if so, what. I mentioned Rosa of Lima and Mariana of Quito. Before he left that afternoon an agreement was reached and a few days later a contract was signed. I consulted my friends, the Peruvian Ambassador to the United States and Señora de Berckemeyer and found that the project was extremely pleasing to them and that they would be glad to do anything they could to further it. (A promise which was amply fulfilled.) As soon as I had finished the work to which I was already committed, I was on my way to South America with Deanie Bullock, the faithful secretary who has accompanied me on so many wanderings.

In order to take advantage of the best season in both countries, it seemed wise to go first to Ecuador. The voyage from New York on the *Santa Isabel* was one of sheer delight from beginning to end—as were many previous voyages on Grace *Santas* and as I hope many subsequent voyages may be. With the renewal of old friendships and the making of new ones, the brief stopovers in Panama and Guayaquil were pleasant in many ways. I cannot say as much for the motor trip across the Andes, though Deanie's prowess as a chauffeur is comparable to her gifts as a secretary. The scenery, of course, is magnificent and varied, the glimpses of primitive life and strange animals arresting and illuminating. But I advise anyone who is told—as we were—that the roads in Ecuador are just as good as those in the United States to take this information with a grain of salt. However, we arrived, without untoward incident, at Quito, superbly located more than nine thousand feet above sea level among mountains towering thousands of feet higher still; and immediately found ourselves surrounded with the same friendliness and helpfulness that had contributed so much to my enjoyment when I had been in Ecuador before.

"The Ecuadorians are among the most hospitable of the South American people," I wrote then. "And, as they are almost universally land owners and land lovers, this hospitality is not confined to the city. At Tampillo Alto we were able to form an opinion of how ideally suited an Ecuadorian country place would prove for retirement and rest. The house, built of pale blue stucco with a tiled roof, with frescoes running along the outer walls, was long and rambling, with deep galleries, a private chapel, and a great bell which hung above stone steps leading from one balcony to another; and it contained twenty rooms on each floor, all opening into one another with wide doors, and a splendid staircase. But attractive as was the house itself, the garden was even lovelier. Here waterfalls fell in smooth broad sheets over a background of lilies, gleaming white through the translucency; here little placid, curving streams, surmounted by rustic bridges, widened gradually into quiet pools where ducks and turtles swam indolently about; here violets and orchids, forget-me-nots, and roses and every other flower imaginable lifted their colorful fragrance beside the paved paths and hung in bright clusters over the terraces. And as the house and garden had for a setting a sloping verdant valley, and for a background remote and lofty mountains, the beauty of the situation was as great as the charm of the hacienda.

"Tampillo Alto was not the only hacienda which we visited; we also spent a day as guests of the distinguished Mena family, at one of their five haciendas, superbly located in the valley of Los Chilios. There are five brothers—as well as five haciendas!—in this family; and we felt, when we left Quito, that the sum total of our obligations to them was very great. One of these brothers, Señor Eduardo Mena—who, by the way, has an American wife—is an official in the Bureau of Public Works; and it was to him that we owed the trip far out on the new highway, leading to the Colombian frontier, which is now under construction—for road-building is one of the major concerns of the present government in Ecuador. It was to another brother, Señor Alberto Mena, that we owed our first acquaintance with Quitenian painting; for he has a fine collection of both ancient and modern masters. There is such a genuine kindness toward foreigners in Quito, such an evident desire to share with them the natural and artistic beauties which abound there, that there is almost no sense of being a stranger in a strange land; there is rather a feeling of having suddenly enlarged one's circle of congenial friends.

"This kindly attitude is not confined to any one class or condition. You meet with it in your room-boy; you also meet with it in the President of the Republic. This remarkable man, Isidro Ayora, summarily placed at the head of the Provisional Government in 1926, and since then duly elected as Chief Executive in 1928, comes of partly Indian stock, and is as rightly proud of the fact as is our own Vice-President.[4] He had never, until he was called to the highest office in the land, been especially interested in politics; he was a physician whose thorough medical education in Ecuador had been supplemented by years of professional study in Germany, and who had come, with reason, to be regarded as the outstanding doctor in Quito. He was the founder of the Red Cross in Ecuador; he was the head of a renowned private clinic; he was the instigator of many hygienic reforms. Radiating health and wholesomeness himself, sturdily built, clear-eyed, ruddy-cheeked; calm, cheerful, and judicious, his personality was ideally suited to his vocation; and he saw no reason for giving it up, when, as one writer has put it: 'The nation, or that part of the nation which directs politics, grew weary of a régime of graft and incompetence which impoverished the country and retarded its development. So a group of prominent men, with the essential co-operation of the army, looked around for an honest man who was also capable and free from political affiliations. Their choice fell upon the leading physician in Quito.'

"Dr. Ayora decided to continue being a doctor even after he had become President. Only a man secure in the courage of his convictions could have made such a decision; only a man with almost superhuman strength and mental balance would have adhered to it. He mapped out a working day for himself which had no relation to union hours. Rising long before daybreak, he devoted his time until half-past nine to his clinic. From then until his lunch, he occupied himself with his presidential duties; after this, he went back to the clinic again; from mid-afternoon until late evening he resumed his presidential duties.

And the clinic, the country, and the President have all thriven under this rigorous régime!

"I first met and talked with the President in his own private house, adjoining the clinic, and not in the Palace which is his official residence, for Señora de Ayora was not very strong just then, so she and the President and their three children were living as quietly as possible. But they were punctilious about participating in official functions of real importance; and consequently I met them several times after this audience, and my favorable first impressions were confirmed and strengthened with each successive meeting." [1]

So much for impressions recorded thirty years ago. I was especially pleased because the friends I had made then seemed as glad to renew their acquaintance with me as I was to have them do so. Among these were Eduardo Mena and his wife, who first introduced me to the attractions of Ecuadorian *estancias* (country estates) and who now live in a charming sixteenth century house at Guapalo (originally the home of the engineers who built the beautiful baroque church there), also, Isidro Ayora, the surgeon-statesman who was President of Ecuador when I first knew him and who now, in his mid-eighties, is still active in the clinic which bears his name. He and his lovely, soft-spoken, white haired Señora were our fellow guests at several delightful dinners and, again, visits at outlying *estancias* figured pleasantly in our design for living. One of these is the property of Carlos de Mantilla Ortega, publisher of Quito's leading daily; another, the domain of the Plazas, two remarkable women and their even more remarkable brother. (The sisters have established a model dairy farm, the only one in Ecuador, and run it between them, with one as supervisor and the other as marketer; the brother, recently president of his country, has since then been the recipient of the Theodore Brent Inter-American Award for 1960.) The American Cultural Attaché—since transferred to La Paz—and Mrs. Jerry James were tireless in their good offices. Dr. Chiriboga's prediction that I would find all sorts and conditions of people eager and willing to help me in my research was amply fulfilled. I worked regularly with Father Luis Alberto Luna, a learned Carmelite, intermittently with Father Oswaldo Romero, an equally learned Jesuit and was privileged in visiting, at the Jesuit Seminary, Father Aurelio Espinosa, who was then undoubtedly the greatest living authority on Mariana de Jesús.

With this pleasing social and scholastic background, I began the sightseeing which would most logically contribute to an interpretation of the Lily of Quito, namely, the Jesuit Church, or the Compañia, as it is generally called. There is probably no more beautiful baroque church in the world. The facade is so delicately and elaborately carved that not a foot of smooth surface is left. Like the interior, where the carving is no less delicate and elaborate, it is made of native stone; but whereas the facade retains its original color—a soft, though somber, gray—the interior has been completely encrusted with gold leaf. Not an altar, not a column, not an arch, not a vault has been left ungilded. The pulpit, the choir, the portals are all aglitter; and the whole effect is one of such dazzling splendor that, at first, the beholder is almost overwhelmed by its brilliance. Only gradually is it possible to discern the harmony of its exquisitely integrated parts: the grilled gallery, the frieze which runs the entire length of this and also along the upper story of the main altar, the separate chapels in the side aisles. It also takes time to appreciate the details of the carving—the garlands, the cherubs, the Islamic designs in the ceiling. The primary impression is almost wholly one of glorious but general luminosity.

Little by little, the paintings and statues begin to emerge, individually, from the radiant surroundings with which they blend so perfectly that, quite aside from the element of blinding light which obscures them, it is not astonishing that it takes so long to discern them clearly. Glowing canvases, framed by the polychromed wood which is an essential part of the decoration, form the center of many retables; sculptured figures of the Evangelists rise from the pendentives; in some of the chapels the Holy Mother and the *Ecce Homo* are presented in velvet robes, fantastically embroidered. In striking contrast to all this is the statue which is placed just below the great crucifix, high above the main altar: the statue of a young woman, haloed in gold, though very simply robed in black, bearing the emblem of the Jesuit Order, and with a sheaf of lilies in her hand; and a small wooden figure, obviously meant to represent the same young woman, though, this time, in a kneeling position, at the foot of the pulpit. Both represent Mariana, whom the Jesuits are proud to call their daughter and who is buried beneath the high altar of this, their church.

A glorious light illumines her resting place, resulting in a concentration of radiance, even more dazzling than the general brilliance of the interior. The figure above the crucifix, of course, represents her in her present state of glory. The smaller one, by the pulpit, commemorates her daily habit of coming here to pray. At a side altar is still another representation of her, in an attitude of grief. At a second side altar, surmounted by a statue of Our Lady of Loreto, to which Mariana had special devotion, are relics of her, including her guitar and her workbox. These are reverently preserved and still bear witness to the fact that she was a skilled musician and an accomplished needlewoman and used both these talents for the glory of God.

Next in importance to the Compañía comes the Carmelite Convent which was once Mariana's ancestral home and which she herself predicted would some time be used exactly as it is today. Thanks to a special dispensation, I was permitted to visit this and was deeply impressed with its perfect state of preservation and its essential beauty.

I shall have to confess that while I was seeing and doing all this, I did not keep fully abreast of Dr. Giesecke's clippings about Santa Rosa. Not that I was unmindful of her—as I have said before, the devotion to her is almost equally great in Quito and Lima. I had found some wonderful representations of her, both by the same Caspicara who had carved my own statuette and by other sculptors of the Quitenian school; and on her feast day I had gone to a beautiful service, held in her honor, at the chapel which bears her name in the Church of Santo Domingo—a service at which a precious relic had been made available for the tribute of the faithful, and the music was furnished by one of those remarkable male choirs, a double quartet in this instance, for which Quito has been so justly famous almost from the very time of its foundation. However, very properly, Mariana's story and not Rosa's was uppermost in my thoughts and labors just then. I had to make the most of every minute that eminent authorities and kindly helpers were willing to put at my disposal. When I received a large envelope with the letterhead of the American Embassy, I glanced hurriedly at its contents—something about the *santuario* evidently. Well, I would be back in Lima in a few weeks, after another delightful voyage on the *Santa Isabel*, and would go over the material later when I could see for myself what it was all about.

Consequently, I was totally unprepared for what I did see, when I arrived in Lima.

The entire facade of the church had been demolished to provide for a wide highway leading to a new bridge. Only a blank wall remained where once there had been twin towers, impressive portals, sculptured stone. The great door leading directly into the garden from the street was closed off, except to the workmen who had not yet finished their twin tasks of demolition and reconstruction. It was no longer possible to enter the hallowed enclosure from one end and look down the entire length of its flowering expanse with a single joyous glance. Instead, the garden was entered at the side from a modern brick terrace, with modern brick steps leading down to it, and it had been bricked over, too, except for the space occupied by rectangular flower beds, some primly bordered with a low picket fence, others simply surrounded by tubing painted bright green. The informality, the charm, the indefinable quality which is the result of affectionate tending, rather than professional pruning, were all gone. The place which I had wanted, for years, to revisit, which, indeed, had been the main source of inspiration for a new book, no longer existed as far as I was concerned. The sudden realization of this was a great shock.

It took me some days to recover from this. I have always felt that no outsider has a right to pass judgment on changes made in a place to which he does not belong and which does not belong to him; I resent such judgment when it is passed by outsiders on places to which I belong and which belong to me. Unquestionably, the widened thoroughfare and the new bridge were indicated by some civic need with which I was unacquainted and which could not be met by widening a thoroughfare and building a bridge elsewhere. I do not doubt for a moment that this is so, but I had come a long way, both figuratively and literally, to find Santa Rosa de Lima in her garden and now, as far as I was concerned, she was not there and I could not seem to find her anywhere else. Like one of her most sympathetic and gifted Peruvian biographers, María Wiesse, it was here, and through her activities here, that I had always visualized her most clearly and found her the greatest source of inspiration: "Not in an act of passion or excitement, but bending tenderly over the humble little flowers of her garden to give them her fostering care. Thus I visualize the saint of my country: smiling, gentle, simple, amiable, rather than tragic and austere. Her penances reached a more heroic level; nevertheless, her spirit remained childlike and candid. After a night spent almost wholly in prayer and mortification, Rosa went into her garden at daybreak and invited the plants, the flowers and the trees to join her in singing the praises of the Lord. The brightness of dawn, the freshness of the earth moistened by the dews of night, the perfume from the flowers, the song of the birds which flew from tree to tree, the hum of the insects—all these colors, all these scents, all these sounds, filled her being with chaste and serene joy. As she bent over her violets, her lilies, her basil, she gave thanks for them to God." [5]

This was the image which I, too, had of her. I went, conscientiously, to all the convents and churches with which Santa Rosa had been associated, I saw her relics and her letters, I talked with nuns and priests and other learned persons who were recognized authorities on her life. They were all very kind and cordial and helpful. Still, she did not come real to me again. No matter how hard I tried to think of her in other connections, I could associate her only with her garden, which, of course, was not the right way or, rather, it should not have been the only way. But again, though I had undergone a disappointment, I had not really suffered a blow. Somehow, I had a feeling that Santa Rosa herself would have a hand in my rediscovery of her and that I should not try to hurry this. It would come about in her own way and in her own good time.

Meanwhile, I did not lack for congenial company and pleasant occupations. I renewed my acquaintance with Don Pedro and found him, if possible, even more genial than before. His *pisco* sours had actually improved and his museum bulged with new treasures. Of course, I had been eager to see Maggie Conroy again and I found her as sociable, as charming, as alert and as active as ever. With the facility which characterizes true friendship, we were able to resume the old relationship, almost as if there had never been a break in it; we lunched at Las Trece Monedas and Le Pavillon, we shopped and read together, we talked over old times and correlated these with present activities. She gave a little party for me at the Golf Club and my fellow guests, in their turn, extended hospitality and gave me rewarding glimpses of Peruvian life in its most attractive phases. (How beautiful they are, these Limenian houses, the old ones with their balconies and patios, the new ones set in gardens which are marvels of florescence!)

Also, through Maggie Conroy, I learned about the wonderful work of charity (which had succeeded teaching and golf as her major interest) dedicated to the mammoth task of improving living conditions among the less privileged. This is the so-called Misión de Lima, founded by the present Archbishop, "to take the message of Christ to the people in the outskirts of Lima, Callao and Balnearios and to make possible for them a decent mode of existence." The rapid growth of Lima, which has entirely outstripped housing facilities for all but the well-to-do, despite valiant efforts on the part of the government, has resulted in squatter settlements of indescribable squalor. Two hundred and fifty thousand human beings are living under conditions almost unbelievable to anyone who has not seen them; and it is to these fellow creatures that consecrated workers, both clerical and

lay, are devoting time, energy and all the help, both spiritual and
material, at their command, in order to carve a better and brighter
future out of a tragic past and a desolate present. There are now forty
committees of co-operation working in the different *barrios* (districts)
—the one where Maggie serves is the Santa Cruz—and four hundred
volunteers. Among the great undertakings which they are carrying
through, besides the establishment of sanitary stations under the
direction of competent doctors, educational centers under the direction
of competent teachers and nurseries under the direction of competent
infirmarians, is a soup kitchen where eight thousand children of pre-
school age are fed a substantial breakfast every day in the year.

These, of course, are only a few aspects of the Misión de Lima; it
was impossible for me to grasp the full extent of its accomplishments,
especially as Maggie was characteristically modest about telling me of
her share in the work. But I learned as much as I could, with increasing wonder and admiration.

I also developed another major interest as I observed that Lima, on
the whole a very sophisticated city, devotes practically the whole
month of October to a celebration in honor of the so-called "Señor de
los Milagros." Although this celebration started among the poor and
humble, it has now become so general that men and women of all
classes take part in it. Many of them refrain from joining in any sort
of festivities until after the 28th, when the last of the three great processions (not unlike those which take place in Seville during Holy
Week) winds its way through the streets of the city. The background
of this celebration has its origin in a picture painted on an adobe wall
in 1665, by a liberated slave. The wall and the picture have withstood
manifold kinds of destruction and many miracles are now attributed
to the painting, which forms an altarpiece in the Church of the Nazarenes. A copy of this picture has been made which is carried in the
processions—lighted by candles and profusely decorated with flowers—
preceded by censer bearers, accompanied by members of the clergy and
purple-clad members of the *cofradías*, or guilds, which act as a special
guard for the holy image, and followed by countless multitudes. Besides the stops which it makes to permit the change of bearers for the
heavy *paso* [float], the procession pauses in front of the presidential
palace, the city hall and the cathedral, where the President, the Mayor
and the Archbishop come out on a balcony to salute it.

A series of Masses, with special music and special prayers, not only
inaugurate this celebration, but continue throughout the month and

are thronged to the last inch of standing room in the Church of the
Nazarenes. Deanie Bullock—the faithful secretary who was again accompanying me on my wanderings—and I had the great privilege of
attending one of the most elaborate and impressive of these ceremonies, under the guidance of the Dean of the cathedral, Monsignor
Hernando Vega Centano, whom we had the honor of meeting at a
luncheon given by Dr. Giesecke (still Special Assistant to the American Ambassador and still unremittingly kind and helpful as far as my
work was concerned). Before Mass actually began, we had the further
privilege of viewing the miraculous painting from the sanctuary itself,
through the courtesy of the Canon of the Church of the Nazarenes.

   Everything conspired to make the "Señor de los Milagros" "a living
bright reality" to us: the Masses; the processions which we saw from
the best possible vantage point; the purple capes and dresses which
became more and more prevalent in the streets every day, until Lima,
if not like Athens actually "violet crowned," was certainly violet hued;
the wonderful story of Antonia Maldonado, who became *Sor* Antonia
Lucia *de Espiritu Santo* (Sister Antonia Lucia of the Holy Spirit),
Foundress of the Instituto Nazareno (whose history, which I hope to
write in full at some future time, was made known to me by the Prior-
ess and Community of the Nazarenas, *Carmelitas Descalzas* themselves); all the changed aspects, of the city, gay as well as grave, during
the month given over to this special cult. Vendors of mechanical toys,
sun glasses, turtles, birds and all sorts of small animals appeared in the
street, cheek by jowl with the vendors of strange foodstuffs such as
anticuchos (beef hearts skewered on small sticks) *ceviche* (raw
fish marinated in lemon), *picarones* (raised doughnuts made with
honey) and *butifarras* (bread spread with pork, red pepper and onion).
All these vendors mingled freely with those selling highly decorated
candles, silver votive offerings, amulets and scapulars of every description. Topical editorials and verse supplemented the news stories. Photographs and line drawings showing the routes of the processions were
in all the newspapers. A special kind of sticky sweetmeat made of
almond paste and known as the *turrón de Doña Pepa* became a favorite
form of food and conversations centered on such subjects as the following: "I hope you had a good place to watch the procession." . . .
"Did you ever see such multitudes in the streets?" . . . "And such
flowers—every time the *paso* stopped, immense quantities were removed from it to make room for others!" . . . "I don't know how I
resisted the temptation to buy those twin puppies I saw a little boy

selling in the Plaza de Armas" . . . "My husband, my brother and I
are all taking part in the procession—we wouldn't think of letting the
year go by without doing so." . . . "I assure you, my own sister has
benefited by special graces from the Señor and I could tell you of other
instances." . . .

So increasingly did I become absorbed in all the phases of this celebration, that my disappointment over the condition in which I had
found the *santuario* of Santa Rosa might have been assuaged had I
come to Lima only as a visitor, for, as far as interesting things to do
and see were concerned, I had actually an embarrassment of riches in
this delightful city. But I had come here as a writer with a definite
purpose and, what was equally—or perhaps even more!—to the point,
on a definite assignment. I seemed to be getting nowhere with that
and, therefore, would probably have continued to feel thwarted had it
not been for the continued good offices of Dr. Giesecke.

I have already mentioned the luncheon given by him. This took
place at the Club Nacional—still as stately and as elegant as when
I first went there thirty years ago—and not only Monsignor Vega
Centano, likewise aforementioned, but other fellow guests had been
chosen with the specific idea of providing me with willing collabora-
tors during my stay in Lima. Among these was Señorita María Rosario
Araoz, long a leader in Catholic Action and education and, like Maggie
Conroy, a tireless worker in the Misión de Lima. I already knew something of Señorita Rosario's remarkable achievements, among them
the establishment of the first free night schools for adults, recognized
by numerous citations and medals and crowned by the Sol de Peru, the
highest decoration given by the government. I would have welcomed
an opportunity to talk with her, then and there, about the signal
success of these magnificent humanitarian undertakings; but she happened to overhear me saying to the Prior of Santo Domingo, who was
also among my fellow guests, that I was seeking for new light on Santa
Rosa, which had nothing to do with her mortifications and which
would more fully explain to me her claims for holiness, and Señorita
Rosario instantly took up the challenge.

"Why, she was the first great Peruvian social worker! Do you mean
to say you have not thought about her in that way?"

"No," I confessed. "I hadn't. I had thought of her largely as an
ascetic and as a gardener."

"Then you must let me tell you other things. It will be easy for me
to do so. I always think of her as a familiar friend, not a distant saint."

This statement, coming from a woman who was herself long a director of a social service school, had extraordinary impact and for the next quarter hour conversation on the subject became general—and illuminating. Then, as we were leaving the dining room, Señorita Rosario asked me if I would be interested in going to Quives.

"Quives?" I repeated in some bewilderment, for the name meant nothing to me.

"Yes. The mountain village where Santa Rosa's father, Gaspar de Flores, was Administrator of Mines for several years. It wasn't a village then—it was a very thriving town. Now it is only a small Indian settlement. But the little church where Rosa was confirmed by the saintly Archbishop, Toribio de Mogrovejo, and the house where she lived with her family have been rescued from ruin and are in a state of reconstruction. A French missionary priest is doing wonderful work there. I believe you'd enjoy meeting him and seeing the locale. And the drive takes you out of the mist and into the sunshine, through some beautiful mountain scenery."

This information, in itself, was sufficient inducement for undertaking the trip. Theoretically, October is springtime in Lima and the claim of its inhabitants that it never actually rains there is probably true. But neither does the sun shine, except rarely and apologetically, for more than six months in the year; every night a cold penetrating fog envelops the city and its dampness is not wholly dissipated during the day; it permeates your warm woolen clothes and keeps even your hair in a moist state. After weeks of such weather, the prospect of escaping from it, even for a day, is alluring.

We set out at midmorning, with Deanie at the wheel of the station wagon which has become an integral part of our travels. Dr. Giesecke, Señorita Rosario and Sister Rose Dominick of the Maryknoll Nuns, which are doing such wonderful work in Lima, made up the rest of the party. The road was rough and dusty and, at first, it wound its way through dun colored hills, devoid of any special charm. The scattered settlements which we passed were invariably depressing and, in one case, actually heartrending. (This was the Pampas de Comas, where thousands of human beings are living in the squalid conditions which have made the aforementioned Misión de Lima such a crying necessity.) But little by little the valley became wider and more verdant. Fine herds of cattle were grazing in the green pastures. Industrious workers—first Chinese and then Indian—were cultivating the thriving fields of vegetables and cotton. Every now and then, at the turn of a road, we came upon a small wayside shrine, decorated with flowers and lighted with candles. Presently, the mountains began to take on new majesty and the mist which had obscured them gradually disappeared; they towered against a sky of bright and cloudless blue.

Only once did we pass a country house of any pretensions and this had obviously seen better days. Long ago, so we learned, it had been the headquarters of the great General San Martín, during the War of Independence. Dashing officers in brilliant uniforms had come galloping up to it; portentous dispatches had been anxiously read and hastily answered in the candlelight of its drawing room; toasts had been drunk, standing, to the success of the Army of Liberation. Now the historic house seemed to drowse in the sun, its windows shuttered, its galleries deserted, its courtyard used for a poultry run. Only in the neighboring barns were signs of human life and human activity visible; but at least there was no sign of misery there, as there had been in the slum settlements.

Villages were few and far between and they all followed much the same pattern, consisting of a cluster of long low buildings, divided into tiny tenements and teeming with Indians, surrounding a bare and dusty square. Sometimes, but by no means always, the tenements were supplemented by a primitive schoolhouse, a stark little church and some open stalls where fruits and beverages were sold. As we approached one such village, which had the stalls but no church and no schoolhouse, Señorita Rosario pointed excitedly to the tiny chapel on the hillside far above it.

"That marks an important stopping place in the old post road—the one which Santa Rosa and her family traveled on their way to and from Quives," she told us. "Father Dalle comes here regularly now to celebrate Mass. Of course, the chapel itself is barely large enough to hold more than two or three worshipers, so the congregation foregathers on the hillside; and since there is no bell, he uses an accordion to summon the people, who come in droves. Essentially, they are very good, these people. But they have much to learn, particularly about their own special saint. They have kept confusing her with the Blessed Virgin because, like Our Lady, she is so often represented with a baby in her arms—of course, in her case, the symbol of her charity. We are teaching the people to watch for the Dominican habit, which Santa Rosa always wears, whereas the Virgin never wears black, except as the Mater Dolorosa, when, of course, she is not carrying the Divine Child, but mourning Her crucified Son. But after all, that is only a detail, compared with the many more important things they must be taught and which Father Dalle is teaching them."

Until I heard about the accordion, this French missionary priest had been merely a name to me; now he began to have a personality and an appealing one. In the next village to which we came, I made his acquaintance.

The Indians living in this village were eagerly awaiting a *paso* bearing a copy of the picture of the "Señor de los Milagros," which they had been promised would be sent up from Lima and which should have reached them by eleven o'clock. In preparation for its coming, they had decorated the entire village profusely with flowers and erected a floral arch at the entrance to it. Only a few of the native women had been able to achieve a complete purple outfit, but all had done the best they could with scarves, blouses, skirts or ribbons. The men had followed suit with purple ties and purple vests. Headed by two members of the local police, they crowded around the station wagon and inquired with eagerness whether or not we had seen the *paso* and, if so, when and where along the way. Sadly, we were obliged to give a negative answer. Just then, a distinctive figure detached itself from the Indians at the rear and came forward.

The first impression he gave was that of the military man rather than a missionary priest, as we generally visualize these. He was tall, slender and very erect. He was wearing a white coverall, neatly belted around a slim waist and fastened so high at the throat that if he were wearing a clerical collar it was not visible. His hair, worn slightly *en brosse*, was cut very short and he was noticeably clean shaven. His color, though healthy, was pale rather than ruddy and his features were very clean cut. His blue eyes were keen and as he smiled in greeting they softened and his parted lips revealed very fine teeth. If you had not known that he had been a prisoner at Buchenwald after he was already a seminarian and that Quives was not his first charge, you might have set him down as under thirty. Actually, as you later learned, Father Dalle—for it was he—was just under forty.

He would return to Quives at once, he said; and when we demurred, saying we were sure his parishioners in this village wished him to remain until the arrival of the *paso*, he laughed and replied that if we had not seen it on our way, there would be plenty of time for him to come back before it reached there. Then he nodded and was off, in the rattling jeep which serves him as transportation over most of the mountain roads—some, which are too steep for it, he has to cover on horseback or muleback; still others, which are only trails, he covers on foot. But in one way or another he reaches more than five thousand persons, scattered over an immense territory, and acts not only as their priest, but as their physician, their counselor and their friend.

The jeep bounded on ahead of the station wagon. When we reached Quives, Father Dalle was already standing beside the so-called "haunted house" which serves as rectory and community center—a box-like, two story structure which he had found in a dilapidated condition and had rebuilt largely himself, because the Indians shunned it after a large snake, which they were sure was the devil in disguise, had been discovered in the debris of its foundations. ("They are very superstitious," he said, "that, as well as their ignorance, is something we have to combat all the time. But we are making progress!") For the rest, there were the usual teeming tenements, the usual barren square and, on either side of it, a small stone building which gave evidences of current construction. That was all. This was Quives, the place we had traveled sixty miles over the mountains to see.

"You must be very hungry," Father Dalle was saying. "Come in, come in! We will have lunch and afterward we will do our sightseeing." He led the way into a narrow corridor and opened a door at the right of it, which, in turn, led into a kitchen, perhaps six feet wide by nine feet long. There was a small china cabinet near the door, a sink with an oil stove under it at the other end, a table in the middle. It was spotlessly clean. Sister Rose Dominick set the table with Father Dalle's dishes while Señorita Rosario unpacked our baskets. She had brought avocado pears, fried chicken, vegetables and bread. Dr. Giesecke had brought wine and cakes, and Deanie and I wine, sandwiches and mineral water. Spread out before us, it looked like a feast. There was just room between the walls and the table for our chairs, drawn up very close. Father Dalle asked a blessing and we sat down.

Conversation progressed easily in three languages—English, Spanish and French. I had been told that Father Dalle was one of eleven children, six of whom had become either priests or nuns; I wanted to hear more about this extraordinary family, what part of France they lived in and so on. Proudly, we were shown a picture of the entire group, both lay and clerical. Their home was at Prinsuejols, a small village near Clermont-Ferrand in central France, we were told, but he had studied for the priesthood at the Sacred Heart in Chateaudun, about thirty miles south of Chartres. These studies had been interrupted when he was summoned to Germany to minister to some young

Frenchmen who had been deprived of all spiritual direction. There he attracted the attention of the secret police who arrested him as a dangerous element. This arrest was almost immediately followed by imprisonment; but he had finally been ordained at the end of the war.

Having been informed on these points, I next wanted to hear how Father Dalle had happened to come to Quives. He made it sound very simple and natural that a man of such outstanding character and superior education should have chosen—for obviously it had been a matter of choice—as a parish an Indian settlement whose inhabitants were practically all illiterate and which lacked almost all means of communication with what we call civilization—telephone, telegraph, plane service, train service, even regular mail and bus service. "I was teaching in Lima at the College of the Recollect Fathers," he said, "and one day I brought my pupils here on a picnic. Of course, long before that, the *santuario* and the *ermita*—the little church where Santa Rosa was confirmed and the house where she lived with her family—had been declared national monuments, as a result of their discovery in ruins, by Father Francisco Arámburu. And you must not give me too much credit for their reconstruction—that had been begun before I came here. I felt Quives was a place my charges should see and, by chance, the day set for the picnic proved to be St. Rose's feast day, though I had not thought of that beforehand. And I myself was born on the Feast of St. Dominick. The two seemed to go together. When the Archbishop created this territory into a parish for the first time and gave it the name of Santa Rosa de Quives, the presence of a resident priest was clearly indicated. I resigned my teaching position and came here."

"It was predestination," Señorita Rosario said with conviction.

As the afternoon wore on, I became increasingly sure of this myself. We went over the premises, all as spotlessly clean as the kitchen. Fitted into the wall beside this was a gleaming white refrigerator, which operated with oil and produced cubes which would be a credit to any such appliance, though there is neither gas nor electricity in Quives. Behind the kitchen was a bathroom of sorts. The stairway led to a large open loft, empty except for a flat-topped desk and a book case at one end, in a corner back of the stairs, and some long tables and straight-backed chairs scattered over the main part of the room. This served as the priest's study when he was alone and as his community center when he gathered his parishioners together. There were no pictures and no statues, only a crucifix to relieve the bareness of the wooden walls; but the windows looked out on the mountains and I thought of the psalmist's verse, "I will lift up mine eyes to the hills from whence cometh my help."

After we had had coffee, we crossed the dusty square to the little church which had stone walls, soundly cemented, a sound new roof and a new belfry; it would not be necessary here to call worshipers to Mass with an accordion! Inside, like the "haunted house," it was very bare and there was little in evidence to remind us of Colonial times: only an ancient statue of the *Inmaculada* (the Immaculate)—always a favorite among Spaniards, whether at home or abroad—which had somehow survived the centuries and a *paso* on which it could be carried in processions on feast days. Yet here, for the first time since coming back to Peru, I began to feel very close to Isabel de Flores, whom the saintly Archbishop called Rosa as he confirmed her when she was a little girl of twelve, though hitherto that had been only a nickname, bestowed on her by her mother and her nurse, because of her flower-like looks, and over the protests of her grandmother, whose namesake she was. I could see the little family—father and mother, brothers and sisters—proudly foregathered for this great occasion, dressed in their simple best; the sponsor, the two little boys, sons of other Spaniards stationed at the mines, who were confirmed at the same time, the Indians, some merely puzzled by the strange ceremony, others actively antagonistic. I was no longer groping in vain for something I could not find. I had begun to discover my heroine as a human being, at one of the great moments of her life, and this was what I had to do before I could rediscover her as a saint.

The feeling of reality increased as we crossed the square to the other little stone building—the one that had been the family home. Temporarily, this was used as a chapel, though later it was to be the community center, for its arrangement—two small rooms, two large ones and a patio—make it eminently suitable for this. But until the renovation of the original church is completed, the Blessed Sacrament will be here, and we all paused to pray before starting back to Lima.

Most of the time on the return trip, I was less mindful of the countryside than I had been in the morning, for I was deep in thought; and though twice I was diverted, these interruptions only served to give me further food for reflection. The first revival of awareness to my surroundings came as we approached the village where we had previously found everyone patiently waiting for the arrival of the "Señor de los Milagros"; now the fragrance of incense and the sound of singing were wafted toward us and, presently, the little procession came into sight: the sacred image on its flower-banked and candlelighted *paso*, the acolytes, the purple-clad men and women. There was no censer to serve as a container for the incense; instead, a girl, walking backward, in order to face the image, lifted an earthen vessel high above her and from this the scented fumes arose. Indian children, drawn up on either side of the road, were strewing flowers in the pathway of the procession; the vendors in the little fruit stall had left their counter to join in the singing; only the oldest and most infirm were taking no active part in the celebration; but lame, halt and blind as they were, their exaltation transcended their crippled bodies, their sightless eyes and their ragged garments.

The entire scene was infinitely moving. Lacking the majesty and the multitudes of the great ceremonies in the city, it somehow seemed to surpass them in this single-heartedness.

The second diversion came as we approached the little chapel high on the hill. Instinctively, Deanie slowed down the car; she knew we would all want to look at it again, that it would have more meaning for us now that we had spent the day in Quives and had seen for ourselves something of the work done by the man who, undaunted by the lack of a bell, calls his people to worship at the shrine of their saint with an accordion. Somehow I believe that, when this Mass begins, she is close in spirit to the place where she paused as she trudged along on the hard road between the "City of Kings" and the mines and the mountains. As far as that goes, she seemed very close to me as I went back to Lima that afternoon.

The second episode which led to my rediscovery of Santa Rosa was quite different.

Late one afternoon, I received a telephone call, asking if I would be willing to see "for five minutes" a man who was a total stranger to me, but who said he believed he had in his possession material that would be important to me. There was every reason why I should have said no. In the first place, I learned long ago that no conference of any kind can be satisfactorily completed in five minutes, least of all one of importance. In the second place, though of course material on some given subject has been offered to me over and over again, as it is to any professional writer, only once in my whole life had such material been of value to me, and then the offer had come from a very old friend, well acquainted with exactly what I was trying to find, which could not be the case in this instance. In the third place, I was exhausted; I had been up very early that morning to see one of the great processions and, after that, a series of appointments, some of them resulting in a state of great confusion, had come piling on top of each other. Now I was awaiting a visit from Dr. John Leddy Phelan, a Professor of History at the University of Wisconsin, who was currently in South America on a Guggenheim Fellowship. He had been doing research in Ecuador at the same time I was and we had discovered mutual interest in the same historical character. We were planning a further discussion of this dignitary's attributes, so that the results of our work would complement each other's. Even this was more than I felt I should attempt when I was nearly frantic with fatigue. In spite of all these good reasons to the contrary, I felt impelled to say yes to the request for a five minute interview.

Dr. Phelan had already arrived when the stranger, who introduced himself as Malcolm Burke, was announced. He brought with him a large envelope and, without waste of words, informed me that it contained a manuscript—on which he had been working for years—that was based on the testimony given during the Process which resulted in the beatification and canonization of Santa Rosa, whom he had set his heart on making better known. He had done his research with the greatest care in the Archives of the Archepiscopal Palace and he was convinced that he had succeeded in unearthing and setting down facts of value which were either unknown to many of her biographers or disregarded by them. But he had not succeeded in convincing any publisher that his manuscript would make a readable book. He had reached the sad conclusion that he was not destined to interpret this saint to the public after all, and as he hoped I might be the one to do it, he had come to offer me his material. If it would be of any help to me in my work, he would be very glad. If I could not use it, that would not matter, since it was clear to him that no one else would use it.

Almost with one voice, Dr. Phelan and I urged him to go on trying to place the manuscript himself. We could both assure him, from sad personal experience, that sometimes material, after being turned down over and over again, eventually found not only a receptive publisher, but a responsive public. Mr. Burke reiterated he was sure this would not be so in his case; anyway, he was through trying. I then appealed to him on other grounds: I did not feel I could take the responsibility for his manuscript (though I would try to give it every care); sometimes there were accidents as lamentable as they were unexpected. Hotel chambermaids had been known to throw away material left around for reference, even when they had been cautioned that nothing on a desk should be touched. There was always the possibility of fire. Even publishers, who had every facility for safeguarding material, were wary about promising to do so and, indeed, often refused to.

These arguments also left Mr. Burke quite unmoved. It would not matter, he said, if the material were lost or destroyed; he had a copy. But even without this, he would not care. It was hopeless as far as he was concerned.

The futile discussion had lasted nearly an hour when he deposited the envelope on the coffee table and rose to go. It was obvious that nothing would swerve him from his purpose and I was distressed. I was still more distressed the following day, when I received a note from him, saying he would not intrude again, after having once forced himself on me; as far as he was concerned, I could throw away the manuscript. It was easy to tell from the tone of the note that I must have appeared to him both very ungracious and very unco-operative when, as a matter of fact, I had tried, despite my exhaustion and preoccupation, to receive him courteously, to listen to his story and, having heard it, to give him encouragement to persevere himself. It seemed tragic to me, considering my own realization of the amount of work he must have done, that he should not receive the full benefit for it himself. In my answer to his note, I tried to explain all this again; then I settled down to read his manuscript.

Whether by accident or design, letters from two of the publishers who had turned it down had been left among the sheets. I had read only about twenty pages before I came to the first of these and, even then, I thought I recognized the reasons why it had been written as it was. By the time I came to the second letter, I was sure I knew. This was not a biography, in the usual sense of the word; that is, it did not give the story of a life with events and experiences chronologically arranged; it was not, strictly speaking, a narrative. This being the case, it probably would not have been considered as such, even if it had been prepared and presented in the form upon which busy and important publishers are more and more insistent: that is, with careful pagination and complete uniformity of margin, with impeccable punctuation and spelling, without typographical errors or handwritten interpolations. Unfortunately, it did not meet such requirements; and in these days publishers and their readers are impatient, wanting everything presented to them in such perfect form that they will not have to hunt for sequences or puzzle over penmanship. I truly believe that they are the losers by this. The merest glance at the manuscripts of some of the greatest writers who have ever lived shows that someone must have had to work hard to decipher them; it also shows that such labor had rich rewards.

I read on, with the sad but growing conviction that what Mr. Burke had told me was true: his manuscript was not likely to find favor with any publisher, at least in its present form, and whether or not he could write it over as a neat and readable narrative, I had no way of knowing, without learning more of his capabilities, not only as a creative writer, but as a typist and a copyreader. But for his capabilities as a researcher, I quickly came to have the greatest respect. He had investigated the testimony of every witness in the Process for Canonization and had listed each one separately, in chronological order. This part of the manuscript alone had immense value as source material, but it represented only a small portion of the whole; it was supplemented by twenty-one chapters, each one clearly titled as to its content—Posthumous Miracles—Perseverance, Active—Perseverance, Passive—Lyrics—Signs and Wonders—Clairvoyance—Home Life. In all the chapters the witnesses were quoted at length, with annotations in the order in which they had appeared, thus facilitating cross reference, and to these quotations were added Mr. Burke's own comments—sometimes very serious, sometimes half jesting, sometimes colloquial, but always thoughtful and intelligently expressed. As far as I was concerned, his script was a treasure trove. I spent the better part of two nights going through it, then I wrote him as follows:

"Thank you for your letter of October 18th, written shortly after you left here.

"I am sorry you feel that, in coming to see me, you were 'forcing yourself and your manuscript on my attention.' I did not feel that way at all. It so happened, however, that I had had a very full day on Tuesday and that I was already exhausted when you telephoned and I already had a professional appointment with Dr. Phelan ahead of me. You did seem urgent and as you said you would need to be here a few minutes, I thought I might wedge in one more conference. The mistake was mine; I should have waited until you and I could talk at leisure, for I should have learned, long before this, that nothing of importance can be settled in five minutes.

"Moreover, Dr. Phelan and I were both completely sincere in saying that we felt you should persevere in the attempt to market your script yourself. Having had a great many discouraging experiences, as I told you, which in the end brought about good results, I hoped the same might be true of you. However, now that I have read the letters you have received from two publishers, I am forced to agree that, in its present condition, your manuscript would probably never be published.

"This does not mean, however, that you have failed to perform a work of great value. I have read the manuscript from start to finish and out of the 278 pages which, according to my count, it contains, there are no less than 90 on which I have found some item which would be of value to me. In some cases, this only gives me an idea; in other cases, it is only a sentence; in still others, it is a complete paragraph. I should welcome the opportunity of talking with you about these items, but, as I am very far behind in my working schedule and am still trying to finish dealing with the material I expected to complete in Quito, I should rather wait until that is done before talking with you about your work and the part it might play in mine. I estimate it will take me about ten days more to get in the clear and, with your permission, I will write you again at that time.

"No reputable writer, at least in my experience, accepts reference material from another without paying for it, both in cash and in kind. Certainly, if you permit me to use your material, your name should be mentioned in the Author's Note as having provided the source. Just how much you should be paid for it is something that would have to be a matter of mutual agreement, but I hope and believe we could reach this without too much difficulty.

"Let me thank you again for putting at my disposal this very valuable material."

This letter resulted in a prompt and pleasant answer from him and then in a series of conferences.

Unfortunately—that is, from my point of view—Mr. Burke was soon to depart on an assignment for the *Peruvian Times*—a periodical to which he regularly contributes travel articles and photographs—that would take him from Lima to navigable Ucayali and then to Iquitos, Belém, Pará and New York. So these conferences could be neither as frequent nor as leisurely as I would have wished, for both professional and personal reasons. I knew he could open up many more avenues of information, which I was having difficulty in exploring and, besides, I found him agreeable company. I would have welcomed him as an out and out collaborator in my work, as well as an invaluable contributor to it. A Yale graduate and an ex-naval officer, he first came to Peru thirteen years ago on a one year contract with the State Department, to direct the Instituto Cultural Peruano-Norteamericano; and—as in the case of Dr. Giesecke—the country proved to have a lasting attraction for him. He has delved more and more deeply into its history, while using it as a base for various types of writing, including articles for *Reader's Digest* and staff work for *Vision*. He has had two books published, one in English and one in Spanish. His industry must be prodigious; of his talents there can be no possible doubt. It would have meant much to me to take advantage of both.

Nevertheless, I was at last on the right road, thanks, in a measure I have tried to indicate, first to María Rosario Araoz, then to Father Dalle and, finally, to Malcolm Burke. I was no longer limited, as far as a happy conception of her was concerned, to Santa Rosa as she appeared in her garden, or to an unhappy conception of her as an ascetic. I could see her as a child in the mountains, an industrious social worker, a talented poetess and musician, a rapt mystic, and a ministering angel. Now I must try to make others see her in all these beautiful and inspiring aspects.

But to accomplish that, I could not begin with her. "Accustomed as we are to see saints in the sky, we forget that their origin was the earth. Saints have never been persons wholly of legend. They were born in a certain country, they belonged to a certain city, they developed in a certain social medium, they represent a certain epoch and, because of all this, it is of historical interest to become acquainted with their families. These can tell us the why and wherefore of many things which would otherwise be obscure in hagiography. So let us become acquainted with the father of the first American saint, and place him definitely in his social order." [6]

This is good advice, as far as it goes. But I do not think we can "place him definitely in his social order" until we know more about that social order than can be learned merely by identifying Santa Rosa's father, Gaspar de Flores, as a dashing Puerto Rican who, after long and varied military service, became an *arcabucero* [harquebusier] in the Viceroy's guard, eventually married a Limenian younger than himself and sired thirteen children. In fact, we must go all the way back to Spain, find the route to Lima, learn who took it and how and why and then we must discover what manner of city it was and how it became such a city and why, toward the end of the sixteenth century. And to do all this, we must first make the acquaintance of a runaway swineherd, who escaped from his repugnant task, boldly set out for Seville from Estremadura, and leaped aboard a caravel that was about to sail for the New World.

The name of this swineherd was Francisco Pizarro.

BOOK I

The Rose

PROLOGUE

1

F RANCISCO PIZARRO was the illegitimate son of Gonzalo Pizarro, a Spanish captain of infantry, who had served with some distinction in the Italian Wars, and Francisca Gonzalez, a poor peasant woman who had somehow attracted his transient attention. Although the captain did not deny the paternity and does not seem to have begrudged his bastard the use of a name which, on the whole, was an honorable one, neither does he appear to have done very much for the boy otherwise, and his mother did even less. According to at least one historian,[7] she actually abandoned him, as a newborn infant, on the steps of a church, whence he was rescued by a humble passer-by, who could provide nothing better than a sow as a wet-nurse for the unfortunate little foundling. Perhaps this story has not much more foundation than the similar one about Romulus and Remus, though its origin is not as obscured by the mists of time (reckoned by centuries); and Francisco's youthful occupation seems a logical link with such a tale.

Be all this as it may, he certainly grew up in miserable surroundings, untaught and uncherished; but somehow stories of the gold, recently discovered in the New World, and the glory which went with its discovery, seeped through to him and fired his dormant imagination. He made his getaway from Trujillo, found the road to Seville, boarded a caravel there and eventually landed in Hispaniola.

From the first, he found opportunities for exploits to suit his venturesome spirit, and revealed rare qualities of resourcefulness and endurance, as well as daring; while the names of the persons with whom he managed to associate himself are outstanding in the pages of history.

After taking part in an expedition to Uraba in Tierra Firme under Alonso de Ojeda, we find him in Panama, first with Balboa, "silent upon a peak in Darien," and later attached to the forces of the governor, Don Pedro Arias de Avila [commonly known as Pedrarias]. The governor sent him on various military missions and "his name became conspicuous among the cavaliers who extended the line of conquest to the north. And there, while engaged in collecting his booty of gold and pearls from the neighboring islands, as his eye ranged over the shadowy line of coast till it faded in the distance, his imagination may have been first fired with the idea of, one day, attempting the conquest of the mysterious regions beyond the mountains." [8]

At all events, when Pascual de Andagoya, who had already been sent to explore "the mysterious regions" which lay to the south, returned to Panama with "more copious accounts than any hitherto received of the opulence and grandeur of the lands that lay beyond," though he had penetrated only to the Puerta de Piñas, a relatively short distance from Panama, "southern expeditions became a common topic of speculation among the colonists." This was enough to convince Pizarro that he himself should be on his way south before some still bolder spirit beat him to the draw; and though he was already fifty years of age and far richer in glory than in gold, these obvious disadvantages did not daunt him. He succeeded in firing the imagination of two boon companions: Diego de Almagro, a fellow soldier of fortune who, like himself, had started life as a foundling, but who, also like himself, was personable and persuasive; and Hernándo de Luque, a highly respected and far-seeing Spanish priest, "who exercised the functions of vicar at Panama." [9] Two small vessels were purchased, a crew assembled, of something more than a hundred hangers-on in the colony, and, in November, 1524, Pizarro set sail in the larger vessel, with the understanding that Almagro would follow as soon as possible in the smaller.

Almost from the first, the expedition seemed doomed to disaster. It had hardly passed the points already familiar through the voyages of Balboa and Andagoya—the Isle of Pearls, the Gulf of St. Michael, the Puerta de Piñas—when its troubles began. In his ignorance of climatic conditions, Pizarro had chosen the worst possible time of year for putting to sea. His progress was impeded by contrary winds and his ship lashed by tempests. When he ventured ashore, conditions were even worse: vast swamps and impenetrable forests were all he and his men found. They were bogged down by the rains and overpowered by the heat; worst of all, they found absolutely nothing to eat in these dank depressing regions except some berries which proved to be poisonous. Inevitably, most of them lost heart, complaining that they had been misled by promises of rich rewards and instead were facing death and destruction. They clamored for a return to Panama.

With a less indomitable leader, they would certainly have had their way. "But Pizarro was prepared to encounter much greater evils than these, before returning to Panama, bankrupt in credit, an object of derision as a vainglorious dreamer, who had persuaded others to embark in an adventure which he had not the courage to carry through himself. *The present was his only chance.*" Yet, after using "every argument that mortified pride or avarice could suggest," [9] he consented to a compromise: he himself would remain at one of the ports where they had put in for water and wood, and send his lieutenant, Montenegro, back to the Isle of Pearls for provisions; those who preferred to go with him, instead of remaining with their leader, were at liberty to do so. About half the company eagerly took advantage of the opportunity thus presented and Montenegro lost no time in weighing anchor.

Weeks passed and still there were no signs of his returning vessel or of the second one, which had been left behind at Panama in charge of Almagro. There was more and more sickness; there were more and more deaths. Finally, a vague rumor reached Pizarro that a light had been seen somewhere in the distance, through an opening in the woods, which seemed to suggest that it might mark an Indian settlement. He had already tried to penetrate the forest without success, but now he decided to try again. This time, he was rewarded. After thrashing and chopping his way along, he came to a small village, whose inhabitants promptly fled in fright; but they had not run so fast that the Spaniards, who possessed a keen eye for such details, failed to note that the crude ornaments these Indians wore were made of gold. What was more, they had left provender behind them, in the form of maize and coconuts. The starving explorers fell to and devoured everything in sight. When the fugitives, somewhat reassured because no violence had been offered them, began to creep back, some kind of communication was established between the two groups, by means of sign language. How much Pizarro actually understood is open to doubt; but he convinced his followers that they need press on only a little further south before finding the rich land they were seeking; and, fortuitously, Montenegro finally returned with fresh supplies before the impetus given to the spirits of the men had lost its force. They were now ready and eager to go on. When they left the place which Pizarro had appropriately named Puerto de Hambre—Port of Hunger—and again headed south, it was with renewed hopes and renewed zest.

Unfortunately, two subsequent landings, though resulting in the acquisition of gold as well as food, were disastrous in other ways. In one, the Indians, who deserted their village as the Spaniards approached it, left behind them the dreadful telltale signs of cannibalism. It was the explorers' turn to retreat, as rapidly as possible, and in their haste to reach safety, they did not realize that there was literally little to choose between the devil and the deep blue sea. A raging tempest so battered their poor little craft that it was obviously unfit for weathering further storms; so again they landed and, this time, they encountered not cannibals, but warriors. Far from fleeing at the strangers' approach, the male Indians, having removed their women and children to a place of safety (thereby providing the Spaniards with an interval in which they could help themselves to the golden trinkets which had been left lying about) returned armed with poisoned arrows. Again, Pizarro showed his extraordinary skill as a leader; calling on his men to follow him, he rushed forward to meet the enemy on their own ground. He was easily recognized as the chief, singled out for the most furious attack and, despite his armor, wounded in seven places. But he fought on and on. Even when he slipped and fell, he regained his footing so fast that the Indians were not able to take advantage of his fall and dispatch him. On the contrary, he succeeded in striking down two of them at the same moment when Montenegro came rushing up from the rear with reinforcements. The battle was over and the Spaniards had won.

It was, however, a Pyrrhic victory. Pizarro made light of his own injuries, but he had not the heart to do so in the case of the others who had been wounded, and it was clear that it would not be safe to keep them where they were; the Indians might return at any time and attack again. Moreover, there were no facilities available at Pueblo Quemado, as Pizarro had named this place,[10] for restoring the ship, and as it could not be expected to withstand any more furious gales it would have to go limping back to the first place which offered some prospects, however slender, of salvage. Pizarro still could not make up his mind to face the governor with a story to which he could not give glamour, no matter how hard he tried; but at last he consented to go back as far as Chicamá, a place on the mainland not far from Panama, and from there to dispatch his treasurer, Nicolás de Ribera, to His Excellency with such gold as had been collected—enough to show that, after all, the land at the south was not devoid of promise.

It was while he was impatiently waiting de Ribera's return at Chicamá that Almagro at last made connections with him. The former had an exciting tale to tell: he had been able to locate the places where Pizarro had stopped by a method of identification on which they had long since agreed: that of notching trees. At Pueblo Quemado, Almagro, too, had been attacked and he, too, had wrested a hard won victory from the Indians, at the price of a javelin wound which eventually blinded him in one eye. Then he had continued to cruise southward, and had been struck by signs of a greater degree of civilization than he had hitherto observed, as well as by the beauty of the countryside. He had also been rewarded with considerable booty in gold. But when he failed to find further notches on trees and realized that his friend had not gone as far south as he had, he became anxious as to the fate of the first expedition and turned back. The reunion at Chicamá was a joyous one.

Nevertheless, glad as they were to see each other, the two explorers agreed that they should not waste too much time in exchanging adventurous stories. With the gold which Almagro could show the governor, added to that with which de Ribera had already departed, it should not be too difficult to convince Pedrarias that another expedition should be outfitted, especially if they could again count on co-operation from de Luque. Leaving Pizarro, who still steadfastly refused to plead his own cause, though the alternative was to remain in uncomfortable quarters where he was almost devoured by insects, Almagro left for Panama, and Pizarro settled down to await the return of his partner and his treasurer.

2

The governor, who had been experiencing annoying reverses in a campaign in Nicaragua and was in an irritable frame of mind, failed to lend a willing ear to de Ribera and Almagro; but he was at last won over, largely through the good offices of de Luque, who was as enthusiastic as ever on the subject of further exploration. Pedrarias, however, made several conditions in giving his consent. One of these was that Almagro and Pizarro—who had left his retreat at Chicamá and come to Panama as soon as negotiations took a turn for the better—should have equal rank: a provision that sowed seeds of jealousy in the latter's heart and was eventually to have disastrous consequences. The governor next stipulated that he should be paid a thousand pesos in gold as the price of his good will. This being settled, the three directly concerned in the enterprise—Almagro, Pizarro and de Luque—subscribed to a solemn pact, in which they agreed to divide equally all conquered territory. Two ships were bought, bigger and better than those in which they had started out before, with larger crews to man them, and a greater store of foodstuffs, as well as more ammunition and a few horses. Then the two captains, each in his own vessel, set sail, under the direction of Bartolomeo Ruiz "a sagacious and resolute pilot." [8] Without stopping at any of the points which they had touched before, and of which their memories were anything but happy, they steered directly to the Rio de San Juan. This was the southernmost limit previously reached by Almagro, which had made such a favorable impression on him before, and which now more than fulfilled its promise, in the form of both gold and prisoners. The two chiefs decided to split their forces again. As usual, it fell to Pizarro's lot to remain on shore. Meanwhile, Almagro went back to Panama to report progress, with visible and tangible signs of this, and to seek more recruits, which he was confident he would now have no trouble in securing; while Ruiz took the other vessel and reconnoitered to the south.

Ruiz first cast anchor at the small nearby Island of Gallo, next proceeded to what is now called the Bay of St. Matthew, and eventually advanced as far as Punta de Pasado, a feat which earned him the distinction of being the first European to cross the equatorial line. He was encouraged by everything he saw: the countryside, more and more rich and fertile; the inhabitants, more and more cultured and elegantly dressed; the rafts which the natives called balsas, ingeniously made of reeds and light wood; the woolen cloth, the embroideries and the ornaments of gold and silver. He returned to the Rio de San Juan, with his favorable report only shortly before Almagro came back from Panama with one equally favorable.

It was high time. Pizarro had experienced nothing but bad luck during their absence. If the pleasant country they had been promised they would find in the locality really existed, then it was beyond his reach. The forests were almost as impenetrable as those they had tried to forge through in the course of their first expedition; and whereas the others had been empty of all animal life except insects, these teemed with shrieking birds, chattering monkeys and horrible reptiles. Many of the Spaniards had perished miserably, the victims of alligators and boa constrictors; others had been cut off by hostile natives when they ventured out in a canoe and were stranded on a riverbank; still others had starved to death, for again there was nothing wholesomely edible in these malign regions. The survivors could not get aboard ship fast enough to suit them, though the sight of new recruits and abundant food and the good reports brought by both pilot and captain temporarily silenced the renewed clamor for a return to Panama. They were willing to go on.

But this mood did not last long. Terrible storms drove them to take refuge and repair their ships on the Island of Gallo, where Ruiz had stopped before; and though eventually they reached the Bay of St. Matthew and the coast beyond, to be impressed, as he had been, with the beauty of the land and the evidences of culture and wealth among the inhabitants, it soon became clear that these not only intended to fight, but were well equipped to do so. Again mutiny seemed very near among the Spaniards and, this time, a hot dispute between the captains added fuel to the flames. Almagro was proposing an arrangement similar to those which had been successfully tried before: that is, he would return to Panama with good reports and secure more and more recruits; Pizarro would withdraw to some safer place and await his return. To this, Pizarro retorted that he had had enough of being left behind and watching his men die like flies while he was powerless to help them. He refused to be placated even when Almagro offered to reverse the previous arrangement and stay behind while his fellow captain went back to Panama. Dauntless as he was in all other respects, Pizarro recoiled from the very idea of facing an indifferent governor and begging him for assistance. The two had almost come to blows when Ruiz succeeded in separating them, and the disastrous effect of their quarrel on the morale of the men was inevitable. Besides, a safe place to withdraw to did not seem easy to come by; when one that might serve the purpose was finally found, it was not anywhere on the pleasant shore, but on the insignificant and barren little Island of Gallo. The men whose lot it was to be left behind hastened to write all their friends, saying they were being futilely sacrificed for avarice and ambition; and Almagro, suspecting that something of the sort was taking place, ordered all letters on board his ship destroyed.

This was not only a dictatorial and inhuman procedure; it was also completely illegal. "Letters were sacred and uncensored, a Spanish tradition for which the *Cortes* of Castile had stood firm, from mediaeval days. In 1386, the *Cortes* of Segovia remonstrated with King John I over some cases of postal censorship. The royal orders which extended this principle to the Indies laid it down that letters were to be respected and that 'no one was to steal or open them, nor to hinder the liberty everyone had to write and send letters to the King our Lord and to his Royal Council, as and whenever he might wish.' As

early as 1509, the Crown warned Diego Colón, the second Admiral of
the Indies and heir of the Discoverer: 'That he should not prevent
anyone from writing to Castile, for in this it seemed there had been a
certain amount of oppression.' " [11] Philip II had indeed instituted a
postal system for the Colonies more effective than was then customary
anywhere else in the world and like many another unjust act, before
and since, Almagro's proved a boomerang. A soldier by the name of
Sarabia suspected that something of the sort might happen and hid
his letter in a ball of cotton, which was being sent as a present to the
governor's wife. Naturally, its discovery automatically revealed the order
which necessitated such a ruse. Public indignation ran high and official
action was indicated. The governor angrily declined to listen to Almagro's petitions, or even to look at the treasure he had brought with him.
He would get no more supplies, no more ships; he was not even to
leave Panama. Vessels would be sent out under the command of
another officer, to bring back the wretched survivors of the expedition,
who had been so cheated and abused. As to Pizarro, the governor
washed his hands of that miscreant.

The two rescue ships, captained by a cavalier named Tafur and
well stocked with provisions, reached Gallo safely and promptly, and
nearly all Pizarro's men crowded quickly around it, asking for nothing
better than to board it and be on their way back to Panama. Pizarro
paid no attention to them; he was engaged in reading letters from Almagro and de Luque. Evidently there had been no effort to destroy or
intercept these; perhaps the ball of cotton had furnished cogent proof
that it was better not to tamper with personal correspondence; perhaps
Tafur felt that the instructions with which he left Panama—namely,
that no further help was on any account to be given Pizarro—would
be sufficient to restrain him from any further rashness, whatever the
contents of the letters. Be that as it may, he finished reading them,
pocketed them and stepped forward. Then he drew his sword and
traced a line from east to west in the sand.

"On that side," he said, pointing to the north, "lie poverty and
shame. If those are what you want, go back to Panama. On this side,"
he continued, pointing to the south, "lie wealth and glory and Peru.
Make your choice. I am going south." Without more ado, he stepped
across the line.

Thirteen followed him. "And with them, he began the Conquest of
Peru. Glory was their portion, and the line that Pizarro drew in the
sand has not been effaced by the shifting winds of the centuries." [12]

Such were the circumstances under which the famous Pact of Gallo was made.[13] And seven years later Pizarro, crowned with riches and honors founded the "very noble, very illustrious and very loyal City of the Kings which they called Lima." [8]

3

It had been no part of Pizarro's original plan to place his capital where he eventually did. But San Miguel de Piura, the site of his first settlement, was too far up the coast to meet his purpose; and Cuzco, the ancient capital of the unfortunate Incas whom he completely subjugated, was too far inland and doubly inaccessible because of its location high among the Andes. After judging that both were unsuitable, he came upon the fruitful valley of Pachacamac, and after giving this consideration, decided on the still more pleasing valley of Rimac, through which flowed a beautiful river; and on the banks of this, a short distance from its mouth, which widened to join the sea in a fine harbor, he founded the city which he called the *Ciudad de los Reyes* (City of the Kings), because its site was determined on Twelfth Night—January 6, 1535.[14]

So far, Pizarro, who had achieved the title of Marquis during a brief visit to Spain and had brought his brothers, Hernándo and Juan, with him to profit by his good fortune in the New World, had revealed himself not only as an adventurer, explorer, and leader, but also—sad to say—as a destroyer. In his greed for gold and power, he had ruthlessly stolen from the defenseless and trustful Incas, slaughtered them and razed their monuments. This is a dark chapter in his story, one which cannot be denied and should not be ignored. But unlike the record of his exploration and the Pact of Gallo, it has no direct bearing on the story of our heroine; so having sadly admitted its truth, we may proceed to the next phase of his self-revelation, which was that of a builder.

Lima was laid out "with great care and sagacity. The area of the city was divided like a chessboard into 117 islands or squares. Each block of 18,762 square yards was divided into four lots. The broad, straight streets were laid out from southeast to northwest so that at every hour of the day there would be shade on one side, and at the same time the trade winds, which blow steadily from the south, would enter obliquely, to ensure a moderate circulation of air. This wise arrangement of the streets adopted by the Marquis, at the advice of 'experts and people of understanding,' made it possible to see the countryside from the *Plaza Mayor*, and, in the distance, the sea. History has handed down to us the names of those who shared in the founding of the city with Pizarro. Thirteen they were, including himself, the same number that followed him on the Isle of Gallo.[15] Apparently this was his lucky number. The names of the founders of Lima were: Nicolás de Ribera the elder and Juan Tello, the two first mayors; Alonso Riquelme, comptroller; García de Salcedo, supervisor; Nicolás de Ribera the younger; Rodrigo de Mazuelas, Ruiz Díaz, Alonso Martín de Don Benito, Cristóbal Palomino, Diego de Agüero, Antonio Picado, secretary to the governor, and Alonso Tinoco, who was the first priest of Lima. In addition to the founders there were thirty Spaniards who had come from San Gayán and twenty-five Indians from Jauja. Building sites were apportioned to these settlers, for which, in the absence of money, they had to pay a number of chickens annually, an arrangement which was modified five years later.

"Thus laid out and divided, the new city began to grow and become populated with an urge for life and grandeur. . . . What it lacked in wealth, which the horn of fortune was not yet pouring out upon it but was depositing in the powerful hold of Spain-bound galleons, it made up for, from its birth, in honors and heraldic pomp. Charles V. in 1537, magnanimously allowed it to display on its coat of arms crowns, which are the symbol of royalty; columns, in tribute to its unswerving loyalty; and a star, to preside over its brilliant future. . . . During its first century the broad and silent city grew about the *Plaza Mayor*. Without pomp and without vanity the humble facades of the houses arose. . . . The only thing on which the city laid special emphasis was its churches. Piety erected churches without interruption and every year a new tower reared itself aloft, from which yet another bell might call to endless prayer. Pizarro himself had begun them, laying 'with his own hands the first stone and the first beams' of the church which later was to be the cathedral of Lima, consecrated to Our Lady of the Assumption. Hernándo Pizarro a little later ordered the Convent and the Church of La Merced built. This was shortly followed by that of San Francisco, in 1535; the Chapel of Vera Cruz, endowed by Pizarro, in 1540; the *Sagrario* in 1541. . . . Meanwhile the city was devoid of palaces and avenues. . . . But the city gladly suffered these shortcomings for the sake of seeing more stone-carved church porticoes and the silhouettes of more slender towers rising above the flat surface of its buildings.

"The city indulged its leisure with another whim, according to Friar Reginaldo de Lizarraga and Father Cobo,[16] in the laying out of the large, perfumed gardens with which it surrounded its buildings. The heavily fruited branches of the trees displayed their verdure and their fragrance above the high adobe walls. Father Cobo, with his eye for detail, says that 'all the houses are roomy and large, with great patios, barnyards, orchards, and gardens.' And Friar Reginaldo, in flowery phrases, says that 'from the outside it does not look like a city but a grove, with its many orchards filled with orange trees, grapevines, pomegranates and other fruit trees of the kind that grow there, and the irrigation ditches that crisscross it.'

"Sixteenth-century Lima put its heart and soul into its churches and its gardens. It was built of rough materials, devoid of all improvements, without water, police, light, or sanitation, lacking in civic pride and the, as yet unknown, pleasures of comfort; yet it could boast that the melancholy sound of its bells soothed the soul and the wafted perfume of its honeysuckle and jasmine intoxicated the spirit.

"The phrase of José Galvez has a twofold musical and floral meaning: 'Lima, the city of church bells and flower bells.' " [17]

From the beginning, the government of Lima was planned on a majestic scale and when the first Viceroy,[18] Blasco Núñez Vela, arrived in 1544 it was ready to receive him with all due ceremony. "He entered in great state, under a canopy of crimson cloth, embroidered with the arms of Spain, and supported by stout poles or staves of solid silver, which were borne by the members of the municipality. A cavalier, holding a mace, the emblem of authority, rode before him; and after the oaths of office were administered in the council-chamber, the procession moved towards the cathedral, where *Te Deum* was sung, and Blasco Núñez was installed in his new dignity of Viceroy of Peru." [8]

It would appear, to the average observer, that he should have been wholly worthy of such a welcome. He was a Knight of Avila, where, to this day, his memory is held in the greatest reverence and his palace carefully preserved; he came of a great Castilian family, and had already filled various official posts to the satisfaction of the Emperor, Charles V. In person, he was handsome, carrying his advancing years well, and in character, he was brave, compassionate, loyal and devout. Unfortunately, however, his conception of duty was such that it "precluded all discretionary exercise of authority, even when the public good demanded it"; [8] and he was arbitrary, irritable and suspicious. These qualities had antagonized many of his associates when he was still as far distant as Panama from the seat of his legal authority; before he actually reached Peru, an uprising against him and the measures he advocated and meant to enforce had been skilfully organ- ized and as skilfully put into action by Gonzalo Pizarro, the brother of Francisco (who had come to a violent and untimely end three years earlier).

The new Viceroy did not, at first, take this uprising very seriously. He contented himself, if not his few faithful followers, by sending a message to Gonzalo at the latter's camp, calling attention to the supremacy of Viceregal powers and ordering that the rebel forces be disbanded at once. Understandably, this slap on the wrist had little effect on a leader whose strength was increasing by the minute; and presently the Viceroy came to the unwelcome realization that mili- tary measures were necessary for the protection of Lima, against which Gonzalo was steadily advancing. The good will of the Judges of the *Audiencia*,[19] whose support would have been invaluable, had already been jeopardized in Panama, whither they had gone to meet the new Viceroy, and now they thwarted him at every turn.

Blasco Núñez next made a mistake which was fatal in the literal sense of the word: during a heated argument, he struck with his poniard a cavalier by the name of Suarez de Carbajal, whom he suspected of disloyalty and whom he had summoned to the palace for a conference. The Viceregal attendants took this accidental blow, which was prompted by rage but not by murderous design, as a signal to dispatch the visitor, whose corpse was hastily removed and as hastily buried. It was impossible to hush, for long, such a horrible secret. Carbajal's grave was found and his mutilated body disinterred. "From this hour, Blasco Núñez was held in universal abhorrence." [8]

His next action, though certainly less criminal, seems inexplicably cowardly, for otherwise his career was at least characterized by courage. Instead of pursuing either one of two logical courses—that of march- ing out to meet the enemy or continuing his defense of Lima with every means at his disposal—he decided to withdraw the government to Truxillo, sending women, children and supplies by sea and himself leading a destructive army overland. The *Audiencia* opposed such a plan as illegal; and supported by the populace, deposed the Viceroy and dispatched him to a desolate island, there to await transportation, first to Panama and then back to Spain.

He was saved from this final humiliation by a change of heart on the part of one of the Judges that enabled him to board a ship from

Santa Rosa de Lima. Spanish School. Prado Museum, Madrid.

Well in Santa Rosa's Garden.

Entrance to Santa Rosa's Garden.

Hermitage in Santa Rosa's Garden.

As it appears today.

QUIVES

Church where Santa Rosa was confirmed.

Entrance to the Convent of the Nazarene Nuns, Lima.

House of the Flores family in Quives.

Harbor of Lima, as seen from Callao.

Plaza de Armas, Lima.

Paseo de Aguas.

LIMA

Old Bridge.

Ladies of Lima saying their Rosary.   Ladies of Lima out for fun.

Coach of a Judge in the Royal *Audiencia*.

STATUES OF SANTA ROSA DE LIMA

In the room where she died. Sculptor unknown (Presumably Chinese, from its style).

In the Quito Cathedral. Sculptor unknown.

Two statues in the Church of San Francisco, Quito. Both by Caspicara.

which he disembarked at Tumbez and headed toward Quito, gathering new forces as he went. Meanwhile, the *Audiencia* had been having its troubles: Gonzalo had been successful, not only in reaching Lima with his revolutionists, but also in making short shift of the *Audiencia's* pre-eminence by getting himself proclaimed Governor; and he then proceeded to pursue the unfortunate Viceroy in hot haste, catching up with him at Añaquito. Fighting bravely on and on, against terrible odds, Blasco Núñez, who was already wounded, fell stunned to the ground, when a blow on the head from a battle-ax struck him from his horse. He was finally decapitated by a black slave, as a final mark of degradation, after he had been recognized by the Licentiate Carbajal, brother of the man whom the Viceroy had so fatally attacked at the palace. Gonzalo expressed himself as greatly shocked at such vengeful indignities; ordered the body of his enemy interred with all honors in the cathedral and attended the funeral clad in elegant black, as chief mourner at a state funeral. "It was usual with the Pizarros," Prescott (the historian) drily observes, "to pay these obituary honors to their victims."

Gonzalo doubtless felt he could well afford to take the center of the stage at such a spectacle now that his only visible rival for supreme power was eliminated; and, as a matter of fact, he showed gracious clemency to those of the Viceroy's former followers who now flocked to follow him. He could well afford to do this, too, for his star was on the ascendant. When he returned to Lima, his entry was quite as impressive as the one made by Blasco Núñez. "A procession was formed of the citizens, the soldiers, and the clergy, and Pizarro made his entry into the capital with two of his principal captains on foot, holding the reins of his charger, while the archbishop of Lima, and the bishops of Cuzco, Quito, and Bogotá, the last of whom had lately come to the city to be consecrated, rode by his side. The streets were strewn with boughs, the walls of the houses hung with showy tapestries, and triumphal arches were thrown over the way in honor of the victor. Every balcony, veranda, and house-top was crowded with spectators, who sent up huzzas, loud and long, saluting the victorious soldier with the titles of 'Liberator, and Protector of the people.' The bells rang out their joyous peal, as on his former entrance into the capital. . . .

"Gonzalo Pizarro was now undisputed master of Peru. . . . His forces were on an excellent footing, including the flower of the warriors who had fought under his brother, and who now eagerly rallied under the name of Pizarro; while the tide of wealth that flowed in from the mines of Potosí supplied him with the resources of an European monarch. The new governor now began to assume a state correspondent with his full-blown fortunes. He was attended by a body-guard of eighty soldiers. He dined always in public, and usually with not less than a hundred guests at table. He even affected, it was said, the most decided etiquette of royalty, giving his hand to be kissed, and allowing no one, of whatever rank, to be seated in his presence. . . . It is certain there were not wanting those who urged him to throw off his allegiance to the Crown and set up an independent government for himself. . . . But Gonzalo Pizarro shrunk from the attitude, in which this placed him, of avowed rebellion. Notwithstanding the criminal course into which he had been, of late, seduced, the sentiment of loyalty was too deeply implanted in his bosom to be wholly eradicated. Though in arms against the measures and ministers of his sovereign, he was not prepared to raise the sword against that sovereign himself." [8] Instead, with naïve optimism, surprising in one so habitually shrewd, he was preparing to undertake a mission to Spain. It was his purpose, once arrived there, to vindicate the course he had taken and ask for confirmation as the successor of his brother, in the role of supreme ruler of Peru.

In making this pleasing plan, he neglected to reckon with his host, which, in this case, was not the Emperor Charles V, who was temporarily absent from Spain, but Charles' son, Philip, acting as Regent for his father and holding Court at Valladolid. Philip who, years later, when an infirm old man, was to state with quiet conviction that he could sit at his desk and rule the world with two inches of paper, had already begun to show the sagacity which was to stamp him as the foremost monarch of his time and among the foremost of any time. "He called together a council of prelates, jurists and military men of greatest experience, to deliberate on the measures to be pursued for restoring order in the colonies. All agreed in regarding Pizarro's movement in the light of an audacious rebellion; and there were few, at first, who were not willing to employ the whole strength of government to vindicate the honor of the Crown,—to quell the insurrection, and bring the authors of it to punishment. But, however desirable this might appear, a very little reflection showed that it was not easy to be done, if, indeed, it were practicable. The great distance of Peru required troops to be transported not merely across the ocean, but over the broad extent of the great continent. . . . Nothing remained, therefore, but to try conciliatory measures. The government, however mortifying to its pride, must retrace its steps. A free grace must be extended to those who submitted, and such persuasive arguments should be used, and such politic concessions made, as would convince the refractory colonists that it was their interest, as well as their duty, to return to their allegiance. But to approach the people in their present state of excitement, and to make those concessions without too far compromising the dignity and permanent authority of the Crown, was a delicate matter, for the success of which they must rely wholly on the character of the agent. After much deliberation, a competent person, as it was thought, was found in an ecclesiastic, by the name of Pedro de la Gasca—a name, which, brighter by contrast with the gloomy times in which it first appeared, still shines with undiminished splendor after the lapse of ages." [8]

4

Pedro de la Gasca was born in Barco de Avila, a small village not far from the capital of the same province whence Blasco Núñez had come. Both had the proud heritage of a noble Castilian background; but whereas Blasco Núñez had seemed a favored child of fortune until near the tragic end of his life, Pedro de la Gasca, though also of distinguished lineage, had been early orphaned and left without means of support. He owed his education to the kindly offices of an uncle. This education, pursued first at Alcalá de Henares and later at Salamanca, was the best obtainable and young Pedro proved to be an outstanding student. He also revealed military talents which had little or nothing to do with his priestly training. This was the period of the *Comunidades*—the revolt of certain Castilian cities against imperial power— and, as usual, many students were ready and eager to join against civic authorities in such an uprising. Gasca, acting as the leader of an opposing force among them, seized the gates of the city, secured the help of the royal troops, checked the rebellion and assured the Crown of the future allegiance of the erstwhile rioters. "This act of loyalty was probably not lost on his vigilant sovereign," Prescott remarks, in another of those delightful statements with which he epitomizes a dramatic situation.

Nevertheless, the escapade seemed, at the time, more or less episodic to most observers, very few of whom were as vigilant as the sovereign. Gasca resumed his studies and eventually received the degree of Master of Theology, with the highest possible honors. He next distinguished himself in scholastic disputation and, after managing various important affairs of an ecclesiastical nature, became a member of the Council of the Inquisition. In this capacity he was sent to Valencia in 1540, to examine alleged cases of heresy; and he proved so successful that he was next appointed to the highly responsible position of *Visitador* by the Cortes,[20] in which he was equally successful. His military genius again came to the fore when Valencia was threatened with invasion by Barbarossa. It was largely through Gasca's efforts that the populace was calmed, the military and naval forces reorganized and the city's defenses strengthened; and he showed himself equally adept as a conciliator and a strategist. It was at this point that Philip and his advisors, reviewing both his past and his present record, decided that Gasca was their man to go to Peru.

He accepted the commission with respect, but with reservations: if he went, it must be with full ambassadorial powers; the situation did not lend itself to leisure for consulting Spain. Moreover, he must go without fanfare of any kind, without ostentation and with the smallest possible retinue. There was some hesitation about accepting his conditions; but when it became obvious that Gasca did not intend to undertake the superhuman task assigned to him on any other basis, the Court had no choice but to yield; reports from Peru indicated all too clearly that Gonzalo was becoming daily more arrogant and more powerful.

Gasca had previously been offered a bishopric and had intended to accept it. Now, despite urgent advice that it would give him added prestige, he declined it on the ground that he could not fulfill the duties of his office during his absence, and that if he never returned "the consciousness of his inefficiency would lie heavy on his soul in his last moments." [8] He did, however, accept the title "President of the Royal *Audiencia*," which carried with it full authority in all civil, military and judicial matters throughout the colony. With a modest retinue, which included Alonso de Alvarado, who had served with such distinction under Francisco Pizarro, he sailed from San Lucar in May, 1546, and arrived in July at the port of Santa Marta, in what is now Colombia. It was there that he first learned of the Battle of Añaquito, the death and defeat of the Viceroy and Gonzalo's latest acts of insubordination.

Every port, as well as all outlying country, was now in the hands of the rebels and Nombre de Dios, which Gasca decided would provide his most auspicious point of entry, was held by a strong force captained by Meixa, one of the ablest and most aggressive of the rebel officers.

However, Meixa was not shrewd enough to see that an emissary whose manners were gentle and friendly, who dressed like a simple priest, and who had no companions except a few followers even less imposing than himself, could possibly prove a menace. But he had hardly dispatched messages to Gonzalo, saying that they did not even bother to notice this new governor who had been sent out from Spain, than he began to change his mind. Gasca pleasantly explained that he had come upon a mission of peace; that all who submitted to the government would be pardoned; that it was his purpose to proclaim a revocation of the ordinances which the people had found unbearable; and as this meant that the insurgents had already succeeded in their purpose, any further resistance would be not only futile but senseless. All this was said so persuasively and so agreeably that Meixa listened, at first reluctantly, then willingly and, at last, gladly. He promised to co-operate and to advise other officials to do the same.

The next step was to win over Hinojosa, the Governor of Panama, for Pizarro's navy of twenty-two vessels lay in the harbor there. This proved a much longer, harder and more complicated task. Besides being genuinely attached to Gonzalo, Hinojosa enjoyed his post and had no desire to lose it through a change in government. He played for time and Gasca seemed willing to give him as much as he wanted, so he dispatched letters to Gonzalo, asking for advice as to what course he should pursue. But Gasca was sending out letters, too. He wrote to Gonzalo himself and with his own letter he inclosed one from the Emperor; he entrusted their delivery to a cavalier who had accompanied him from Spain, by name Paniagua, together with various manifestoes and other documents, which he suggested should be rather widely distributed throughout Lima. The general purport was the same as that of his initial talk with Meixa. He also secured the services of a Dominican priest who had opportunely taken passage on this mail boat. The Dominican undertook to visit a number of ports between Panama and Lima, scattering messages as he went. Very few of them fell on barren ground.

Gonzalo, after due deliberation, concluded that Gasca's mild methods were somehow too persuasive for the well-being of the new emissary's antagonists and reverted to his plan of sending his own representatives to Spain, while he continued to rule as Governor. He also wrote courteously. But he informed the new President that the latter had come too late to settle any problems, as the overthrow of the Viceroy had already disposed of them all and Peru was at peace under his, Pizarro's, guidance. His ambassadors had already set out, not to sue for pardon, but merely to ask for official confirmation of authority. Meanwhile, the arrival of a soi-disant ambassador would only confuse both the people and the issue. He was sure Gasca would see that it would be superfluous for him to remain in Peru.

Gonzalo had chosen able representatives—the Bishop of Lima, a cavalier by the name of Aldana, and several others; they believed in his cause and had no doubts concerning the success of their mission. But when they reached Panama, where Gasca had been patiently waiting all this time, they were appalled to find that he now had a very extensive and very important following—indeed, so many persons had been convinced his purpose was just, that they urged him not to delay any longer, but to depose Hinojosa and seize the fleet. This he had declined to do, still calmly maintaining that his mission was a peaceful one; but that he could have done it, had he so chosen, was all too obvious. Moreover, he had not only achieved this immense popular following; but he was in possession of royal warrants to act in any way he saw fit. The King and the Courts, as well as the people, were on his side and all were ready to prove it. Aldana and the Bishop hastily decided to go no further than Panama, to accept the pardon of the Spanish government and to help the new President settle the affairs of Peru. Hinojosa, convinced that Gasca's was now the winning side, quickly assured him that the fleet was his to command.

The surrender was marked with great ceremony. A free pardon for all past offenses was proclaimed by a herald mounted on a platform in the main square of the city. Hinojosa and his captains placed their resignations in the hands of the President and vowed allegiance to Castile. Gasca greeted them as loyal subjects of the Crown and at once restored their commissions. The royal standard was hoisted over the squadron. As far as this stronghold was concerned, Pizarro's power was gone forever.

Among those who took part in this dramatic surrender was a young Puerto Rican by the name of Gaspar de Flores. It has taken us quite a long while to reach him and place him in his exciting environment, but it has seemed to me worth the time and trouble. For he was destined to be the father of a saint and, as such, to play a very important part in our story.

CHAPTER I

INFORMATION REGARDING the date of Gaspar de Flores' birth is con-
flicting. Most biographers state that he was twenty-three when he
arrived in Peru. However, according to the Archives of the Indies,[6] he
was born between 1531 and 1538. The latter date can almost automatically be ruled out, for it is inconceivable that he would have come
alone from Puerto Rico to seek his fortune elsewhere at the age of ten,
or that he could have been a member of the armed forces at that age.
In the midst of all the contradictory data, one fact seems to stand out
clearly: he had arrived in Peru by 1548, and it is conceivable that he
might have come at the age of seventeen.

The records of San Germán, Puerto Rico, state that he was the son
of Hernándo de la Puente and María Flores, both citizens of that place.
These same records state that he was born there and he probably was,
though both Toledo and Salamanca have put in claims for the honor
of having been his birthplace, and it is not beyond the realm of possibility that his parents emigrated from Spain when he was so young
that the Puerto Rican authorities assumed he had been born after
and not before their arrival.[21] In any case, he seems to have begun his
wanderings early, for he was already in Panama when Pedro de Casaus
—the predecessor of Hinojosa—was governor; and it is certain that he
was still there at the time the Gonzalista Armada surrendered to Pedro
de la Gasca, for he himself wrote years later, in referring to it, "I
personally know about all this, because I embarked in [one of] those
ships with the President Gasca and saw it all and can bear witness
that it happened thus."

Evidently both military and naval forces were engaged in the surrender, as well as in subsequent preparations for the ships' departure,[8]
for, in so far as we know, Gaspar was never a sailor; and he is definitely
labeled as "a soldier of the King" when we find him in Gasca's Armada
bound for Peru. This left Panama in April of the following year (1547)
and, after a long and perilous voyage, finally landed at Tumbez in June

and proceeded to Jauja, which the President decided to make his head-quarters. He now had a considerable force at his disposal, for besides the "many soldiers of the King," Flores among them, who had accompanied him from Panama, he had been joined by volunteers all along the way and after he landed; and he was now informed that his position enabled him to hold the passes by which Pizarro intended to escape from the country.

However, the pieces of the pattern failed to fall so neatly into place. Before setting out himself, Gasca had sent the faithful Aldana in command of a four ship squadron, to Callao, with instructions to make a last effort to bring Gonzalo to terms. The loss of his fleet had been a severe blow, as he now had nothing with which to give battle to Aldana; but he had been successful in enlarging and equipping his army, and was still determined to hold out, so he withdrew at the head of his army to Arequipa. Then, abandoning a plan of taking refuge in Chile, he took a circuitous route to Juarina, a small town near Lake Titicaca, and there met the loyalist troops led by Diego Centeno, who had his own reasons for hating Gonzalo. To the horror, as well as the amazement, of the Loyalists, Pizarro won a smashing victory. Gasca's cause had suffered its first major setback; and it was not until a year after his departure from Panama, in the battle against the rebels generally called the "rout of Jaquijahuana" that he finally and decisively accomplished the downfall of Pizarro.

His mission fulfilled, Gasca returned to Spain, after settling affairs in Lima and preparing the way for a new Viceroy. He received the royal welcome which he so richly deserved and accepted the bishopric which he had previously declined. To the end of his life he remained powerful, respected and beloved. Though we know, from the Archives of the Indies, that Gaspar fought under him at Jaquijahuana, it is not entirely clear where the "soldier of the King" in whom we are primarily interested spent the next four years. The army was moved about a good deal and its movements were not always confined to one crown colony. Spain treated these in many ways, military and otherwise, much as she did the provinces—(formerly the separate kingdoms)—of the mother country, and a soldier was as likely to find himself first in Panama and then in Peru, as first in León and then in Castile, for instance. However, it seems probable that he was in Peru most, if not all of that time, for when next we hear of him he is leaving Lima for Cuzco with Juan Ramírez Zegarra, the son of Pedro de Casaus—Hinojosa's predecessor as Governor of Panama—and Pedro Luis de Cabrera, for whom he later became armor bearer. When they arrived in the Valley of Pincos, they learned that there had been an uprising, hostile to the *Audiencia*, under the leadership of one Francisco Hernández Girón, a former lieutenant of Pizarro, who preferred to leave to others the conquest and catechization of uncivilized Indians. Unfortunately, there had been an interim between the departure of Gasca and the arrival of the new Viceroy, Antonio de Mendoza. During such a period, the Governor, who was also the President of the *Audiencia*, and the *oidores*, (judges) who were his fellow members of this body, automatically had supreme authority; and now that they were no longer restrained by Gasca's pacific policies and tactful treatment, they antagonized the people by the manner in which they dealt with the payment of debts and the redistribution of land—a method highly disadvantageous to the rebels, who had expected treatment more favorable to themselves. The *encomenderos* (the agents who had hitherto controlled land grants and reduced the Indians to serfdom) willingly gave their support to the new movement, hoping to gain time by taking advantage of conditions epitomized in the old saying that fishing is good in troubled waters. Assured of their backing, the rebels very quickly gained the upper hand.

With the intention of warning the capital, which had not yet received the news, Flores and his companions returned to Lima; but the revolt did not amount to much after all. The new Viceroy, Antonio de Mendoza, a kindly, cultured man, who followed Pedro de la Gasca's example of apparent simplicity, had a calming effect upon both factions, largely by declining to listen to either one; and when peace was restored between them, Flores started back to Cuzco with Cabrera.

Unfortunately for all concerned, the temperate Viceroy lived only a year and, while awaiting the arrival of his successor, the *Audiencia* resumed its unwelcome policies and equally unwelcome power. In one of the many eastern villages where troops were stationed, Gaspar heard from wayfarers, stopping at the local inn, of another mutiny. He doubtless had many opportunities for gleaning information without much effort, for the chroniclers tell us that the soldiers spent days and days in polishing armor and saddling chargers; and since such tasks would normally have been performed in the courtyard of the inn, this would have been an excellent vantage point at which to pick up gossip.

Turmoil was typical of the times and Flores throve on it. His activities in Gasca's Armada and invading forces had given him that taste for blood which is hard to appease and he now belonged to an army of conquerors who were also swashbucklers and marauders; but, unlike many of his companions, he was not triggered to rebellion. This explains why, in traveling from Lima to Potosí in 1553, he did not himself turn to Francisco Hernández Girón, the leader who again incited Peru to revolt. On the contrary, Flores enrolled himself in the troops of the *Audiencia* and, since he was with them in the encampment on the outskirts of Lima, must have been present at the arrival of the conquered army in Chuquinga. But, after a short time, he was forced to leave camp on account of illness and take refuge in the house of a friend "because he had none of his own." For this reason, he did not take part in the capture of Toribio de Galíndez, a soldier who had planned to join in the mutiny of the fleet and help deliver it to the rebels. As Flores explained later, he could not serve in this capture, "because, on account of his indisposition, he could not leave the house." At the first sign of improvement in health, however, he returned to the camp and from there left with General Pablo de Maneses to fight Girón in the Valley of Villacuri, taking part in this hasty and disastrous action, in which the loyalist troops were engaged for the second time. Flores must have served there in the cavalry, because the infantry did not take part in it. Nevertheless, we do not necessarily see him as the owner of a mount. In those days, the loan of animals for military purposes was often approved by the authorities.

Having returned to camp, Gaspar followed the army of the *Audiencia* to Jauja, afterward fighting—for the first time in this capacity—with the troops of *arcabuceros* in the battle of Pucara, which brought the Gironista cause to an end. Francisco Hernández Girón was beheaded and the smell of gunpowder evaporated. The civil wars of Peru were over.

But, with the coming of peace, the *arcabucero* was left without employment. He was, above all, a man of war and the doors had been closed on his profession; and we are told that Don Andrés Hurtado de Mendoza, Marqués of Cañete and new Viceroy of Peru, "understood this very well." His understanding was apparently based on the fact that "quite aside from being a blueblood of the most exalted rank, he was at one and the same time a stern statesman and a brave soldier." [22]

Bearing all this in mind, it seems quite in character that Don Andrés should have carefully considered what disposition it would be best to make of Flores and that he ended by ordering him to go with Antonio de Oznayo to Jaén de los Bracamoros, the ancient *Pacamuru* of the Incas, territory which still remained to be conquered. Flores left

Lima in the direction of these regions, knowing beforehand that they were far away, that the terrain was rough and mountainous and that the inhabitants were warlike Indians.

The entire march to Jaén de los Bracamoros was made hard and painful not only by the presence of Indian archers, but also by the inclement and unhealthful climate. However, the most perilous point of the expedition was the meeting with Juan de Salinas, the captain who maintained that this territory was his by right of conquest. He came toward de Oznayo's troops with the intention of barring their way. The two factions were ready to destroy each other when Juan Ramírez Zegarra, the friend of our *arcabucero*, arrived in their midst with stern orders that harmony must be restored. As Gaspar de Flores wrote long afterward, he realized that the coming of the Commissioner had been most opportune, adding that Juan Ramírez rendered notable service to God Our Saviour and to His Majesty, because, if he had not arrived at that juncture and brought about peace, serious trouble would have ensued, since these headstrong captains each had a well-organized troop of brave soldiers.

The mission of Juan Ramírez being accomplished, de Oznayo ordered Flores and other soldiers to escort him far enough to place him beyond the range of the Indians' weapons and, eventually, having traveled along a road lined with ambushed archers, they emerged at the coast.

Gaspar's military life did not end here. Not long after his return to Lima, his labors were rewarded by a place among the *arcabuceros* of the Viceroy's guard. Autobiographically, he has referred to himself, later on, as "a resident of this city and a gentleman in the harquebusiers of the guard of this realm." But his name does not appear in the lists and musters of the lances and harquebuses of any company serving under Don Diego López de Zuñiga y de Velasco, Conde de Nieva, who followed Don Andrés Hurtado de Mendoza, Marqués de Cañete, as Viceroy; so it seems probable that he obtained the new office during the time that the Licentiate, Lope García de Castro, acted temporarily as provisional governor, after the departure of one Viceroy and before the arrival of another. One thing is clear: when Francisco de Toledo became Viceroy, Flores already had his place as harquebusier.

Such a position in such a place was certainly a contrast—and probably a welcome one—to that of combat in Jaén de los Bracamoros, where life was "hard and painful." The viceregal guard was a body designed for decoration rather than defense. Its members were gorgeously attired in uniforms which might well have been designed for theatrical performances, with red trousers and blue coats, both profusely orna-mented with gold braid. They did not even carry their harquebuses except when they were on parade: all weapons were kept in the armory and distributed for use only at such grand occasions as flag drills, reli-gious processions and parades at which the Viceroy presided and when, accompanied by his guard, he visited seven churches on Holy Thursday or went to Vespers at the cathedral on the Eve of Twelfth Night. To be sure, there were intervals of more active and sober service; when Francisco de Toledo made his famous visit to the *Sierra,* Gaspar was one of the soldiers chosen to escort him and the great geographer, Sarmiento de Gamboa. Before the return of the expedition, which covered considerable territory, there was some intermittent fighting. But association with this Viceroy, even in a humble capacity and under trying conditions, was rightly regarded as a privilege by practically all who served him, Flores among them. Andrés Hurtado de Mendoza, the nobleman who was at one and the same time a stern statesman and a brave soldier, had filled his post with ability and distinction; but Philip II felt that the members of the *Audiencia,* who had again re-joiced in a period of power, were more concerned with the direction of the Council of the Indies than with their monarchs. Theoretically at least, the "Viceroys were above all images of the Kings of Spain" [11] and if they did not always attain this ideal, it was not for lack of either foresight or desire on Philip's part. Therefore, he now decided to send to Peru a "noble patrician" who had been attached to his own person; and with the arrival of Francisco de Toledo, "the colony had entered upon its most interesting and sound period of its maturity." . . . "The Cortes of Spain had at last found a man of the stature for great enter-prise. His spirit was exalted, his mentality all embracing, his military exploits comparable to those of the Dukes of Alba. The loftiness of his character made him worthy of a throne. He was the real ruler of Peru." [22]

No wonder that Flores, like his fellows, entered heart and soul into the service of this paragon and it was his most rewarding experience. Moreover, the periods of daily struggle, privation and peril were over; the whole pattern of life was altered and now designed along less rugged lines. The thoughts, ideals and desires of the once hard-bitten campaigner who, after becoming a seasoned soldier, had been trans-formed into an ornamental guardsman, also underwent a change.

The holy state of matrimony had held no attractions for him, either

in his tumultuous youth or during the forceful days of his early man-
hood; indeed, he had never so much as given it serious consideration.
Now, when he was past middle-age,[23] he suddenly and surprisingly
found himself deeply in love with a high-spirited girl young enough
to be his daughter.

Her name was María de Oliva, her birthplace was Lima and her
background was creditable, if in some respects now indeterminate. Both
her parents have been described by biographers as "limited as to fortune, but honorable." Her father, Francisco de Oliva, also a native of
Lima, seems to have been a rather colorless character; at all events, it
was his wife, Isabel de Herrera, who dominated the family scene. She
came—just when or why, we do not know—from Tomaiquichua, a
tiny town across the Continental Divide, situated in the rich Valley
of Huanco, a five days' journey by muleback from Lima; and, according
to her own sworn statement, she had been born there, shortly after
the conquest of the Incas, when Pizarro's soldiers comprised practically
all of the valley's white inhabitants. It can be safely assumed that one
of these bold and lusty men was her father. It is less safe to guess at
the identity of her mother. We know that she was wilful, opinionated
and short tempered, and, withal, energetic, self-reliant, self-respecting
and high-spirited, all of which qualities were inherited by her daughter
María. Of her genealogy we know nothing.

By the time Gasper de Flores came courting their daughter, Francisco and Isabel had managed to give her a better education than most
girls of her period and station in life—good enough, in fact, so that,
later on, she was able to add to her husband's salary by giving lessons
to gentle-born girls. María herself did not belong in that category and
made no such pretensions. Nevertheless, the witnesses at her wedding
in the Parish of the *Sagrario* (the oldest in the city) were all persons
of some social standing and at least one of them, Captain Juan Maldonado de Buendía, was an officer of considerable distinction. Both
bride and bridegroom had every reason to feel gratified with everything
about the ceremony and set off for their new home with great elation.

For all their natural impetuosity, they had chosen this with careful
forethought. It was situated on the Calle de Santo Domingo, a quiet
street in one of the less fashionable quarters of the city, but it was
large enough not only for their immediate needs, but for the sizable
family which they confidently expected and without which marriage
would have seemed more or less meaningless to them both. Gaspar
would have considered it a reflection on his virility if he could not still

have sired vigorous sons and daughters; in like measure, María would
have considered barrenness a reproach and fecundity an honor; so,
from the beginning, despite the handicap of their limited means, they
provided space for as many children as might be born to them. There
was also space enough for the accommodation of as many friends as
could visit them. Gaspar had not forgotten how much it had meant
to him, when he was first enrolled in the troops of the *Audiencia* at
their encampment near Lima and had fallen ill, to find shelter and
welcome in a friend's house, when he had none of his own. Now he
and María together gladly received, among others, the paymaster Juan
de Cáceres and Gaspar's old companion in arms, Juan Ramírez Zegarra,
who had attained an important position as Mayor of Arequipa, already
the second city of Peru, and had married the daughter of the Commissioner Bernardino de Romaní. There had always been great devotion
between these men and their reunion would have been a source of
joy under any circumstances. Gaspar would have been less than human
if he had not also derived satisfaction from the consciousness that
close connections with persons of such important official standing represented, for him, an ascent of the social scale. True, he and María
did not belong to the closely knit viceregal circle of aristocrats; they
were not entitled to coats of arms. But, despite the ambiguity of
María's maternal ancestry, no one questioned their right to call themselves *cristianos viejos*—that is, free from any suspicion of Moorish or
Jewish strains. They had attained the position of *hidalgos de segunda
fila*—gentlefolk of secondary rank. For this reason, as has been frequently pointed out, they probably remained unaware of the very
existence of a small mulatto, by name Martín de Porres, who was born
shortly after their marriage in a house on the street next to the one
where they lived.

Like many houses of the period, theirs was built in the form of a U,
with the entrance at its base, a wall closing in its open end and
a series of rooms on both the long sides. The bridal couple were not
concerned because they could not furnish it luxuriously or even adequately at the moment; they did not need all those rooms as yet, and by
the time they did—well, they could worry about that later. Meanwhile,
they could congratulate themselves on the fact that their house and the
wall at its rear formed an ample enclosure not only for a large patio,
but a garden, an orchard and a corral; and though they had probably
not given this aspect of their new property any particular thought
beforehand, they could not have been other than pleased to find that

the garden plot, though naturally lacking any formal cultivation, was already productive. Besides the attribute of spaciousness, the property had additional advantages provided by its location.

It was adjacent to the property of the famous hospital known as the Supremo del Espíritu Santo, one of the most important institutions in the city. The origin of this was arresting, the development extraordinary. A public-spirited citizen by the name of Miguel Acosta, who was a Greek by birth, became concerned about the dismal lot of the sailors who had met with accidents or fallen ill in the course of their long voyage to Callao, or who were incapacitated in some way after they reached there. "As they were, for the most part, foreigners, no one would care for them or console them." He therefore decided to give them such help as he could, and began his mission by taking them into his own house; but as he had neither the space nor the means to carry on a work of such magnitude as this soon became, "he conceived the idea of founding a hospital with this in view and such was the origin of the Hospital of the Holy Spirit." [24]

Once the idea was conceived, it did not take Acosta long to get into action. He secured the support of commercial establishments to help finance his undertaking. But he was too practical to depend entirely on this. He stipulated that each ship which came into Callao should help, too, its quota being determined partly by the size and importance of its home port, partly by the distance it had come and partly by the wage scale of its crew. On an average, about eight thousand pesos were obtained in this way, a sufficient amount to support the seventy beds with which the hospital was at first provided. In addition to its wards, its dispensary and its surgery, it contained a chapel large enough to accommodate seven altars, "which enjoyed special privileges on the part of the Holy Father"; [24] and later, as it expanded, a classroom where pilots were instructed in mathematics (the earliest of its kind in Lima, antedating even those of San Marcos University). It was the first hospital in which the sick were classified by profession and not by sex or race. On the land partly occupied by its garden and partly by the garden of Gaspar de Flores and his wife María, grew the first roses that ever flourished in Peru.

For some unknown reason, these had not thriven when Lima was founded, despite its natural florescence as far as lilies and jasmine and many other flowers were concerned. "The years went by"—according to a Jesuit chronicler—"without the city having enjoyed the beauty of the rose. But in 1552, a good citizen with the soul of a poet brought in the seed and, greatly desiring that it should grow, planted and tended it with the utmost care. In those days, nothing was attempted without asking the blessing of God, and this was especially true when seed was sown, since everybody knows that 'it is not he who plants nor he who waters, but only God Himself Who gives increase.' A Mass was celebrated with the rose seed on the altar, so that the priest's blessing would assure success; and thus it came to pass." [25]

The place where the "good citizen," whose name, unfortunately, has not been preserved to us, planted the seed "and tended it with the utmost care" was on that plot of land later occupied partly by the Espíritu Santo Hospital and partly by the bridal pair. So the neighbors of Gaspar and María were priests and doctors and men who sailed the seven seas. From the beginning, their married life was brightened and blessed with flowers; and, as they had hoped, it was soon brightened and blessed with children: a girl, Bernardina; a boy, Hernándo; another girl, Isabel; and after her Juana, Andrés, Gaspar, Antonio, Matías and some whose names and history are lost to us. Among these were several who died very young, probably including the earliest, for Bernardina, the first of whom we have definite information, was born in 1581 and after that the data are fairly complete. But it is in Bernardina and Hernándo and Isabel that most of our interest is centered.

Especially in Isabel, who was named for her grandmother, but who, much to that determined woman's displeasure, was given the nickname of Rosa while she was still a baby, because this seemed to suit her so perfectly. To be sure, it was just a nickname—until the saintly Archbishop Toribio called her that when he confirmed her and thus made it official.

But that is getting ahead of our story.

CHAPTER II

THERE HAVE been even more differences of opinion, expressed with even greater acrimony, over the exact date of Isabel de Flores' birth than over that of her father's. In her case, however, it is only a question of days in the same month and not of years in the same century. Her mother, María de Oliva, in the Process for Canonization; her confessor, Fray Pedro Loaiza, who was also her first biographer; and Fray Leonardo Hansen, generally conceded to be the "most celebrated and diligent" historian of her life and times, who examined all the documents relating to the Bull of Canonization, give April 20, 1586 as the date, and their testimony would seem to this biographer conclusive. However, many other authorities insist that Isabel's birthday was not the 20th but the 30th, and back up their claims to accuracy in various ways. Since the 30th is the widely celebrated feast day of Catherine of Siena, who was to prove Isabel's lifelong ideal, and the 20th the somewhat neglected feast day of the far less venerated and famous Santa Inés de Montepulciano, it is easy to understand why it would seem more arresting to link the baby with the former rather than the latter; and, after all, do ten days really make so much difference? Can we be accused of carelessness as to detail if we merely say, "She was born the latter part of April," and let it go at that? I do not think so.

No such controversy rages as to the date of the baby's baptism. This is firmly fixed as the 25th of May, which was the Feast of Pentecost. The place was the Church of San Sebastian, the godparents Hernández de Valdes and María de Orosco, the officiating priest Antonio Polanco. On the margin of the baptismal certificate, which is still carefully preserved, and which gives the baby's name as Isabel and those of her parents as Gaspar de Flores and María de Oliva, the priest wrote, "*Hija de estima*"—"esteemed daughter." The usual wording, under the given circumstances, would have been "legitimate daughter." Something must have prompted him to make his statement more emphatic.[26]

The baby quickly became the darling of the household. Her sister, Bernardina, and her brother, Hernándo, respectively five and two years her senior, adored her; the Indian maid of all work, Mariana, was her willing slave. It was Mariana who, in voicing her fond admiration for her charge, was responsible for little Isabel's nickname.

The baby was lying quietly in her cradle and, as Mariana lifted the light veil which covered the little face, to see whether Isabel was awake or asleep, the maid was enraptured by the loveliness of what she saw. It far transcended the pink and white prettiness of any well-fed, well-tended infant; there was a freshness to it, a delicacy, a clarity that had a flowerlike, rather than a human, quality. Spontaneously, she expressed her consciousness of this. "Our beautiful baby looks just like a rose!" she exclaimed.

The elder children had been hovering near by and now they came closer and nodded in smiling agreement. María, who had been otherwise occupied, also heard the exclamation and came swiftly to the side of the others. A single glance at the baby revealed the reason for Mariana's rapture; the mother, as well as the servant, could recognize the supernal freshness embodied before her. She lifted the slumberous child from the cradle and held it close to her as she murmured words of love and wonder. "Life of my life, soul of my soul! You are indeed my little rose, my Rosita, and as long as God gives me life, you shall have no other name than that!"

This impetuous declaration was characteristic of the rapidity with which María usually spoke and acted. Very often, her sober second thought took a different turn; but on this occasion, it was followed by a decisive order: not only did the baby's mother intend to call her Rose from that day forward; everyone in the family, everyone in the household, everyone in their circle of friends was to do the same. María gave as her reason for this that in the baby's flowerlike beauty they would all find their comfort and well being; and she said this with such conviction that all her hearers, save one, were quite willing to believe her and follow her wishes in the matter.

The exception was the baby's grandmother, Isabel de Herrera.

She had now come to live with her daughter and son-in-law, so it may be presumed that her husband, Francisco de Oliva, apparently a colorless figure at best on the otherwise glowing arras of the times, had now been gathered to his fathers, since there is no further mention of him. Isabel de Herrera was not a young woman any longer, as age was reckoned in those days, though even so it is quite probable she

was Gaspar's junior; but she had lost none of her essential vigor, deter-
mination and spirit and, indeed, she was to retain these for years to
come. As her daughter had inherited many of her qualities, it is not
strange that there was frequent conflict between them. They were
too much alike to dwell together amicably and this lack of harmony,
which pervaded and corroded their surroundings, was never more pronounced than it became over the question of the baby's name.

It is impossible not to feel considerable sympathy with the older
woman. Her name was a beautiful one, which had been borne by the
great queen whose faith and generosity had made possible the discovery
of the New World and who was universally revered there. Isabel de
Herrera had been proud to bear it herself and to feel that her granddaughter was to bear it after her. Besides, a namesake seemed closer
to a woman than a child whose sponsors in baptism had not taken
family ties into consideration; little Isabel's christening had marked a
red letter day in her grandmother's life, whereas she had experienced
no such sense of rejoicing when Bernardina and Hernándo were taken
to the font. Now this self-willed María proposed to defraud her of her
pride and happiness. And why? Just because an ignorant Indian woman
had said the baby looked like a rose! What did they expect her to look
like, for heaven's sake? A periwinkle? What was even more to the
point, how could they legally make such a change? A baptismal certificate was an official document.

Very probably, María herself suffered some qualms concerning this
point of legality, which was not settled for good and all until some
years later. But meanwhile her orders were carried out: everyone except
Isabel de Herrera called the baby Rosa or Rosita; her father, who had
adroitly avoided being drawn into the discussion (he was beginning
to feel his age, though he hated to admit it, and he had had his fill of
turmoil long ago); her sister and brother, who thought Rosa a much
easier name to pronounce quickly than Isabel and a much prettier one
anyhow; Mariana, who swelled with pride because she was responsible
for such an important suggestion; and the friends who came and went
and listened to the story of how the suggestion had come about and
complimented Mariana on her perceptiveness, causing her pride to
increase still further. In the midst of this ready and general acceptance
of María's verdict, what did it matter if one stubborn old woman felt
aggrieved?

If she had been old enough to understand when the arbitrary change
took place, Isabel de Flores, who had now—however unofficially—

become Rosa de Flores, might have thought it mattered, because she
had been blessed not only with a lovely face, but with a tender heart,
and she would have done and said what she could to comfort her grandmother, to whom she was devotedly attached. But though she may
sometimes have been vaguely puzzled because this elderly lady, who
seemed to be unhappy about something, did not address her in the
same way that everyone else did, it is doubtful if she could have
attached much importance to this, though she was a precocious and
intelligent child, as well as a brave one. The family physician was
amazed at the uncomplaining fortitude with which she bore the pain of
a crushed finger and, later, of an ear infection, and his treatment of
both. She taught herself to read with very little help from her mother,
for María had scant patience with book learning, except in as far as
her own slight store of it enabled her to teach other people's children,
for which she was paid, while of course she was not paid for teaching
her own. With only the help of Hernándo, Rosa built herself a little
leafy "hermitage" in the quietest part of the garden and to this she
loved to retreat. "If you cannot find Rosita, look for her in the
hermitage," the members of the family told each other and they were
usually right. She did not care for noisy games, and her gentle spirit
must often have been troubled by the unconcealed friction between her
grandmother and her mother; her corner of the garden seemed a natural
refuge to her. Unquestionably, she had learned to pray, as she had
learned to read, to sew and to sing at a very early age; and prayer was
not to her merely a patter. It was an utterance that came from her
heart and which was equally fervent whether it took the form of a
petition or a thanksgiving. But it is doubtful whether she would have
prayed so earnestly and so much at such a tender age if she had not
found in prayer a means of withdrawal as well as of worship, nor would
her thoughts have turned so early to fasting and penance, much less to
chastity—the very word for which is not included in the vocabulary
of most children—if in all respects her life had been one of unclouded
and unpuzzled happiness. She began to refuse the appetizing fruits
and vegetables which appeared on the family table. Even with the need
for strict economy, oranges, plums, avocadoes, plantains and the deli-
cious tropical fruit known as chirimoya, of which we have no exact
equivalent, were served as a matter of course; they were wholesome
and nourishing and much cheaper than meat. Why on earth did she
not eat her fill of them, María wanted to know, rather crossly. Rosita
tried to explain that she was keeping a fast and found that the explana-

tion did no good. Rather than argue, she withdrew to her *ermita*.

Her beauty was not confined to her coloring, her face and figure; she also had very beautiful hair. Her brother told her teasingly that, when she grew a little older, she could ensnare any suitor she chose with this. She promptly cut off the long locks and, despite her mother's anger, said she would never allow them to grow again. She had made her vow of chastity as early as she had made the one of abstinence and she was resolved that nothing would tempt her to break either one. Moreover, it is quite likely that she was delighted with so opportune an occasion for imitating a similar action on the part of St. Catherine of Siena, with whose story she was already familiar. Catherine, too, had been dowered with very beautiful blond curls, which she hacked off as soon as her first serious suitor appeared on the scene. A woman's hair was then still considered her crown of glory and a shorn head an insurmountable obstacle to romance. Catherine's mother, whose heart had been set on an advantageous alliance for her youngest daughter, raged helplessly at the wreck of her carefully laid plan. Hernándo, who had only meant to jest with his sister, was not angry; he was stricken. Yet for a time, though she went willingly to church with him—he was always her chosen companion when she left the garden for Santo Domingo—she was withdrawn in other ways. She spent more and more time in the *ermita*, less and less in the family circle.

Still, by and large, she was not a sad child, much less a morbid one. She loved flowers and had a great gift for making them grow. She also loved animals of all kinds and with these, too, she had a gift. She talked with them and insisted that they understood her. There are countless stories founded upon this aspect of her activities. The most famous one is probably the one of the bird which had strayed into the poultry yard, but which never sang there. With characteristic impatience, María declared that they might as well eat it; it was good for nothing else, but it could help to make a meal. Rosa captured it and held it close to her heart. "Sing, little bird, sing, if you do not wish to die!" she whispered. And the little bird burst into song.

Only a legend? Very well. But it is the sort of a legend that makes her akin to Francis of Assisi. After all, he preached to the birds in the forest and claimed that they listened; and in that same forest, he admonished a wolf to mend its cruel ways—and it did. Or so we are happy to believe.

I am equally happy to believe that the little bird sang for Rosa de Lima.

CHAPTER III

W<small>HEN HIS</small> daughter Isabel—so soon and so definitely to be known as Rosa—was a baby, Gaspar de Flores, as we have said before, was probably already beginning to feel his age, though he continued to serve in the Viceroy's guard. Ten years later, under the ninth Viceroy, Don Luis de Velasco, Marqués de Salinas and Chevalier of the Order of Santiago, he was still doing so. He was almost seventy now and, truth to tell, he would have been quite content to sit for endless hours basking in the sun and, between naps, to recall the days of his great exploits, whether to himself, his wondering children and his neighbors or the convalescent sailors at Espíritu Santo. The surrender of the Gonzalista Armada at Panama—the defeat of Pizarro and his rebels at Jaquijahuana—the Andean expedition led by Francisco de Toledo—the mere memory of these quickened his thinning blood, the recital of them made a stirring story. In retrospect, Gaspar's belligerent days were tinged with glamour and his present occupations—presenting the colors, standing at attention during a state visit paid or received, visiting seven churches on Holy Thursday—seemed tame by comparison. He was probably gratified, rather than disturbed, when told that he had been appointed superintendent of the silver mines at Quives and that his duties in the viceroyal guard were at least temporarily suspended.

Quives was a thriving town of some three thousand inhabitants, located in the rich Province of Canta, among the more approachable ranges of the Andes, about twenty leagues from Lima. It was blessed with a much pleasanter climate than the capital, where the sun shone for only a few months in the year, and where heavy mists, which took the place of rain, enveloped the city every evening and lasted well into the following day, drenching it with perpetual dampness. In Quives, on the other hand, the air was clear, dry and sparkling, the skies a radiant blue. The silver mines were richly productive [27] and the lot of the miners, on the whole, much better than it was in Europe at the same period, thanks to Don Francisco de Toledo, who had done much to

improve their erstwhile miserable condition by a wise and humane
code. A small, but suitable, stone house, located on a plaza directly
opposite a stone church, was provided for the superintendent and the
salary was adequate for his needs, no small consideration for a man
with a rapidly increasing family. Besides, a superintendent was a person of authority, the direct deputy of the Viceroy; the position carried
considerably more prestige than that of a private in the guard, even
though it was less showy. Gaspar had every reason to be gratified and
the children, of whom there were now seven, were all delighted with
the idea of living in the country, especially at the prospect of seeing
and perhaps even owning the strange animals which they were told
they would find everywhere—long-necked llamas, silky vicuñas, shaggy
alpacas. The Indians not only used them for beasts of burden; their
pelts were used for cloth. Hernándo thought it would be wonderful
to have a llama for a pet; Rosa gave thoughtful consideration to helping her mother make garments of vicuña cloth.

It is probable that Isabel de Herrera and María were less pleased
with the prospect than the youngsters. They were not interested in
strange animals and the old lady, having shaken the dust of one Andean
village from her feet, presumably for good and all, can hardly have
welcomed the idea of going to live in another, even though Quives
was much more accessible than Tomaiquichua and boasted more
Spanish families. María was loath to leave her pupils, for the money
she earned from teaching was essentially hers, (even though she spent
most of it for the good of her family) whereas Gaspar's salary would
be handled by him. Besides, even though there were other persons of
their race and class in Quives, they were few indeed compared to the
number which now made up the circle of her friends in Lima; she
could expect to be lonely, with her husband at the mines all day, her
children playing outdoors and her mother no kind of company. Besides,
what did Quives, a mere mining town, have to offer in a general way,
compared to Lima, a cosmopolitan city?

If María asked this question, as it seems almost inevitable that she
must have, the honest answer would necessarily have been, "Very
little." Lima, as the sixteenth century drew swiftly toward its close,
more than fulfilled its promise of becoming a great religious center
and also a metropolis of charm, culture and sophistication. The celebrations of the church followed each other in quick succession. Some
were obligatory only to Spaniards, others to both Spaniards and Indians.
The Viceroy, the members of the Tribunal and of the *Cabildo* attended

those which were de rigeur. The processions achieved an extraordinary splendor when sacred images, many of them made of silver, were carried through the streets. They were accompanied by all the various Orders and Communities, by the civil authorities and by the populace, while Negroes in grotesque attire danced and acted the buffoon along the way. From time to time, the bonfires of the Inquisition blazed in the *Plaza Mayor* and the green cross, the friars with blazing torches, and the condemned heretics, clad in their yellow penitential robes—the *sambenitos*—staged a scene of stark tragedy in their majestic surroundings.

Such pious practices alternated with bullfights, guild festivals, public games, contests for university prizes and the investiture of the Knights of Santiago, Calatrava and Alcántara. The very rich rode in magnificent coaches; those slightly less opulent contented themselves with so-called *calesas*, constructed to accommodate four persons and drawn by a mule; but even these *calesas* were gilded all over. They were in harmony with the standard of living that had become more and more luxurious as more and more gold and silver poured into the coffers of the colonists. They had, indeed, come to the land of their fondest hopes, their wildest imaginings. "It is worth a Peru," was a common saying, meaning that such and such an object was more valuable than tongue could tell.

At almost every street corner, a sacred image, with a vigil light burning at its feet, had been enshrined in a niche, and the portals of almost every house were engraved with devout inscriptions: Blessed be the Most Holy Sacrament—Honor and Glory to the Immaculate Conception. The gardens were glorious and their choicest flowers were saved for the adornment of altars.

Through the narrow streets filed Dominicans and Mercedarians in their white habits, Franciscans in their rough brown serge and eminent ecclesiastics in voluminous black capes. Among them walked grave gentlemen with pointed beards and finely chiseled features, who wore starched ruffs above their velvet doublets, and who were by no means always meditating on points of theology as they moved along. As for the elegant young gallants, who uncovered their heads and murmured a prayer as they approached a church, they were apt to linger outside of this, instead of helping to swell the congregation inside. For the *tapadas*, the beautiful semi-veiled ladies who never missed going to Mass and confession and saying novenas, gave such young gallants, even when these were strangers, shy sweet glances as they came out into the street after attending to their Catholic duties; and—their fingers still wet with Holy Water—they accepted flowers and even slipped love letters into their bosoms, with the delicate ease of long practice. The sound of bells did not drown their false promises, though these were whispered, and the fragrance of the jasmine with which they adorned their hair mingled with the odor of incense escaping through the open doors of the church.

It availed nothing for the clergy, from the Archbishop to the lowliest priest, to denounce these *tapadas*, or for the Viceroys to forbid the wearing of the sheer black veils with which the ladies of fashion covered their heads and half their faces, thereby attaining a pseudo-anonymity which permitted them to carry on their love affairs without danger of open scandal. Undisturbed by fulminations, undaunted by threats of fines and imprisonment, serenely confident of defying inescapable detection, they went their wilful and seductive way. Their undergarments were so lavishly bordered with lace that there was little room left for linen; their slippers were made of satin, their stockings of sheerest silk; their dresses were of the richest possible fabrics, velvets and brocades in the most gorgeous colors; their jewels were fabulous. But it was their black veils, seemingly so simple, actually so destructive, to which they owed their designation and which made them a menace to morality and a dazzling ornament to society.

Lima was the city where they reigned supreme, even while heroic virtues flourished in the shadow of the Cross. Lima's atmosphere was at one and the same time animated and indolent, restrained and romantic, practical and mystic, saintly and sensual. It was a heady mixture.

It was the mixture which made up the milieu in which María had always lived and had always wanted to live. When she went to Quives, she was wrenched away from it.

CHAPTER IV

THE JOURNEY itself, from the foggy coast to the wild sunshine of the wintry Andes, must have been extremely trying. The Incas had built wonderful roads, but the Spaniards, though they had utilized these for triumphal marches, had failed to recognize the importance of their maintenance in the same degree of perfection as the conquered people. Climatic conditions and neglect had contributed to rapid disintegration. The countryside through which these roads wound their way was rich in cattle and cotton, oranges and mangoes and, in its higher reaches, potatoes and barley; and the landscape was as varied as its products. However, it is doubtful that the wayfarers paid much attention to either, though the children kept a sharp lookout for the llamas and vicuñas which they had so greatly anticipated seeing. The accepted mode of travel was, of course, on foot, except for the cavalry of the army and personages of great importance. Gaspar's family, journeying toward their new home, were provided with mules to convey their household effects, since beasts of burden for such purposes were taken for granted; but, except for the youngest children, they themselves must have walked, carrying not only the babies, but such extra clothing as they possessed, in bundles on their backs. It was a long hard trip, especially for the youngsters who were old enough to walk, but not yet old enough to keep up easily with their elders, and for Gaspar and Isabel de Herrera, who were now well along in years; and when they reached the end of it, in a state of exhaustion, they were cramped and crowded in the small stone dwelling that awaited their occupancy. Hitherto, they had actually had more space than they needed, rejoicing in the amplitude of their house, patio, garden, orchard and corral. Now they had only four rooms, two large and two small, and a small patio, in which to accommodate ten persons and their belongings. The prospect was far from rosy.

It was rendered even darker by the inimical atmosphere of the place. True, the few Spaniards who were living there proved friendly and

congenial. Some of them had planted and nurtured gardens where
fruit and flowers grew abundantly, and these they were willing and
eager to share with the newcomers. Their traditions were much the
same as those of the Flores family and, for the most part, they, too,
had connections with the mines; so in these, as in religious observances,
there was a common interest. In addition to the residents, Quives attracted a certain number of Spanish visitors, who were drawn to it by
its climate or who found it a convenient stopping place on their way
to and from Lima, when they traveled through the Andes. Their brief so-
journs gave variety to an otherwise monotonous design for living. But
none of these new acquaintances meant as much to the Flores as their
neighbors at Espíritu Santo and on the Calle de Santo Domingo, or
the wider circle of friends to whom they had become more and more
close with the passage of years. Moreover, the great majority of Quives'
inhabitants were hostile natives. The Indians of Canta Province, like
those of nearby Huarochirí, had resisted the Conquest with all their
not inconsiderable force, and they still seethed with rebellion against
Spanish dominion, both lay and clerical. Witchcraft, idolatry and revolt were rampant among them; neither the parish priest in Quives,
Francisco Gonzalez,[28] a gentle Mercedarian, nor the well-intentioned
foremen at the mines could convert or control them. Their hostility
and the menace of danger carried with it, permeated and poisoned
the air.

Hernándo acquired his llama, to his great satisfaction, and Rosa
learned to weave cloth from vicuña pelts, which pleased her. But, since
she was such a sensitive child, it is not strange that she sickened under
the generally adverse conditions of her new home. She went, with
touching faithfulness, to the little church on the further side of the
plaza from her house and she even succeeded in building a small shrine
in the house itself, using a stone for a kneeling bench; but she did not
play much with neighboring children, partly because she was disinclined to do so and partly because she was ill a great deal and, when
well enough, was needed to help with the housework and the care of
her younger sister and brothers—Juana, Francisco, Andrés, Antonio
and Matías. Her elder sister, Bernardina, who would normally have
undertaken the greater part of these tasks, was in even poorer health
than Rosa and could not help their grandmother and mother at all,
requiring constant attention herself; and, despite all efforts to spare
her and to find effective remedies for her condition, nothing seemed
to avail. She continued to grow weaker and weaker. Before long, it was

all too evident that there could be but one outcome to her illness. Her death was a shattering blow to everyone in the family, but especially to Rosa.

The general gloom of the situation was only once really brightened: by the prospect of a visitation from the Archbishop, Toribio de Mogrovejo. This dedicated and compassionate man was revered as a saint by all those with whom he was associated, long before his formal canonization. He was a native of León and, like Pedro de la Gasca, the scion of a noble family, who had distinguished himself both as a soldier and a scholar and had held numerous positions of great responsibility and honor before coming to Peru. There he gave added distinction to his exalted office and though his courage, learning and executive ability all commanded a degree of respect amounting almost to awe, it was, above all, for his devotion to God and his boundless charity to his fellow men that he was beloved. He was accustomed to retire, periodically, to mountain fastnesses for prayer and meditation; and he also made it a practice to visit every part of his archdiocese, even the most remote, to assure himself of his people's well-being, both temporal and spiritual, and to administer the Sacraments. When, in the course of these pastoral travels, he reached Quives, he was told by Father Gonzalez that his coming had been awaited with even more than the usual amount of anticipation by a little girl who was thoroughly grounded in her catechism and had eagerly prepared for Confirmation. There were also two little boys whom the parish priest could recommend for the same rite.

Very naturally, the Archbishop had hoped for more; three seemed a very small number out of three thousand. Very possibly, he voiced the disappointment he must certainly have felt. Of course, he did not know that, for almost the only time in history, a saint was privileged to confirm a saint. At all events, his chagrin formed the basis for a legend, which it seems suitable to include in our story.

According to this legend, when the Archbishop left the chapel after the ceremony of Confirmation, in order to return to the house where he was being entertained, the hostile Indians crowded about him, not to show him reverence, but to hurl insults at him. His eyes filled with tears and, instead of lifting his hand to bless them, he murmured sadly, "Unhappy creatures! You will never exceed three!"

Those who believe in numerology—and there are many intelligent and upright people among them—do not fail to observe that, within three years after the historic Confirmation, the glowing prosperity of

Quives was at an end and calamities of every kind overtook it. Earthquakes, cloudbursts, conflagrations, failure of harvests and landslides in the mines followed each other in swift succession. Illness was fatal in many families which the elements spared. Others, fearing further disasters, found pretexts for leaving as soon as possible, if they did not actually desert their homes and posts and flee. At the end of three years, only three families remained. This number was never increased, as long as Quives was listed in the official census.[29] "So great is the belief of the indigenes in St. Toribio's prophecy that no fourth family will settle in Quives," one chronicler asserts, "they are convinced that in a short time they would perish miserably." [30] The cry, *"Esquive vivir en Quives"*—"Avoid living in Quives"—had become as much of a byword as, "It is worth a Peru."

The Flores family was among those who left Quives when three years had passed, though whether this was by accident or design we do not know. Obviously, the mines were less productive than they had been, and it is quite possible that the services of Gaspar as superintendent were no longer needed. Whatever the reason for departure, this was certainly made without regret; the improvement in finances, so sorely needed, so greatly hoped for, had not been realized. The climate, presumably so invigorating, had proved just the opposite; one little girl had died and another had become more and more fragile. And those hostile, idolatrous Indians! If they would insult the Archbishop, there was no knowing what they would do next. Isabel de Herrera and María were not afraid for themselves, because it was not in their nature to be afraid of anything or anybody; but when it came to a question of young children. . . . Their feet fairly flew over the welcome road back to Lima, the same road where the going had seemed so slow and hard when they went to Quives.

It was good to be back, among their own kind, in their own home, which had come to no harm in their absence. Indeed, the orchard and garden had become increasingly productive; their yield would more than suffice to fill the family needs. Fruit could be sold and Rosa felt that flowers could, too. She would undertake to do this to help to salvage the fallen family fortunes.

She was then only fourteen, a slight pale girl who looked as if a strong breeze would blow her away. She had always been quiet and docile, deferring to her elders and seldom voicing an opinion of her own, but now she spoke with authority and conviction and, though her hearers were astonished at her tone and manner, no one interrupted her or contradicted her. Even her grandmother admitted that, perhaps, Rosa had a good idea. Isabel de Herrera addressed her as Rosa now, the way all the others did. For that was the name by which the Archbishop had called her when he placed his holy hands upon her in confirming her and, henceforth, she would be known by no other. If the stay in Quives had accomplished nothing else, it had at least put an end to wrangling on this subject.

Not that plenty of others did not still remain to be settled.

CHAPTER V

THE MATTER of merchandising fruit and flowers was not the only one about which Rosa was adamant. She refused, with a degree of will power surprising to her elders, to consider the question of marriage or to permit them to consider it for her.

She had been a delightful baby and a pretty child, and now, as a young girl, she was becoming increasingly lovely. When her health improved, after her return from Quives, color came to her pale cheeks and curves to her slender form. Her face was a delicate oval in shape, her features regular, her eyes dark and dreamy, and fringed with long lashes. To please her mother, she had allowed her abundant hair to grow again and it was the color of ripe wheat. Like most Limenians, she had beautiful hands and feet, carried herself with dignity and moved with grace. In short, she was extremely attractive and eligible suitors quickly began to present themselves. As far as Gaspar and María were concerned, they were very welcome; as far as Rosa was concerned, they could not be discouraged or dismissed too quickly.

She took her childhood vow of virginity quite seriously, again copying, unconsciously or consciously—but quite probably the latter—her beau ideal, Catherine of Siena, as well as following her own inclination and the dictates of her own conscience. She regarded a promise made to herself quite as binding as one made to anybody else, and though her heart was overflowing with loving kindness to God's creatures, this devotion was of the spirit rather than of the flesh and was so all embracing that she could not confine its limits to any one. There is nothing to indicate—at least, nothing that I have learned about her—that she was deficient in normal human emotions, though these were always under control and completely untinged by sin or sordidness. She instinctively knew how to deal with attentions which were not wholly honorable—in fact, her handling of one such situation was told in detail, years afterward, by the very man, a certain Vicente Montez, who went to her parents' house, ostensibly to order collars, but with ulterior motives. He first approached María, who referred him to Rosa, saying that, after all, it was she who would do the work. Strangely enough, considering the strict supervision usually given young girls, María simply indicated where he would find her daughter and sent him on his way. Rosa, her head bent, was quietly sewing when he entered the room to which he had been directed, and he seated himself, asked after her health and then said he would need at least two or three collars. For the first time, she raised her eyes, not toward him, but toward heaven, and remarked, in a matter of fact way, "Alas, good Jesus, how different from the making of collars are the intentions of a certain person!" Then, facing her unworthy suitor, she added, "Your Grace, be assured that I am the least of God's creatures and, moreover, that all is vanity save in the service of God. So may Your Grace alter his intentions and follow in the way that God commands, for by that road He will bring you to Divine well-being."

Considerably startled, Montez "admitted to Rosa's perspicacity" and managed to say that he would be glad of her help in finding the road that she recommended. After that, a changed man, he frequently returned to visit her—according to one account, "almost daily," though that is probably an exaggeration. Far from causing her further concern, he proved a model of propriety and "as long as she lived" went every week to confession and Communion. He does not state whether or not he continued to do so after she died. But that his devotion to her lasted a long while, and that he contented himself with showing it in the only way she would permit, we cannot doubt.

Another admirer, a silversmith by the name of Diego de Requena, also visited her frequently; but he always took someone with him when he went and, far from addressing her with intent to deceive, apparently became so tongue-tied in her presence that he never addressed her directly at all! After she died, however, he was one of the first to reach her bier; he then kissed her hands, "still as supple as if she were alive," and in awestruck tones pronounced her beautiful. He was certainly the prime example of the medieval lover, who longed through a lifetime and never risked the shattering of an ideal by direct contact or exchange of words. It seems fitting that he should have come from La Mancha, where Cervantes, about the same time, was locating the imaginary heroines who people *Don Quixote*. But the poor deluded knight has always seemed more real to me than they have and I believe that Rosa, who was a very real person, would have been rather bored with Don Diego, if she permitted him to intrude very much on her consciousness, which I doubt. I am sure she found Don Vicente more interesting.

Between these two extremes—the suitor with dishonorable intentions and the one with no intentions at all—there were numerous others: some who were merely passers-by, murmuring inoffensive but extravagant compliments, according to the well-established and well-regarded customs in Latin countries, as Rosa walked quietly through the streets to church; and some who diligently sought her hand in marriage. However, she was deaf to flattery and what might have been conjugal love was to find expression and fulfillment not in blessing a single hearthstone, but in brightening the bleakness of many. Her maternal impulses were to be directed toward every child within the radius of her vision and knowledge who was in need of care.

She could not explain this to her suitors, she could not explain it to her parents, probably—at fourteen or fifteen—she could not explain it to herself. Her thoughts must often have been troubled as she went about marketing her flowers, cultivated the garden where these grew, together with luscious fruits and healing herbs, or sat by her window, doing the exquisite needlework in which she excelled and which included stitchery on fine linen shirts, embroidery in delicate designs, especially of birds, and the fashioning of silken floral decorations for the altar. She was especially successful with carnations and sweet basil, for both of which there was an increasingly large demand, and her handicraft became a second source of revenue for her family. She was delighted that this was so. But she knew what her course must be and she held fast to it. Just as she had let her hair grow to please her mother, she consented, for the same reason, to make and receive visits, to join in the traditional *paseo* (evening stroll) and to wear becoming clothes. It was only when she saw that these practices were leading straight to proposals of marriage that she took wilful steps to make herself seem less desirable and resolutely withdrew to the solitude for which she longed when she was deprived of it.

Such solitude left her free for the reading, meditation and prayer which were so necessary to fulfill her soul's sincere desire. Her faith was an essential part of her being and its normal outlet was in knowledge of God, thoughts of God and worship of God; and, before long, it also began to find expression in song and story. She was naturally musical and her talent developed rapidly as she learned, with ease, to play one instrument after another. She likewise had a natural gift for versifying and, the more she wrote, the more charming her poems became. Fortunately, many of them have been preserved and though they inevitably lose much in translation, their essential delicacy is not wholly destroyed. The tone of these verses is seldom sad, and sometimes it is actually merry, despite its devotional character, as when she makes a play on words with her own Christian name and the surnames of her father and mother, in addressing a poem to the Saviour.

> *"Ay Jesus de mi alma*
> *Que bien pareces*
> *Entre flores y Rosas*
> *Y Olivas Verdes!"* [31]

Very probably Rosa's thoughts would have turned, sooner or later, longingly to the cloister, even if so much pressure had not been put upon her to accept one of the wealthier, more personable and more distinguished applicants for her hand. In a convent she would have had not only release from the strain caused by her parents' importunities, but she would have been free to spend all her time in the ways most congenial to her. In any event, when she received a definite and appealing invitation to enter one, she felt irresistibly drawn to it. Doña Grimanesa de Mogrovejo, the sister of the Archbishop who had confirmed her, was among the sponsors of a new Foundation, a Community of the Poor Clares. It seemed to Rosa to offer an ideal opportunity. But such a clamor arose that, after tentatively accepting the invitation, she reluctantly withdrew, on the ground that her parents could not do without the money from the sale of her needlework and her flowers. (We cannot help wondering whether or not they would have expected her to carry on her merchandising activities after her marriage. Once she had left their home and gone to one of her own, it seems logical to suppose that her husband would have wanted her to give all her attention to that, which would have deprived Gaspar and María of her assistance in any case. But they seem not to have thought of this.)

Later, a similar opportunity arose: she would be welcome at the Convent of the Incarnation, which was under the direction of the Augustinians. It had been founded by Doña Mencia Porto-Carrero and her mother, Doña Leonor, and this foundation was of special interest to the Flores family, just as the one started by Doña Grimanesa de Mogrovejo had been, though for a different reason. Doña Mencia was the widow of Francisco Hernández Girón, against whose forces Gaspar had fought in the King's Army, and when people began talking about this new convent, it revived many memories of his military career, on which he loved to dwell. He was not horrified because, after the bloody execution, Girón's body had been placed in a sack and tied to a horse which dragged it through the streets; Gaspar felt the traitor had only met his just deserts, and his public disgrace would be a warning to others who plotted against their lawful ruler. But wasn't it a terrible thing, María asked, that Girón's widow should be obliged to see the whole dreadful punishment? Yes, Gaspar supposed so. And wasn't it both natural and noble of Doña Mencia to feel she wanted to spend the rest of her life praying for Girón's release from Purgatory? To be sure, he had died a common criminal, but God in His mercy could pardon even such a malefactor as Girón; it was not certain that nothing could save him from everlasting fire. Doña Mencia and Doña Leonor hoped—they *believed*—that their prayers might help to do that. So they had gone to the Prior of the Augustinian Monastery and he had given them permission to found a convent. Some people, María among them, thought they should have waited until more money and more helpers were available. But those two pious ladies went straight ahead, thinking only of Girón's immortal soul, and not of impediments to saving it.

It was inevitable, in the light of her father's reminiscences and her mother's arguments, to both of which Rosa constantly listened, that her interest in this convent should have been awakened. She consulted her spiritual adviser, a Dominican by the name of Alfonso Velásquez, and he urged her to embrace this second opportunity, for Doña Mencia and Doña Leonor had told her they would welcome her with open arms. Rosa decided that this time nothing should swerve her from her purpose. But, before entering the convent for good and all, she wanted to pay a final visit to the Church of Santo Domingo and pray before the altar of Our Lady of the Rosary that her novitiate might be blessed.

The image therein enshrined was one of the most venerated in Peru. It had been brought to the Indies by the Conquistadores and given a place of honor in the first church built in Lima, that of the Dominicans. Many miracles were attributed to it and an Archconfraternity, with four branches or subdivisions, had been founded in its name. Devotion to it was general, and members of the Archconfraternity vied with each other to provide the statue with gorgeous garments in which it could be robed on such occasions as great festivals. Rosa grieved because she was not rich enough to contribute one of these.

As far as the embroidery was concerned, she could have matched her needlecraft with that of any woman in the city; but the brocade or velvet on which the work must be done was costly, the gold and silver thread even more so. Realizing this, with reluctance and humility, she had "offered a robe woven of prayer and penance and the Virgin had rewarded her with graces and mercies." [5]

As usual, her brother Hernándo accompanied her to church when she went to ask the Virgin's blessing on her novitiate. As she knelt on and on, without showing any disposition to leave, he hesitantly reminded her that the hour at which Doña Mencia and Doña Leonor were expecting her had already passed and they should be on their way to the convent. She whispered back that she realized this, but that she could not seem to move; it was as if something were holding her back. He tried to help her rise, at first by gently taking her arm and then by tugging at her. His efforts were also quite unavailing.

At last, Rosa became convinced that there was some reason why she should not carry out her plan, that a force more powerful than her own was preventing her from doing so. She raised her eyes to the altar and again addressed the Virgin of her fond devotion.

"Señora, I promise that if it is not Your wish I should become a cloistered nun, I will return to the home of my parents. I will continue to serve them, but I will also serve You. Their house shall be my retreat and Your sanctuary."

She had hardly finished her prayer when she found she could move without difficulty. She sent a message of respectful regret to the Augustinians and calmly left the church, with Hernándo walking joyfully at her side. He had not been able to reconcile himself to the idea of her departure, though he had no ulterior motive in wishing to keep her with him; she was infinitely dear to him, as she always had been and always would be. That was all.

Her grandmother, who was now bedridden, was the only other member of the family in whom Rosa had confided. She had been afraid to tell her father and mother what she meant to do lest, a second time, they should overwhelm her with their reproaches. But the stern old lady, who, like Hernándo, loved her only for herself, was trustworthy. She had grieved at the decision of her most cherished grandchild, but she had not tried to deflect her from it, nor had she betrayed Rosa's intention to anyone. Now tears of joy ran down her withered cheeks at the sight of her darling.

Rosa sat beside her bed and comforted her. But another plan was already taking form and substance in her mind. She would stay at home, as she had promised. (Here was another promise to be kept, not made to herself this time, but to the Blessed Virgin.) She would continue to sell her needlework and her flowers and thus add to the family income. She would care for the helpless old woman who loved her so much and whose love she returned as well as for anyone else in the family who was ill and for the younger sisters and brothers who still needed supervision. (Three more children had been born since the return from Quives.) She would—and she knew she should—take time from her reading, meditations and prayers to do all this. But she must find some way of excusing herself from making and receiving social visits and from constantly changing one pretty dress for another, if she were still to seek a retreat and found a sanctuary. Again she prayed that she might be shown what to do and, as she glanced at the statuette of her favorite saint, enshrined in a nearby niche, the answer came so quickly that she was startled by it.

She would join the Third Order of St. Dominic. That was what St. Catherine of Siena had done, that was what she herself should do. She wondered why she had not thought of it before. She knew this Order had been founded expressly to provide for "the religious life in the bosom of the family." Since its institution, four centuries earlier, it had produced saints in all walks of life, from the throne to the humblest cottage, among all sorts and conditions of men and women from kings and queens to peasants, and in such abundance that the cloister might well envy it. Women especially had escaped the tyranny of unwelcome positions by wearing the habit of St. Dominic. The monastery had come to them since they had not been free to go to the monastery. Probably Rosa did not say this to herself in exactly those words. Nevertheless, they carry the purport of her rushing thoughts. The monastery would indeed be coming to her—the retreat, the sanctuary for which she had so longed. And, though she would not be obliged to wear a habit, she would be entitled to do so. She would never wear anything else as long as she lived.

Still gazing at the statuette of St. Catherine, she murmured a prayer of thanksgiving. Then she turned and looked through the narrow window by her grandmother's bed into the garden where the birds were singing and the insects humming. She could see the flowers that she loved, and butterflies flitting over the flower beds. One of them fluttered through the open window, settled lightly on her breast and spread its wings: a black and white butterfly.

She had often heard that butterflies were a symbol of immortality, of life after death. Now, in this one, she saw a symbol of life on earth, her life as a Tertiary of St. Dominic.

B.T. Sanctam Rosam Confirmat et nomen imponit.

Quis dubitet Zephyrum te dicere Numinis alti,
Dum Dinam mulces, nomine, rore, Rosam!

Confirmation of Santa Rosa de Lima.

Colonial Era. Anonymous.
Property of the Convent of San
Francisco, Lima.

As interpreted by the Cuzco School. Prc
erty of Don Pedro de Osma, Lima.

Colonial Era. Anonymous. Casa de Ejercicios de Santa Rosa.

obably 17th Century. Anonymous. Prop-
ty of the Monastery of Rosa de Santa
aría, Lima.

Santa Rosa de Lima as interpreted
by Francisco Laso (1828-1869).
In the City Hall, Lima.

Don Francisco de Borja y Aragón, Viceroy of Peru at the time of Santa Rosa's
death.

Santa Rosa de Lima as interpreted by the Cuzco School. Anonymous. Property of Don J. Tijero, Lima.

Santa Rosa de Lima. Italian School. Anonymous. Property of Don Fernando Rincón, Lima.

Cross of Santa Rosa de Lima. Preserved in the room where she died.

Garden of Santa Rosa de Lima.

atio of the house of Doña María de Uzatégui and Don Gonzalo de la Maza where
nta Rosa de Lima spent her last years. Now the Monastery of Rosa de Santa María.

Glorification of Santa Rosa de Lima by Gonippo Raggi (1918). In the Church
of Santo Domingo, Lima.

CHAPTER VI

Rosa was twenty years old when her confessor, Alfonso de Velásquez—the same who had encouraged her to seek a cloistered life—clothed her in her habit.

The ceremony was a simple one, attended only by María and a few young women who had already joined the Dominican Order. But it was celebrated with great solemnity before the altar of Our Lady of the Rosary; and Rosa's face was radiant as she knelt and heard Father Velásquez begin the ceremony of reception:

" 'O Lord Jesus Christ, Who didst vouchsafe to clothe Thyself with the garment of our mortality, we beseech Thee, of the abundance of Thy great mercy, that Thou wouldst be pleased so to bless this kind of garment, which the holy Fathers have appointed to be worn in token of innocence and humility, that she who is to be clothed with it may be worthy to put on Thee, Christ Our Lord.'

"Rose looked up at the garment Father Alfonso was blessing. It was the Dominican habit of white wool, spread out now upon the altar. . . . In a few minutes this white habit would be hers to wear, instead of the fine clothes of her mother's choice. . . .

"She shut her eyes in sheer happiness as Father Alfonso sprinkled her with Holy Water and continued the prayer:

" ' May the Lord also sprinkle thee with hyssop, who art now going to be clothed with our garments, that thou mayest be made clean, so that being thus cleansed and made whiter than snow in thy soul, thou mayest so appear outwardly in our habit. . . .' " [32]

As the service continued and Rosa joined in the ritual prayers, she gazed at the image enshrined above her and her heart was filled with thanksgiving. True, it was St. Catherine she was trying to emulate, by every means in her power, and it had been while wondering how best to do this that the way had suddenly become clear to her; but if she had not first found herself unable to proceed to the Augustinian Convent because she had been rooted to this very place until she renounced

the vocation of a nun, she would not have been vouchsafed that clari-
fying vision. It was primarily the Virgin who was responsible for her
present overwhelming happiness. For the Virgin had not only paved
the way for the investiture but had signified Her approval of the new
tertiary's wish to call herself henceforth not Rosa de Flores, but Rosa
de Santa María. The young girl was permitted to couple her own name,
officially bestowed on her by the great Archbishop Toribio, with that
of the Queen of Heaven.

It was, perhaps, inevitable that this overwhelming joy should not
last. In the history of almost every saint, there are chapters which
dwell on "aridity" or, as St. John of the Cross has so beautifully expressed it, "the dark night of the soul." Rosa had experienced intermittent periods of such aridity during her adolescence, but they had
not troubled her deeply. This was partly because she could attribute
them to the fact that she was prevented from spending as much time
in seclusion and prayer as she would have wished, and therefore she
did not seem close to Christ and the path of righteousness was not
clear to her. It was also partly because the intervals of really deep depression were brief. Most of the time she was happy in the consciousness of her Saviour's Presence, whether He were seen or unseen, and
in the guidance of her guardian angel.[33] Now that no impediment was
placed in her way, that she was free to order her days exactly as she
thought best, she had expected that the bleak periods would disappear
entirely, that the smiling angel would always be visible beside her, and
that the radiance of Christ's Presence would so illumine her life that,
since she frequently saw Him with eyes of the spirit, it would not matter whether or not He were otherwise visible.

Instead, she could not see the angel, she could not feel the Presence
of Christ; and this was no longer a brief and intermittent experience;
it was a frequent one. "In spirit and heart, the Divine Majesty sometimes suspended the union which she had experienced with God and
left her feeling that she was deserted in such a way that she knew
neither God nor God's creatures."

She would have needed wisdom beyond her years to realize that this
desolation was, in a sense, exactly what she should have expected, that
it was irrational for her to suppose that, by merely changing her daily
routine and putting on a habit, she could command supernatural privileges. She still needed to learn that a true devotee is always ready to
receive the Lord, but does not take His favors for granted; to acquire
the great qualities of patience and resignation; to accept the discipline

of enforced self-confidence, so often a gift of God. In short, she still needed to grow in grace. And because she did not do this rapidly, her dark night of the soul lasted for several years.

Meanwhile, she taught herself to do with less and less sleep, less and less food, with the conviction that normal rest and normal nourishment were impediments to sanctified living, a conviction, we should not fail to stress, that she shared with almost every saint whose life is a matter of record, until Ignatius Loyola counseled a different approach to godliness. What was more—and what was worse, from the modern viewpoint—she redoubled her penances, which, from childhood, had already verged on the extreme. To her, discipline still meant self-inflicted bodily suffering, bravely borne and, as far as possible, secretly practiced. If she had succeeded in joining a cloistered Order, even the most rigorous, she would have been permitted no such excesses as those in which she now indulged. She was no longer satisfied with a knotted cord, but scourged herself with a chain; she locked an iron belt around her waist and threw its key into the well, so that she might never be tempted to unfasten it when its spikes dug into her flesh. She changed the position of her pewter crown of thorns every day, so that its points would continually make new wounds. All of her early biographers and some of her later ones dwell on these practices with seeming delight; to this writer, they exemplify the least appealing aspect of her character. But we cannot give a complete picture of her unless we mention them and, in so doing, recognize that, at the time she lived, they were highly esteemed and widely praised, even when some effort was made on the part of priests or physicians to mitigate their severity.

Fortunately, there are other aspects of this period of aridity which also help to give a complete picture of her and which are pleasanter to contemplate. She continued to be a dutiful daughter, a skillful seamstress, an inspired gardener and a successful wage earner; and her natural aptitude for service was beginning to embrace not only her family, but the needy among her neighbors, especially their destitute children and their ailing elders. We do not know exactly when she first asked for permission to set aside one room in the house for the care of such unfortunates, which later became her main preoccupation, and which is, in the eyes of many, the outstanding reason for her claim to canonization; but it must have been early in the period of aridity. Also, like many another soul in distress, John of the Cross among them, she found an outlet for her emotions in writing, and some of her most touching verse springs from her sense of abandonment. One she addressed to her guardian angel who, she believed, was still hovering near, even though she could not see him.

> *"Fly, O swift messenger,*
> *Fly to our Lord!*
> *Oh, haste to our dear Master adored!*
> *Ask why He delays, and remains*
> *Far from our side.*
>
> *Tell Him I cannot live*
> *Parted from Him:*
> *My life then no happiness knows:*
> *In Him only my heart can repose,*
> *Or pleasure can find.*
>
> *Fly, noble messenger, fly!*
> *Tell Him when He is not here*
> *I languish alone.*
> *Tell Him His Rose must her sorrow bemoan*
> *Till the moment when He shall return."* [34]

Although Rosa led a secluded life, leaving her hermitage, her cell-like bedroom and her garden only to attend Mass and sell her flowers, it was inevitable that she should become an increasingly conspicuous figure. An attractive girl who dismisses a succession of eligible suitors always has been and probably always will be the subject of neighborhood gossip, and this has a way of spreading. When such a girl not only declines to marry, but steadfastly refuses to mingle in society and dresses like a religious; spends hours on end in church, even when no service is going on, and leaves the altar rail in a state of apparent rapture; and sets aside part of her home as an infirmary—she actually called it that—where she works herself, gossip about her soon ceases to be confined to a neighborhood, but spreads through all the streets of a city and then through the length and breadth of a land.

Rosa made no parade of her austerities. Quite the contrary. Her crown of thorns was hidden by the wreath of roses which her mother had insisted she should wear over her veil, when she was being decked out for the matrimonial market, and which Rosa, for her own reasons, had continued to wear since with her Dominican habit; but there were sometimes telltale drops of blood on her forehead. She had been forced to appeal to Mariana for help, when the agony of her belt became too great even for her superhuman endurance and she found she could not undo it. It is unthinkable that, even if Mariana had held her tongue about excessive fasting and minor mortifications, she would have done so about the condition in which she found her *amita's* ("little soul") delicate flesh, or the further damage that was done when María was heard approaching and an effort was made to remove the belt so rapidly that this meant literally wrenching it off. As far as that goes, María probably did some indiscreet talking herself. She still felt aggrieved because her daughter had not made a brilliant match; and as for all these paupers on the premises, any sensible housewife would resent them; there were probably thieves among them; certainly there were repulsive cripples and dotards in the last stages of loathsome diseases. Yet Rosa insisted that in ministering to them, she was ministering to the Lord, that there was actually something in Holy Writ—María could not remember just what—that gave authority to this. As far as that went, Rosa pretended she did not even need to read a book to know what she should do: the Lord had told her Himself, her guardian angel had showed her the way.

It is not surprising that with the widening spread of gossip, to which a faithful servant and a girl's own mother gave the ring of truth, Rosa should now have attracted the notice, not of eligible young gallants, but of the Inquisition.

Fortunately, before this happened, the worst phase of her aridity was over. She *had* grown in grace, and was again rejoicing, much of the time, in the consciousness that she was close to Christ and that her guardian angel was leading her. Moreover, she was mercifully not required to appear before the Inquisition's Tribunal. Instead, at its instigation, eminent theologians—at first, only two and, later, a larger group—came to question her at home in the presence of her mother and a certain Doña María Uzátegui, almost the only acquaintance whom Rosa accepted as a close friend. One of the first interrogaters was the greatly revered doctor of medicine, Juan de Castillo (since declared a Venerable by the Church) who would now doubtless be classed as a psychiatrist of the first order, and who was considered as well versed in theology and mysticism as he was in diseases of the mind and body. The other was Father Juan de Lorenzana, a leading professor at the University of San Marcos and Prior of its Convent, Vicar General of the Province of San Juan Bautista and, furthermore, its Provincial and *Visitador*. Rosa could hardly have been confronted with a more formidable pair; there is no doubt that if she could not have answered them to their entire satisfaction, the questioning would have gone no further and their report to the Inquisition would have been disastrous to her.

She faced them without abashment, but with humility and with a candid confession that she lacked learning. She spoke in moving terms of her desolation of spirit when she did not feel close to God and of her joy when she had a sense of reunion with Him.

"The examiners pressed her again, asking if, after having thus separated from God and suffering eclipse of His light, she did not receive some compensating consolation. To this she answered that, when God entered her soul again, it was with a brilliant light which enkindled so great a love in her will that it grew all inflamed with ardor. Then she felt herself, she said, to enter into the very bosom of God, where she was transformed into her Beloved, so completely that not all the temptations of the world, the flesh and the devil could ever separate her from His love. Again questioned, she said that she had attained so perfect a union with God that she found it impossible to turn her thoughts from Him, so that none of her external occupations could divert her attention, nor could the ailments she suffered, painful though these were. She gave them a conviction that she could find no pleasure on earth except in the contemplation of the divine mercy.

"Those before whom she had been summoned were learned men. . . . All were astonished when, upon being asked if she had never read any books of mystical theology, or any teaching a method of prayer by which the unitive life might be attained, she answered that she did not know that such books existed. And when asked what efforts she made to resist evil inclinations, she could only tell them that, by the grace of God, she did not remember ever to have found in her soul any opposition to virtue; that, on the contrary, she had had from her infancy a strong inclination to piety, and that this had made her joyfully embrace its practices. 'I do not mean,' she added, 'that I have not perceived in myself involuntary movements; but as soon as I applied my mind to the presence of God, they vanished so promptly that I usually did not have time to resist them.' Finally, when they wanted to know if she did not find some trifling satisfaction in earthly things, when her mind was relaxed after being extended in prayer, she said that she could not possibly take the least pleasure in them, and that her mind suffered inconceivable pain when, if only for a moment, it was unoccupied with God. . . . What could these learned men conclude but that this girl, who was quite untaught from books, was a mystic of a high order? Deeply blushing at revealing her secrets, and in a faltering voice, she let them know that Christ often appeared to her, now as a child, and again as a man thirty years old. She added that the Blessed Virgin and her guardian angel also came to console her.

"They went on to question her about the dogmas of faith, and were surprised at the way she spoke of the Holy Trinity, of the hypostatic union of the two natures in Christ, of predestination and grace, and other matters of theology. It was plain that she had learned all this not from study but from infused knowledge. What they could not understand was how Rose, contrary to all systems of mysticism, should have attained the unitive life with very little of the laborious methods of the purgative. Seemingly they did not take into account her ascetic practices, about which in modesty she said as little as possible. These had never been to purge out the 'old leaven' in herself but had been for others. A public statement was issued in the name of the priests who had examined her that she was actuated in her conduct by the impulses of grace." [35]

After that, there was nothing the Inquisitors needed to say to Rosa or that she needed to say to them. She "heard the voice of the Lord God walking in the garden in the cool of the day," as she went quietly among her flowers, her guardian angel at her side.

CHAPTER VII

"The poor called her their mother, the wretched, the corrupt, the dregs of humanity blessed her name." This statement is made by one of Rosa's most understanding and accurate biographers [5] and it is coupled, in the same paragraph, with a question: "What would have availed her prayers, her fasts and her vigils, without her love of the poor, without her flaming charity, without her compassion for suffering mankind?"

The answer, as far as many of us today are concerned, is, "Very little." At the same time, we should by no means overlook or forget her other great qualities. Her gifts as a mystic, for example, entitle her to be classified not only with her beloved Catherine of Siena, but with Teresa of Avila and John of the Cross. To be sure, she did not have their genius for sharing their experiences with others in writing. Her verses, though delicate and charming, cannot compare with St. John's immortal poetry. The few letters she wrote, though clear and gracious, cannot compare with Teresa's voluminous correspondence, much less with *The Interior Castle* and other similar great works; and no one has ever produced anything comparable, of its kind, to Catherine's *Dialogue*, which was composed in five days. But her attainment of the "unitive life" and the extent of her "infused knowledge" certainly point to mystic powers of a high order. So many examples of these are available that it is with the greatest difficulty I have decided upon one among them as an example of their symbolic splendor. But it seems to me that her own account of a dazzling vision is the most compelling and inspiring of all.

"I saw a great light which seemed a thing infinite and, in the midst of it, a rainbow, very beautiful and very large, of many and varied tones, and above which there was another, equally beautiful, and above the second rainbow, I saw a cross whereon Jesus Christ had been crucified, and, under the first rainbow, I saw Our Lord Jesus Christ with such grandeur and majesty and beauty that I can not, nor know how to, explain.

"And I saw Him face to face a very long while. And His Divine Majesty was served to give me forces to be looking at Him so long a while, face to face, all entire, from feet to head.

"And from His face and body, there came to my spirit and my body rays and tongues of glory so that I thought myself ended with this world and in glory itself.

"Then, I saw how Jesus Christ took a weight and scales. A great number of angels came, very beautiful. They knelt to Him and did Him reverence. Afterward, there came a great number of spirits. And then the angels began to weigh and to measure in the scales works and more works. I saw that Jesus Christ did not trust the angels and took the weight and the scales in His Own hands and distributed works and more works to the spirits. And I saw also that He imparted unto me a very great work. After this, I saw that Jesus Christ again took the weight and the scales in His hands, and the angels began to weigh in those scales graces and more graces. I saw that Jesus Christ did not trust the angels and took the weight in His Own hand and distributed to the spirits graces and more graces. And I saw that He imparted unto me more and more graces. . . .

"And Jesus Christ declared to me and said unto me, 'May all know that, after works, comes grace, and that, without works, there is no grace; many works are necessary to augment it; and, let no one be mistaken, this is the scale of heaven, and there is none other.'" [36]

The spectacle of the rainbows and the cross is one of the most striking which I have found in mystical literature; but the parable of the scales with which the vision ends is even more impressive: "without works, there is no grace; let no one be mistaken, this is the scale of heaven." This unequivocal and magnificent statement brings us back to the question, previously quoted, "What would have availed her prayers, her fasts and her vigils, without her love of the poor, without her flaming charity, without her compassion for suffering mankind?" It also answers this question for us.

Her gifts as a prophetess were less remarkable. To be sure, in the opinion of some writers, she predicted the peaceable departure of a buccaneering band, about which we shall hear more presently. But it is more probable that, as far as these pirates were concerned, the wish was father to the thought in Rosa's mind, rather than that she was divinely inspired—at least, in this writer's opinion. The same is true of her prophecy regarding the foundation of a convent dedicated to St. Catherine of Siena and the repeated conviction that her mother would eventually be there, a prediction which María greeted with derision, exclaiming, "Yes, when elephants fly!" Both these prophecies were fulfilled, but, great as was her faith in the Lord, Rosa herself had left no stone unturned to see that they came true. In fact, for the only time in her life, she stepped out of character to the extent of taking part in a public display with the hope of arousing general interest in building such a convent. She persuaded eight girls, clad in the Dominican habit, to join her in a procession on Christmas Eve. According to her mother, the girls gathered around Rosa's cell, wherein there was an altar with a statue of the saint, adorned with palms, garlands and silver ornaments and surrounded with candles. Rosa instructed each and all to pray to the Child Jesus "in such words as God should dictate, and so they did with much joy." At Matins bell they took candles and set out for St. Dominic's, accompanied by María. Each girl wore a veil and carried palms and garlands to be laid before the altar of Our Lady of the Rosary; each confessed and received Communion. At dawn a second procession was formed and they all returned to Rosa's house. The whole proceeding was engineered by Rosa who explained, "Thus it will be understood in the city that a convent, dedicated to Catherine of Siena, needs must be founded."

She was right in believing that a flurry of excitement would follow this demonstration. Women began to throng the house, asking if it were true that she believed such a convent could be founded and Rosa calmly replied that she did. Her mother, considerably annoyed, reminded Rosa of the expense that would be involved and of their lack of wealth. To this, she also made a calm reply: "Mother, it grieves me to see you so distrustful of God's mercy, for I have faith that the work of men can be done if guided by God. I repeat that you will see this convent, that you must see it. Just when, I do not know, but I do know that you will."

Most of Rosa's other predictions were of minor matters: a priest would not be sent to an unwelcome post; an invalid should be of good cheer because there was no present prospect of death; a friend would send her a pitcher of hot chocolate to refresh her after a fast. There is no doubt that she was clairvoyant and the exactitude with which she foretold the day and hour of her own death does point to supernatural perception of natural events; but her powers in the field of prophecy are not to be compared with her mystic powers, still less with her powers of prayer.

I use the word power advisedly, for prayer is not only an act of worship; it is an agent of vast achievement. It does not come naturally to everyone, either as an act of worship or as a vital force. The ability to pray is, in itself, God given, whether in unquestioning adoration, in petition or in thanksgiving. When it approaches or attains perfection, it is the evidence of the faith which can move mountains.

Rosa had a program of prayer covering many things. She prayed for souls in Purgatory. She offered all her devotions for specific intentions. For the saving of even one soul, she stood ready to give her life. She prayed regularly for everyone in Peru, with special stress on the idolatrous Indians. Three times a day—in the morning, at noon and at night —she declaimed over and over again the words, "Thanks be to God, thanks be to God." Other hours of the day she set off for the various forms of contemplation, offerings and petitions, both public and private. While she was sewing or cultivating, she prayed silently and continuously. But in moments of less intensive activity, when she had a sense of work well done and rejoiced in it, she joined the birds in her garden and burst into song. One charming story is told by a friend who found her addressing a nightingale which had come to perch on a nearby tree.

"Little nightingale, let us praise the Lord"—Rosa was singing— "praise thou thy Creator, while I praise my Redeemer."

The little bird and Rosa sang back and forth, antiphonally, until the church bells began to ring for Vespers. Then the nightingale flew away and Rosa marked its flight with another song beginning, "Blessed is God, my little bird has left me. . . ."

She prayed neither from fear nor from hope of reward, but from pure love. Nevertheless, though she did not seek Divine favors, they were unquestionably granted her. In fact, when she was once questioned as to whether or not she had received them, on a given occasion, she replied quite simply, "Father, I always do."

We may say that many persons and by no means always persons who have been recognized as saints have spent as much time in prayer as Rosa, that they have done so with as little self-seeking and that they have received as many direct answers to their prayers. I agree that we could do so quite truthfully. But I would still say that I do not happen to know of many who have so fully realized the value of prayer, both as a form of worship and as a vital force, or have achieved so complete and so perfect an understanding of it. Rosa came to comprehend that her form of petition was, indeed, a prayer of union with God. Each time she set herself to pray, she recognized His Presence in her spirit. This recognition enabled her to give an inimitable reply when asked the question, "What is God like?"

"Like ocean infinite or like infinite cloud."

Could any simile be more beautiful or more meaningful, coming from a girl who lived in a mist-veiled city between the great Andes and the trackless ocean?

Having granted all this and having also considered Rosa's industry, humility, purity of thought and action and dedication to the Divine, it is still a source of constant wonder to the modern chronicler why we are not invited to learn more about Rosa's infirmary and less about her mortifications. It is now a matter of conviction, in her native land, that she was both the originator and the supreme exponent of social service in Peru, just as the same thing is said of Mariana in Ecuador; and as the latter was outspoken in her indebtedness to the former as an example, it is no exaggeration to say that the Dominican Tertiary was responsible for the awakening of humanitarianism in what are now two countries, though, at the time the two consecrated young girls were living, Peru and Ecuador were both part of the same viceregal province. Yet, elsewhere, we hear very little about these activities. In fact, one of Rosa's biographers, who has beautifully and eloquently interpreted her mystic powers, says that he does not touch on her private charities because they were not conducted on a scale that was "particularly noteworthy"! With all due respect to his views, which I know are sincere, I believe that, in this, he is mistaken. Certainly, the Peruvians of both sexes, who are now devoting their lives to social service, recognize and hail Rosa de Santa María not only as their patroness, but as their model and their inspiration. They stress her talent for organization and her knowledge as an herbalist. They insist that she was "the brightest light ever to shine upon submerged masses of Indians and slaves, who made up the larger part of Lima's inhabitants," and they still venerate the "Little Doctor"—the *mediquito*—a statue of the Child Jesus which she placed in her infirmary and to which her patients, as well as herself, attributed many miracles.

As the work of the infirmary went on, it was gradually taken for granted, both by Rosa's family and by the citizens of Lima generally, ceasing to seem bothersome to María or eccentric to high-born ladies. But it offered no spectacular elements as far as either was concerned, and the transitory excitement which had sprung from neighborhood gossip and culminated in the probings prompted by the Inquisition, had long since died down. It was not until 1615, when Rosa was twenty-nine years old and had been wearing her Dominican habit for nearly a decade, that anything happened to bring her forcibly before the public again.

Pirates, long a formidable menace, had ceased to harass the Peruvian shores since 1593. Sir Francis Drake—Thomas Cavendish—Richard Hawkins—their very names had once struck terror to those who heard them; but though Drake and Cavendish had done tremendous damage and eventually made off with sizable booty, Hawkins had been vanquished by the Peruvians in 1593 and, since then, there had been no alarums and excursions. Now, word reached Lima that a formidable Dutchman, Jorge Spitberg, had passed through the Straits of Magellan with a squadron of seven ships and, having ravaged the coast of Chile, was now headed straight for Callao.

The Viceroy, Don Juan de Mendoza y Luna, Marqués de Montes Claros, promptly dispatched three warships to encounter the free-booters. The opposing fleets met near Cerro Azul, about halfway between Callao and Cape Quemado, with disastrous results to the Peruvians. Spitberg then resumed his devastating progress.

When the report reached Lima that the dark sails of the pirate ships had appeared on the horizon, consternation seized the inhabitants. There was a veritable clatter of coffers, hastily closed and hidden. All the bells tolled, women and children took refuge in churches, *arcabuceros* and lancers met in formation around the *Plaza Mayor* and were swiftly joined by the leading citizens. The Viceroy, fully armed and mounted on horseback, came galloping from the palace, prepared to lead his troops; but the *Audiencia* forbade his departure for the coast. He must remain where he was, they said, to give orders and calm the general hysteria. Reluctantly, he bowed to the authority of his counselors, but, as the expected bombardment began, he commanded that, with the exception of ecclesiastics, every able-bodied male should prepare to bear arms.

Gaspar de Flores was not among the *arcabuceros* who went tramping off at dawn, eager volunteers at their side, together with mounted soldiers armed with glittering lances and cavaliers accompanied by armor bearers and servants. His days in the guard were long since past. He was now around ninety years of age and, except for submitting occasional complaints that he had not been receiving his pension with the regularity he had a right to expect, he was no longer in communica-

tion with the Viceroy. He had become somewhat querulous as he
grew older, at the same time, losing none of the bravado which had
made him such a dashing figure in his youth. By all means, let his
wife and daughters take refuge in a church if they wished; his sons
were already on their way to Callao. He would remain at home alone.
If the pirates wanted him, they would have to come and find him.

Rosa had gone to church with the others, but this was with no
idea of seeking safety. On the contrary, she ardently welcomed the
idea of martyrdom. However, if she were going to die, as she would
have rejoiced to do, it must be in defense of the Sanctuary. She
mounted the altar steps and stood facing the door, which the pirates
could be expected, at any moment, to force. If some priest tried to stop
her, there is no record of this; and, obedient as she habitually was to
authority, it is doubtful if she would have heeded such a command, in
this instance. She was enraptured, not through a mystic trance, but
through ecstasy of another sort. She was at one and the same time
her father's daughter and her Saviour's crusader. And her guardian
angel was at her side.

The marauding band burst into the church and came charging
up the aisle. Then, as suddenly as it had entered and advanced, it
halted. The pirates did not even hear the crying children or see the
cowering women on either side of them. They saw only the figure of
a slender girl, clad in black and white, her arms outstretched to shield
the tabernacle, her face defiant, exalted and radiant. Nor was the
radiance confined to her face; it seemed to flow from her very draperies. There was a quality in it which was, at first, arresting, then blinding, then frightening. The pirates, despite their lust for loot and
carnage, quailed before it. They would have said, indeed often had
said, that they feared neither God nor man. But now they were afraid.

They left the church as hastily as they had entered it. The next day
their dark sails had disappeared beyond the horizon.

There are, of course, many who have sought to disprove or alter
this story. One version has it that the pirates never actually came to
the church where Rosa had gone; in fact, that they never disembarked
at all and that their bombardment had done but little damage—it was
Rosa's *prayers* that had prevented this and she had prophesied right
along that these would be answered. If this were the case, how could
she have consistently hoped for martyrdom? And why should a girl

who, all her life, had shunned public observation have taken a dramatic stand before the altar?

Another version of the story is that the pirates probably intended no harm anyway. This seems to me open to even more serious doubt. If Rosa were not responsible for their abrupt departure, then I think we should consider this one of those mysteries that has never been explained, just as Hannibal's retreat, when he was at the very gates of Rome, which he had sought for years to conquer, has remained unexplained through the centuries. But that Rosa, single-handed, should have accomplished the defeat of the marauders seems to me no more unbelievable than that Catherine of Siena should have persuaded an errant pope to leave the "Babylonian exile" of Avignon and return to the Vatican in Rome; and that is not a matter of legend, it is a matter of history. In each instance, all that could be seen was a frail girl, clad in black and white—in Catherine's case, a girl standing engulfed by the tall stone columns of a vast and gloomy audience chamber; in Rosa's case, a girl with her back to the Holy of Holies. In each instance, the girl was confronted by enemies and surrounded by weaklings; in each instance, the girl proved stronger than all the powers of darkness arrayed against her.[37]

Whether or not we personally believe it to be true, there is no doubt that Limenians, both then and thereafter, regarded Rosa as the saviour of their city. If she had not won martyrdom, she had won something else that was to have a profound effect on her own history and the history of her people, even if she did not realize it. Of course, it is quite possible that they should have felt she had preserved them merely through the power of prayer, as she stood at the altar, and had thus averted catastrophe. Now that her supernatural gifts had taken a striking form, witnessed by multitudes, the people achieved a deeper realization of her other attributes, and, withdrawn as she had always preferred to remain from close human relationships aside from those of her family and her patients, from the day she defended the altar, she found it easier to return this affection she herself compelled and to admit that friendship could and should have its proper place in her design for living. This was especially true in the case of Doña María de Uzátegui, the noble lady who had been present at the interrogation of Rosa by ecclesiastical authorities; of Doña María's two daughters, Doña Micaela and Doña Andrea; and of their father, Don Gonzalo de la Maza.

Don Gonzalo was a distinguished man and the position he held was an important one. The wealth pouring into Spain from the New World was literally fabulous, but the methods of handling it were realistic and practical in the extreme. The Viceroy was assisted in his administrative duties by skilled accountants, royal officials who acted as bookkeepers, and ministers and other personages who seemed especially adapted by training or nature, or both, to finance. Don Gonzalo had been entrusted by that astute monarch, Philip II, with the task of visiting the so-called *Tribunal de Cuentas*—the Commission of Audits—in Spain; and as a result of the information thus gleaned and the talent he had showed in using it to best advantage, he had next been appointed to establish the *Tribunal de la Cruzada,* a colonial counterpart of the commission in the home country.

When he selected a residence in Lima for himself and his wife and daughters, Don Gonzalo was unhampered by straitened circumstances and he and his wife had taste as well as riches. He came from a prominent family in Burgos, she from an equally prominent one in Madrid. Their house in Lima surrounded an enormous and luxuriant patio. The rooms of this house were also enormous and were lavishly furnished. Richly carved tables and *armarios,* chairs upholstered in Cordoba leather, beautifully tooled chests, rich carpets, painted screens, ancestral portraits—all these were there in abundance. The private chapel had gold embroidered velvet draperies, a golden altar, candelabra of wrought silver, a beautiful reproduction of the Virgin of Atocha,[38] and an *Ecce Homo* painted by Angelino Mezos; it was in every way indicative both of its owners great piety and of their abundant means to make their place of prayer one of magnificence.[39]

Apparently Don Gonzalo, who was extremely devout, had heard of Rosa de Santa María even before his wife was aware of the girl's existence. Rumors of her saintliness had reached him at his office and he asked Doña María to watch, in church, for a beautiful girl, clad in the Dominican habit, who gave, at one and the same time, an impression of great dignity and great modesty. Doña María was not long in singling out this paragon. She saw, kneeling close to her, a girl whose veil, as it parted, disclosed a face of such purity and nobility, that the Spanish lady was moved to approach her as soon as the service came to an end and to offer her friendship.

This casual encounter led, with surprising rapidity, considering Rosa's natural diffidence under such circumstances, to an acquaintance which ripened satisfactorily for all concerned. We are fortunate in possessing a delightful account of a visit which Don Gonzalo paid her.

"Once, in the summertime, he went into the garden at the house of Rosa's parents, to see Rosa in her cell. He sat by the door in the shade of young trees. He and Rosa talked; Rosa's mother wandered about in the garden. There were many mosquitoes bothering and biting him, but not one touched Rosa. Her face and hands were free of welts, too. He inquired, 'My Mother, how is it that these mosquitoes bite guests and not my Mother?' Rosa replied in her always charming way, 'My Father, I have made friends with the mosquitoes ever since I've been coming to this cell; so, not only do they not bite me, but they are besides, for me, a great motive for praise of God. For by night, they gather here inside, and great swarms cling to the walls and when, by morning, I come and open the door, they rise, and I tell them we must praise the Lord. And really, my Father, according to my affection, it seems the mosquitoes do just that, in concert of their humming.'

"Rosa carried the discussion beyond mosquitoes to other things of creation: 'Besides, my Father, when, in the morning, I open the garden door, I say to trees and plants and flowers that they [must] praise and give thanks to Our Lord. And, my Father, according to my affection, they seem to do it. They bow down their branches and leaves. They waken and sound in concert, very softly. Look, my Father, whether it be right that all do love and praise this great God Who so many mercies shows us!' "

Gonzalo's wife, María de Uzátegui, reports on the same event as follows:

"Mornings, when she went into the garden, Rosa said to flowers and trees:

" 'Let us praise God.'

And the trees humbled themselves and made extraordinary sound. Something similar happened with the mosquitoes that entered Rosa's cell: told to praise God, they rose and made answering murmur."

María de Uzátegui further reports on a visit she made to Rosa in the cell in the garden. She was stung and asked how Rosa escaped. Rosa answered:

"Mother mine, I have a pact with them, whereby they do not sting me and I do not kill them." [40]

Eventually, feeling that even such pleasant interludes as these did not permit them to see enough of each other, Doña María invited Rosa to be her house guest. The latter accepted without hesitation and soon became almost a member of the family. In fact, for the last few years of her life, she spent almost as much time with her benefactors—for such they were in every sense of the word—as she did in her own home.

Far from objecting to such an arrangement, Rosa's parents were pleased with it. To them, this association with a rich and noble family seemed the next best thing to an advantageous marriage, for the generosity of Don Gonzalo and Doña María was far reaching. To Rosa, the magnificent chapel was hallowed ground. Her devotion to the Virgin of Atocha had always been second only to that she felt for the Virgin of the Rosary; the *Ecce Homo* spoke to her eloquently. The happiness of the hours she spent with them was unalloyed and she also found infinite contentment in her human companionship. She taught the two young girls, Doña Micaela and Doña Andrea to embroider the same delicate designs that she did, to play the same musical instruments, to read the same books.

She had more difficulty in adjusting herself to the general scheme of the social life into which she was automatically thrust. Her parents' congenial friends, like themselves, were persons of limited means and opportunities who could not aspire to places among the seats of the mighty. It was only during the great religious ceremonies, the games and parades, that they were actually participants in the dazzling scene. The rest of the time they observed it with admiration, but with awe, as outsiders. But by birth and breeding, as well as by official position, Don Gonzalo and Doña María were qualified to move in the most exclusive and aristocratic circles and they did; and life at the viceregal court was patterned, as closely as possible, after court life in Spain—at that period, certainly the most formal and probably the most cultured and elegant of any in Europe. The first few Viceroys, though they lived in state themselves, had not brought their wives with them, but, beginning with the administration of the second Marqués de Cañete, this custom underwent a change. His consort, "the very beautiful and very noble" Doña Teresa de Castilla y de la Cueva, came with her husband, accompanied by several highborn ladies in waiting, scarcely less charming and distinguished than herself. She had added a delightful note of femininity to the palace and also endeared herself to the people by her graciousness and her generosity and acted as godmother to several Indian babies, honoring the humble homes of their parents with her presence in the course of the christening celebrations.

The shining example of this very noble and very beautiful lady set a standard which her successors strove to meet, with varying degrees of success. The Marquesa de Montes Claros, Vicereine when Rosa's acquaintance with Don Gonzalo and Doña María began to blossom into friendship, was one of the more successful; and from the moment of meeting their protégée, the Marquesa took a liking to her and overwhelmed Rosa with attentions which embarrassed her. However, Rosa recognized the essential kindliness behind these attentions and tried to think of something she could do to show her appreciation. She had grieved because she could not give the Virgin of the Rosary a rich robe, lavishly embroidered; but it now occurred to her that she might offer the Vicereine a sample of her "horticulture sculpture." She had devised a "Cross of Christ" from three stalks of rosemary and planted these arrangements in small ornamental jars. One of these she had given the Prior of St. Dominic's, Father Alfonso Velásquez, for himself; a second she also sent him, but with the request that it be forwarded by him to the Vicereine.

The Marquesa was as pleased as a child with the original gift. But, though she tended the plant as carefully as she knew how, it quickly began to wither and, with great regret, she returned it to Rosa, asking that something be done to revive it. Father Velásquez was disturbed and puzzled; he could not understand why it should have drooped so soon, if the Vicereine had given it proper attention. The Vicereine was not at fault, Rosa assured him, coming to that great lady's defense; it was just that the cross was the product of a very humble garden, that it was not yet adapted to royal surroundings. She nurtured it again and, within a few days, it was completely restored. She decorated it with a group of figurines—Mary Magdalen surrounded by angels—and sent it back. The Vicereine was enchanted; nothing would do but that Rosa must come and visit her at the palace. The girl could not decline, but she was glad when the visit was over; in fact, she was secretly relieved when Montes Claros—"an enlightened and prudent man who, in Lima, no less than in his native Seville, was considered supremely learned"—asked for permission to resign his post. It was her hope that the next Vicereine would be less demonstrative. Evidently this hope was realized, for—as far as I know—there is no record that the Princess de Esquilache singled her out for special attentions during her lifetime, though the Vicereine was one of the great personages who paid her signal honors after her death.

The Marquesa de Montes Claros was not, however, by any means the only great lady who treated Rosa with excessive fondness. Doña María Eufemia de Pareja, who was enormously rich, insisted on having the girl use her carriage when Rosa went back and forth between her own home and that of Don Gonzalo, or when, instead of going to St. Dominic's, she went to St. Peter's, which was farther away. Doña Eufemia insisted that the cobblestones were hard on Rosa's feet and the dust bad for her to breathe. It did her no good to protest that she had been used to cobblestones and dust all her life; Doña Eufemia had her way. And, to tell the truth, Rosa did not protest as vigorously as she would have a few years earlier, because she could not do so convincingly; walking tired her more and more all the time.

There is at least one recorded instance of an attention which Rosa received with gratitude, untinged by embarrassment. She had always managed to deck her statuette of St. Catherine with jewels, three times a year. But the jewels were borrowed and she had to return them at the end of the special occasion for which they had been lent. She wanted something of her own, something permanent, in the way of adornment for the statuette. It has always been part and parcel of the Spanish tradition to dress sacred images in rich robes, and she had already been disappointed because she could not furnish these for the Virgin of the Rosary. Finally, speaking aloud to St. Catherine, she said, "Thou knowest well, my Mother, that if I only had fifteen or sixteen *patacones* (silver dollars), I should dress thee to my pleasure."

Within two hours, a Negro servant arrived with a note wrapped around silver coins. The note came from a distinguished lady of the Agama family and read, "My dear sister: Since I know you are adorning my mother, I send you these sixteen *patacones*, so that you may secure whatever may be lacking."

Rosa burst out with a happy exclamation and forthwith sent for some white satin!

At the other end of the social scale, Rosa continued her good work. On the days when she did not go home, María, no longer antagonistic, supervised the infirmary for her; but Rosa's patients watched for her return and she did not disappoint them. However, she was obliged to admit to herself—and eventually to others—that she could not devote the endless hours to nursing which she formerly had done. Her strength, overtaxed for so long, was beginning to fail. She was only thirty, but she did not have the physical endurance of her mother, (now in her fifties) or even of her father (in his nineties). She tired easily, and suffered in unexpected and unwelcome ways. She did not need to seek pain any more; it came to her unsought. She accepted it uncomplainingly. Her only lament—and this she tried not to voice—was that her failing health prevented her from nurturing the health of others.

But on the whole, as we have said, she was happy. She was surrounded by the loving-kindness which, all her life, she had shown so lavishly to others. And, on Palm Sunday, when she went to the Church of Santo Domingo, to receive a palm that had been blessed, she herself was blessed beyond her fondest hopes, her fondest imaginings.

The day had not begun auspiciously. Through accident or absent-mindedness, the Sacristan overlooked Rosa as he was distributing the palms. Deeply disappointed, she retired to her preferred refuge before the Virgin of the Rosary and, lifting tearful eyes to the image, she said, "Queen of Heaven, God did not wish me to receive a palm from mortal hands. But You, Who are the Palm of Cades,[41] You shall give me a branch that will never wither, and with this I shall be eternally proud, eternally rich and eternally happy."

As Rosa said this, it seemed to her that the Divine Child, from the arms of His Mother, looked toward the supplicant with such infinite tenderness that Rosa was bathed in rapture. "Rose of My Heart, be My spouse," she thought she heard Him say and then decided that she must have been mistaken, not because she disbelieved the voice, but because she did not grasp the words correctly. "Señor, I am only Your slave, ready to obey Your every command," she murmured. But Mary was confirming the words of the Saviour: "Rosa, behold! My Son is showing you infinite mercy."

After that, there was no room for doubt. On Easter Sunday, Rosa was given her wedding ring, a band of gold on which were inscribed the words she had heard Jesus pronounce. Rosa had ordered it through the medium of her brother Hernándo who, divinely inspired, had designed the ring, placing on it the mystic message in the form of a device or motto. On Holy Thursday, Rosa took the ring to the Sacristan and begged him to conceal it for her. All of Good Friday and Holy Saturday she spent on her knees before the tabernacle; and on Easter Sunday, after she had received Holy Communion, Father Velásquez placed on her finger the emblem of her nuptials. She was now the Bride of Christ.

CHAPTER VIII

For a long time, Rosa had felt that she was already walking in the valley of the shadow of death. She had even prophesied the very day when this would take place: on the Feast of St. Bartholomew, August 24, 1617. Each year she observed this feast day in a very special manner. Her foreknowledge did not depress her; but it did cause her to visit, systematically, the places and people she could not bear to leave without saying farewell.

Though she had continued to supervise her infirmary, even when she could no longer do much hard work in it, she had, of late years, spent less and less time in her garden. Now, she seated herself among her flowers, fruit trees and healing herbs, played her guitar and sang little songs which she composed herself. One of these she addressed to her patron saint:

> "Padre mio Santo Domingo
> Antes que me muera,
> Te encomiendo a mi Madre
> Que sola queda." [42]

María who was working indoors, heard the tinkle of the guitar and caught some of the words. For a moment, she was startled. Then, as she glanced out of the window and saw that her daughter had never looked lovelier, that her attitude and her expression both indicated tranquility, María quickly dismissed her anxious thoughts. It was nothing unusual for Rosa to pray to St. Dominic and it was not surprising that she should ask him to watch over her mother, even if she did word her petition a little strangely or a little prematurely. Why, Rosa was only thirty-one! Of course, she had many years of life before her yet.

After the garden, came the church; the one she thought of as hers. There she met by chance Juan de Tineo, Secretary of the Exchequer and a great friend of Don Gonzalo. She asked him to pray for her, telling him she was sure of her impending death. Like María, he felt she was needlessly apprehensive; surely, she was in the best of health! But, of course, he would be glad to pray for her. She smiled and left him to go and kneel before the Virgin of the Rosary.

At midnight, on the First of August, she was seized with terrible pain. She was at the home of her benefactors, and her cries brought them to her side. At first, she could not describe her sufferings explicitly. Later, she said that a band of iron seemed to be pressing against her temples, a red-hot dart piercing her from head to foot, a fiery poinard plunging into her heart, her bones dissolving little by little and their marrow being reduced to ashes.

It was a grim picture and grew steadily grimmer. The band of iron seemed to restrict her chest as well as her head, her left side became paralyzed. She tried to jest about it; referring to her useless arm and leg, she said, "I wanted to nurse a child for love of Our Lord and His Divine Majesty has given me two—a boy and a girl." But it was hard to make light of her condition, for her fever mounted. The best physicians were summoned, but none was able to diagnose her case successfully. By way of treatment, they forbade her to drink water. There is probably nothing that could have been better calculated to increase her sufferings, for her thirst must have been terrible. She had foreseen this phase of her last illness and, months before, had extracted a promise from Doña María that she should always be given water. Now Doña María broke her promise. She did it regretfully, even tearfully, but she said the doctors must be obeyed. Rosa agreed.

She wanted to see her father. Her mother came and went constantly to the house of Don Gonzalo and, since Rosa's illness, had remained there most of the time. But Gaspar de Flores was an old man now, so infirm that he could not walk or ride to visit his daughter and, hitherto, he and she had both been content to see each other when she was at home. Since she could not go to him any more, it was necessary to find a way in which he could come to her. He was finally brought in a chair, carried by four men, and when he saw that her helplessness was so much greater than his own, he broke down and sobbed, covering his face with his wrinkled hands. Rosa had never seen him give way to weakness before. In her mind's eye, he was still the adventurous soldier, the hard fighter, the dashing guard, the able and energetic administrator. Now, she saw him otherwise. She reached for his hands and kissed them and asked for his benediction. As he gave it to her, his voice grew steady again. He left her strengthened and comforted.

She next expressed a wish in regard to her burial and, to make sure there would not be any mistakes about it later, she did this in writing. She hoped that the priests of Santo Domingo would grant her an alms; she begged to be buried in the cloister of their convent. She entrusted this document to Don Gonzalo, asking him, when the proper time came, to give it to her friend and confessor, Father de Lorenzana. Don Gonzalo approved of her definite statement, not only because her close ties with the Dominicans made her wish seem logical, but also because he knew every religious order in Lima would urge that it be accorded the honor of providing her sepulchre, and any dissension or jealousy could now be avoided.

On the twenty-first of August, Rosa asked for the Last Rites. As the ringing of little bells announced that the Host was being carried through the streets, passers-by stopped, to ask each other where the priest was going and, when they found out, they rushed home to inform their families and alert these for sad tidings. But Rosa herself felt no sadness. Indeed, though one of her spiritual advisers had observed that she was characterized by a "gravity alien to women," she continued to treat her condition lightly as possible. "Give me your blessing, Father," she said to Lorenzana, who had hastened to her side, "for I am invited to a very great banquet tonight and surely I must go to it with gladness!"

Much of the time she held a crucifix clasped in both hands, but, as the end approached, she took it in one and asked for the Candle-of-Good-Death to hold in the other. Then she asked those present to pray that God might "give her quiet in this affair." Evidently, she meant to assure herself that the prayer would be answered, for she next requested that all the women who had gathered around her bedside should leave the room and these included her own mother. But the dismissal was marred by no element of abruptness or discourtesy, for, as they were leaving, she said, "The blessing of the Father and of the Son and of the Holy Ghost, with all its gifts and graces, fall upon these ladies and on all other friends and acquaintances, present and absent, and expand in their welfare so that they may enjoy it eternally."

Only Don Gonzalo and her confessor were with her now. The silence became profound. If she sought for solace or if she suffered at the end, this was revealed only through the way she worded her last prayer, at midnight, on St. Bartholomew's Day:

"Jesus, be with me."

None of the mourners gathered at her bedside doubted that her prayer was answered.

The news of her death had been awaited for three days and, when word of it went forth, this was greeted with the cry, "A saint has died!" Before preparations could be completed to admit clamoring crowds to the house where she had breathed her last, they were ready to batter down the door in their eagerness and impatience to get in. Don Gonzalo and Doña María recognized that devotion was the basis for this impatience and did their best to arrange that as many persons as possible should see and venerate the dead girl. As soon as she was fully clothed in her Dominican habit, she was carried from her bed to a bier which had been erected in the great hall of the house and covered with rich draperies. There she looked as if she were quietly sleeping, her head on a pillow, her rosary interlaced with her fingers, her favorite flowers around her. Her long lashes rested on her cheeks which had not lost their color and her slender form was without rigidity. Candles were lighted around the bier and Dominicans, forming a guard of honor, took up their vigil. Sensing that this was an occasion for rejoicing, rather than mourning, Father Lorenzana began to chant the *Te Deum* and Father Martinez declared that, instead of a Requiem, he would say the Mass of All Saints.

Without being summoned, members of all the religious societies in Lima quickly arrived and adorned Rosa with a silver crucifix and crown. Then the doors were thrown open and the multitude poured in, filling the patios and galleries to overflowing. Great nobles bent over to kiss the hem of Rosa's garments; high ranking ladies touched her hands with their rosaries, their medals and their scapulars; the poor, the aged and infirm wept as they went by; they had lost the friend they called their mother.

The hour of the funeral was set for five in the afternoon, and the Canons of the Venerable Metropolitan Chapter had asked for the privilege of transporting the bier, an honor hitherto shown only to Archbishops. The streets between Don Gonzalo's house and the Dominican Church were already thronged as were the balconies and roof tops. The Canons, attired in their white rochets, carried their precious burden to the corner of the Street of the Students; there the cortege was stopped for the chanting of prayers. Immediately the multitude rushed forward with rosaries, prayer cards and other objects of piety, seeking to reach the bier with these. It was with the greatest difficulty that the cortege was able to proceed.

One religious community after another, nuns with candles in their hands, great administrators wearing the insignia of their office, grave judges, somber Inquisitors, members of the Viceroy's guard—all these crowded around the bier where Rosa lay. After them surged the multitude, devout, exalted, turbulent: *tapadas* with scissors concealed under their veils, hoping to snip scraps from the habit of the Tertiary; cavaliers wrapped in great cloaks, but with uncovered heads; beggars who dragged themselves along, groaning as they went—a motley gathering mingled in a state of incredible confusion. From the balconies above, decorated with priceless hangings as on the days of the greatest festivals, came a rain of flowers.

At the viceregal palace, the cortege stopped a second time. The Prince and Princess of Esquilache with their suite were standing to salute it as it went by. When it finally reached the Dominican Church, the Archbishop was awaiting it. But, by this time, the crowd was so immense and so unruly that it was impossible to conduct funeral services with any degree of solemnity. It was therefore decided to postpone these until the next day and the church slowly emptied. The bier was removed to the Chapel of the Novitiate and there the Archbishop and the members of the *Audiencia* knelt around it while friars, designated by the Archbishop, began a second vigil in a second *capilla ardiente*. But the following day the same disorder prevailed as before. Again it proved impossible to celebrate the Funeral Mass. As a last resort, when the doors were locked, as usual, between twelve and three, with only their murmured prayers breaking the silence, the Dominicans carried Rosa to their cloistered chapter house.

By this time—and certainly not without reason—the Dominicans had begun to fear the frenzy of the populace. Therefore, on the third day after Rosa's death, they buried her privately, only to find that even this extreme measure did not suffice to keep the people under control. When they reached the re-opened church and found that the body was gone, they were enraged. They broke through the doors of the convent, forced their way into the chapter house and carried off the earth from the sepulchre. They invaded the home of Rosa's parents and the mansion of Don Gonzalo, seeking for souvenirs of her. Days were required to restore any semblance of order in the city and it was not until the fourth of September that a Requiem Mass could be held in Santo Domingo, superbly decorated for the occasion. Father

Velásquez, Rosa's confessor, preached the funeral sermon and the service was attended by the Viceroy, the *Audiencia* as a body, the chapters and guilds, both clerical and lay, and all the aristocracy and gentry of Lima. And later, by special dispensation, it was arranged to transfer the sepulchre to a place where it could be more readily accessible to the devout than in the cloistered chapter house, namely to the body of the church. So, again, a magnificent ceremony took place.[43]

Meanwhile, the clamor, stilled in one way, was becoming more and more vociferous in another. The people had considered Rosa a saint long before her death; indeed, ever since she had defended them from the pirates. Now they attributed numerous miracles to her; among them the recovery of a twelve year old boy, a cripple from birth, who had knelt beside her bier and reported that "*La Rosita* had been pleased with his prayers"; he could now run and jump like ordinary children. Another devotee spoke of waking from a sound sleep to see Rosa surrounded with a great light—"shining like the sun"—and to hear her say she had just entered Paradise. As time went on, more and more marvels were credited to Rosa; but this did not permit them to raise her to their altars. They began a vigorous campaign to bring this about and, within a surprisingly short period, considering the length of time such a movement ordinarily involves, Rome took action. At the instigation of Pope Urban VIII, the faithful of Lima were apprised on the fourteenth of April, 1630—Sunday of the Good Shepherd—by announcement from all the pulpits, that sessions were about to begin, inquiring into "the admirable life, sanctity and miracles" of Rosa de Santa María.

All those interested in giving testimony before this Special Inquisition were requested to submit their names within fifteen days and, three days after the promulgation, the first witness appeared and took oath by the Sign of the Cross and the Four Gospels. From then on, sessions were continuous, except for Sundays, feast days and the vigils of feasts.

Because of the uncommon promptness with which this formal investigation was made by the Church, direct testimony was given by many who had known Rosa as intimately as it is possible to know a great mystic. Besides her mother, many of her elders, as well as many of her contemporaries, appeared as witnesses. We have the record, all of it testimony under oath, and oaths were not lightly taken before scribes of the Inquisition. From these sworn statements Rosa emerges an inspiring and vivid figure.

On the twenty-eighth of May, 1632, after one hundred and eighty-eight witnesses had appeared, the testimony thus far recorded was sent off to Rome, there being ready to sail an armada "from this Realm to Firm Land." Further delay would have meant the impossibility of getting the testimony before the College of Rites for another year.

So off to Europe went two copies of this testimony, one of one thousand and thirty-three folio pages, the other of nine hundred and fourteen. The copy that remained in Lima is of nine hundred and twenty-eight folio pages. Difference in page count does not mean difference in content; all three are the same, set down in the scrawling curlicued script of various scribes. Actually, according to later methods of counting, the number of pages should be doubled, for seventeenth century Spaniards wrote on both sides of the sheet.

The Cause for Canonization of Rosa de Santa María was presented at the Vatican in July, 1634. Urban VIII specified that a waiting period of fifty years must be observed, but this edict was ignored by Alexander VII, who ordered the Cause continued in 1664. Shortly thereafter, the College of Rites declared "saintliness of life and virtue, in heroic degree," for Rosa. As the result of a book about her, which had providentially fallen into his hands, Clement IX had conceived a great admiration for the Limenian Tertiary while he was still Cardinal Rospigliosi. He now lent a willing ear to the advocates of her beatification and expedited the preparations for this. In 1667, only fifty years after her death, he issued the Bull pronouncing her Blessed. He died before he was able to proceed with the necessary steps for her canonization, but his successor, Clement X, needed no urging to do this. A scant two years later, he declared Rosa not only the Patroness of Lima and of Peru, but likewise of "all provinces, kingdoms, isles and regions of *Tierra Firme* in the whole of America, the Philippine Islands and India."

The splendor with which these decrees were celebrated in Lima surpassed that of any celebration ever held there before. The Bull of Beatification reached the city in February and, in April, the magnificent ceremony took place. In the streets, through which the procession was to pass, triumphal arches had been raised and altars blazing with precious stones erected. Tapestries and brocades adorned the balconies and a brilliant cortege accompanied the image of Rosa de Santa

María. Bernardo de Caresco, Provincial of the Dominicans, carried the Papal Bull under a canopy, escorted by all the religious communities of the city. Before the holy image marched twelve little girls, clad in the habit of the Dominicans, wearing wreaths of roses and carrying sprays of roses. The Viceroy, the Vicereine, the Archbishop, the Bishop, and all other dignitaries and aristocrats wore diamond chains fashioned in a sequence of clustered roses. The secondary nobility wore golden chains, the Creoles silver chains and even the humblest and poorest had garlands of roses around their necks. The Viceroy himself carried the standard of the Beatified and in the plaza the artillery fired a salute.

The Canonization was celebrated in an even more sumptuous manner. The tapestries were unbelievably gorgeous, the altars sparkled with an even greater variety of jewels and the streets where the procession was to pass were literally paved with silver. The religious ceremonies were followed by a series of bullfights, races, tournaments and poetical competitions. The Viceroy and all his court attended the fights and participated in both the races and the competitions. His Excellency, the Conde de Lemos, mounted on a magnificent white horse, raced with Don Alvero Navamuel, a Knight of Alcántara, who was attired in black with a baldric of brown and silver and a hat adorned with plumes of the same colors. He also composed a roundelay which read:

> "Si es flor de Lima el azahar,
> Hoy con suerte mas dishosa,
> Es flor de Lima la Rosa." [44]

She has been the Flower of Lima ever since.

As we have said before, Rosa emerged from the Cause of her Canonization an inspiring and vivid figure. She was recognized as a saint in her own city and her own time and would be outstanding in any city at any time. She was subject not only to her parents, but to her superiors, her friends and her mendicants; yet she earned money to support her family, operated the first free clinic on the Continent and carried on a public ministry. She led a life of great seclusion and wore a habit as a means of escape from worldliness; yet somehow, thanks to her strong will and her ingenuity, she solved the problem of essential solitude. She was bound to Christ in mind, heart and soul; His life was her life; and it was He Himself Who said, "He that believeth in me, although he be dead, shall live."

Dead over three hundred years, Rosa still lives.

BOOK II

The Lily

PROLOGUE

F ROM THE earliest days of its occupation by the Spaniards—that is, from 1534—Quito, as a whole, was a great religious center, its atmosphere "conducive to mystic contemplation and rare artistic tradition"; [45] and learning and industry were the handmaidens of faith. "It would be difficult to overestimate Quito's contribution to the spiritual and cultural life of South America." [45] The Franciscans and Mercedarians had been the earliest to arrive and on the great terrace in front of their enormous church, one member of the Franciscan Order, a Fleming by the name of Jodoco Ricke (who, incidentally, was a cousin of Emperor Charles V) had planted the first wheat to reach South America. He also taught the Indians to till the soil with wooden plows, opened the first schools for native children and, indeed, gave himself, heart and soul, to the service of humanity, the advancement of learning and the glory of God. Among his companions was another Fleming, Pedro Gosseal, an artist, who started the school of Quitenian art which eventually came to such fine flower under the sculptors, Caspicara and Legarda, and the painter, Miguel de Santiago. Eight years after the coming of the Franciscans, the monastery of the Dominicans was founded. In 1586, the Augustinians founded the first university in Quito, San Fulgencio, and the Jesuits, who arrived the same year, founded the Seminary of San Luis shortly thereafter. "By early seventeenth century the New World is said to have had 70,000 churches and 500 convents of the various Orders." Quito had its full share of these and they "are indeed worthy of heaven. They are on the small side, intimate and devotional; lovely, and decorated as though they were the private dwellings of the blessed; dressing rooms of the Holy Virgin; sentry-boxes of the angels; a glorious cell of St. Francis; a gala pulpit of St. Ignatius, and drawing rooms of the whole celestial court. How beautiful they are, in their harmonious baroque masses, with their cupolas and glazed-tile sky-lanterns, their graceful little towers, perfect cloisters—neither tragic nor frivolous, their perrons and scenographic parapets, their façades resembling a lacework of stone, and their reredoses of flaming gold." [46]

In 1537, within four years of its first occupation by the Spaniards, Quito became the seat of a bishop, the "Venerable Bachelor" Garcí Díaz Arias, who through "his life and doctrine" had already proved himself worthy of so difficult and responsible a post, and who became, at one and the same time, "father, master and defender of his flock. Hardly had he arrived in his immense and desolate diocese, when he drew up a complete statement of everything which could lead to the advantage of the Spaniards rather than the conversion and advancement of the Indians. He did not wish to impose on them [the Spaniards] the burden of evangelization; and he took it upon himself to teach the Indians in person. With the purpose of facilitating [their understanding of Christian] doctrine, he appointed [native] constables, who pledged themselves to help him and to avoid, at the same time, the vices of their fellows, especially drunkenness and witchcraft." [47]

In all his good works, but particularly in the construction of the cathedral, Bishop Díaz Arias was ably assisted by his Vicar General, Don Pedro Rodríguez de Ajuayo. This cathedral was erected "at small cost and in little time, for he and all of the other canons at his request carried the building materials, stones, sand and bricks, on their backs, and even members of the civil government, Spanish as well as Indian, followed their example." [46] So much haste, as well as so much zeal, went into the edifice that it inevitably lacked much of the carving and other sumptuous ornamentation that gave splendor to most of Quito's churches; but "the excellent canon and generous citizens who constructed the cathedral" gave it the best site in Quito and the Bishop, following current custom, made importations from Spain "on a grand scale" with which to adorn it, while the canon provided it with a richly worked ceiling. Moreover, it became, in a sense, the first conservatory of music in the New World; for, far from content with importing ornaments alone, the Bishop brought skilled musicians from Spain for the purpose of teaching Indians to form a native cathedral choir, and thus laid the foundations for a type of choral singing which has become more and more justly famous. "The memory of the good prelate is blessed by all the faithful, and especially by those who understand the role of the arts in the support of the liturgical life." [47]

Salvador de Madariaga reminds us that "the men who explored and conquered America did so with the scantiest material means. Their spirit did it all. Colón had set the example by discovering the New

World with three caravels, the biggest of which was 140 tons. Cabeza deVaca walked through thousands of miles of unexplored country in both the northern and the southern parts of the continent. Cortés conquered Mexico with four hundred men and sixteen horses. Official help was seldom given, in fact seldom asked for, by these men who preferred to go ahead without shackles. They nearly always applied for some official sanction before starting on their expeditions of exploration and conquest, but what they sought at Court was less money, weapons, ships and horses, than the moral force of legitimate authority. No man will ever understand the Conquest who does not give its due value to this feature of it: spirited, undisciplined, anarchical, the conquerors are nevertheless obsessed by the majesty of the law. . . . Why? Because these Spaniards were all imbued with the sense of common fellowship fostered in Spain as in all the Latin world by the twofold tradition of Rome—the Imperial and the Christian. They were, in a word, deeply *civilized*." [11]

No less valiant than the Conquistadores whom they invariably accompanied, the missionary priests of the various Orders established in Quito were often their superiors in both culture and resourcefulness. Private homes were constructed with a sense of the harmonious and the fitting, and residences of lay officials were often palatial in character and design. But the most significant buildings of the Spanish Colonial Period were the churches, convents and universities. It was to the men who built and maintained them, of whom Díaz Arias and Rodríguez de Ajuayo are typical examples, that the Quitenian families looked for spiritual strength and inspiration and, also, for mental sustenance and development. They never looked in vain.

Quito, within less than a century of its first occupation by the Spaniards, had long since passed the stage of a pioneer settlement and achieved the Spanish ideal of becoming a "noble city." [48] It had a pattern for social and cultural life based on that of the mother country for "Spain gave the Indies her best . . . without measure or reservation, and . . . a splendour and a beauty still glows wherever her handiwork is to be seen in the New World." [11] Colonization, though it brought with it the European concept of culture, also absorbed another type of civilization, a very ancient one. Hernándo Cortés, in exploring Mexico, found a highly developed Aztec capital. Francisco Pizarro, exploring Peru, found equal marvels in the Cuzco of the Incas. Pizarro's lieutenant, Sebastian de Benalcázar ("a cavalier who afterwards placed his name in the first ranks of the South American conquerors, for courage, capacity,—and cruelty." [8]), sent forth for further exploration, traveled between the two Inca capitals of Cuzco and Quito over a road "said to be broad enough for six horsemen to ride abreast" [45] and transformed Quito, which actually takes its name from the *Quitu* Indians, according to Spanish standards, on the ruin of still another great pre-Columbian city. He became its first governor and, for the next thirty years, the administration of its affairs was directed from Cuzco and entrusted to a governor selected there. Among these was the younger brother of Francisco Pizarro, Gonzalo, whose fame has been somewhat overshadowed by the exploits of his brother, but who is entitled to recognition because of his own exploits. We are told "He had a brilliant exterior; excelled in all martial exercises; rode well, fenced well, managed his lance to perfection, was a first-rate marksman with the arquebuse, and added the accomplishment of being an excellent draughtsman. He was bold and chivalrous, even to temerity; courted adventure, and was always in the front of danger. He was a knight-errant, in short, in the most extravagant sense of the term, and 'mounted on his favorite charger,' says one who had seen him, 'made no more account of a squadron of Indians than of a swarm of flies.' While thus, by his brilliant exploits and showy manners, he captivated the imaginations of his countrymen, he won their hearts no less by his soldier-like frankness, his trust in their fidelity—too often abused— and his liberal largesses; for Pizarro, though avaricious of the property of others, was, like the Roman conspirator, prodigal of his own." [8] Gonzalo held office for a number of years, sometimes actively and sometimes only nominally, for he was absent from Quito a great deal, entrusting the management of its affairs to able lieutenants. In the course of one such absence, he led the expedition which discovered the Amazon River: a feat which has been compared to the passage through the Straits of Magellan as embodying "impetuous virility, the nimbus of mystery and the magical quality of the human race." [49]

Unfortunately, the governors who succeeded Gonzalo Pizarro were of less remarkable calibre and one, Rodrigo Salazar, actually achieved the position through the agency of assassination. Eventually, the leading residents of Quito, who apparently felt the time was ripe for a change in the administration of the city, met in open council (*Calbildo Abierto*) and sent a petition to the Crown asking that its status might be changed from that of a mere Province to that of a Royal *Audiencia*. In due course, the petition was granted by Philip II, son of Emperor

Charles V, and great-grandson of the so-called Catholic Kings, Ferdinand and Isabella.

The term, *Audiencia,* was used to define both a governing body and the territory under its jurisdiction. In the case with which we are concerned, the territory, which was part of the Viceroyalty of Peru, was a much larger area than that comprising the modern Republic of Ecuador. The governing body, although primarily a superior court of justice, also exercised political and military functions. It consisted of a President, four *oidores,* or judges (except in Mexico and Peru, where there were eight *oidores* in the *Audiencia* and the President was automatically the Viceroy) and a *Fiscal* (Prosecutor), and was responsible to the Viceroy of the colony where it was located, whether in Mexico, Peru or New Granada. "As a general rule, the *Audiencias* of the Indies possessed the same competence and authority as those of Spain, but owing to the distance from the motherland, they had received special powers which in Spain were reserved to the Royal Council of Justice. In particular, the *Audiencias* of the Indies had the right of judicial inspection over local political and judicial authorities, such as governors and *corregidores* [magistrates]. . . . The *Audiencia* had exclusive jurisdiction in legal matters and could even hear appeals against executive action taken by the Viceroy. The Viceroy was required to respect and honour it and its members. In case of the death of the Viceroy, the *Audiencia* of the chief city took over the viceregal powers. One of the *oidores* was required to be always on circuit, hearing and studying local cases and conditions. The *oidores* were forbidden to accept gifts from any party having come before the court within the bygone year. They wore a black gown known as a *garnacha.* Every well-bred citizen, on meeting one of them, dismounted from his horse as a matter of courtesy and offered to escort him on his way." [11] Among Quito's earliest officials were four brothers of the Great Santa Teresa who came from Avila in the suite of the Viceroy, Blasco Núñez Vela. (The fifth, Antonio, was killed in the Battle of Iñaquito.) Lorenzo was a *regidor* (a councilman or alderman); Agustín was governor of Quijos Province, in the so-called *oriente*—the eastern lowlands; and Jerónimo succeeded Hernándo, who had been badly wounded during the same battle in which Antonio was killed, as treasurer of the *Real Hacienda.* Jerónimo was also a member of the *cofradia* (brotherhood), responsible for the foundation of the Royal Hospital—the first in the New World; and Lorenzo's daughter, Teresa, the namesake and favorite niece of St. Teresa, became the first Ecuadorean nun and the first

Ecuadorean writer. Their families—the Ahumadas y Cepedes—were among the most illustrious in Spain; and the men and women who bore these names were, in every way, worthy of them, setting high standards for those who supplemented their endeavors and accomplishments and succeeded them in positions of authority.

Unfortunately, these standards were not always met. Hernándo de Sentillan, the first President of the *Audiencia*, became involved in such heated disputes with the Bishop, Pedro de la Peña, that this eventually led to the former's exile, after a period of great scandal. However, it should be recorded to his credit that he led the movement, in which he was ably assisted by Don Lorenzo and others, for the foundation of the Charity Hospital. In the same administration, the *Fiscal* of the *Audiencia*, Gaspar de Peralta, surprised his wife with a lover and killed them both. The term of Pedro Venegas del Cañaveral, an *oidor* who acted as President *pro tempore*, was marked principally by "ineptitude," and his wife, who carried thrift to extremes, became the object of hatred because of her avarice and harshness. In the official residence she established not only two groceries and a watchmaker's shop, but a factory where she exploited without mercy the unfortunate Indians who did the weaving.

Manuel Barros de San Millán, President from 1587 to 1593, was said to be a man of ungovernable temper, but nevertheless very fair to the Indians; so fair, indeed, as to make enemies for himself among certain of the landed gentry. He ordered an increase of salaries, forbade forced labor, including that for the construction of convents, and commanded the clergy to reduce the number of their servants, which endeared him to the wealthy among them as little as he was already endeared to rich proprietors. His reforms and the taxes he advocated, in order to bring these about, eventually led to revolution among the people and to his own exile; but there is no doubt that, whatever his sins of omission and commission, he was essentially a great humanitarian.

The Royal Commissioner, Esteban Marañon, who dispossessed Barros de San Millán in office and succeeded him in it, was another who governed with "ineptitude," in his case so marked that he was actually thought to be mentally affected and was finally pensioned off by the Council of the Indies. The next President, Miguel de Ibarra—a distinguished Basque, the cousin of Juan de Ibarra, the secretary of Philip III—was one of the best as far as his own personal life was concerned and he greatly extended the territory under his jurisdiction. But his administration was marred by the scandal created by his Prosecutor,

Blas Torres de Altamirano, who ordered a sleeping potion for the husband of his sweetheart. The witch who prepared it made it too strong and the unfortunate man died!

Morga, a native of Seville, who became President in 1615, had already been governor of both Manila and Mexico and headed the *Audiencia* for nearly twenty years. Though gambling was forbidden in Quito, he turned his house into a casino, and almost invariably won at cards. Even when he apparently gave others a chance to do so, he recovered his losses by selling gifts for the wives of the winners. He further increased his ill-gotten gains through the sale of contraband merchandise at a dry goods store of which he was the proprietor, but which was managed by his son.

But, whatever the faults and failings of its individual members, the establishment of such an important governing body as the Royal *Audiencia* inevitably meant that Quitenian society, essentially cultured, enlightened and devout from the beginning and early privileged with a Bishopric for its ecclesiastical center, likewise became formal, elegant and sophisticated. True, as late as the eighteenth century, only the Bishop and the President of the *Audiencia* rode in coaches, "the navigation of which through the steep uneven streets was a special art. . . . Practically everyone went on horseback or on foot—the gentry distinguished by large umbrellas borne by servants." [45] But the transportation difficulties did not prevent the circulation of impressive processions during Holy Week and on Corpus Christi or attendance at the other elaborate ceremonies connected with the feast days of the Church. Weddings and First Holy Communions were also great occasions and, prior to a girl's entry into a convent as a nun (even in a strictly cloistered Order), a large number of splendid entertainments were held in her honor. Festivities of this character dominated the social scene, for "the idea that religion is one of the multifarious activities of man, usually shoved out of the way and relegated to the idle Sunday, is a modern invention. . . . The human and the divine have always been closely intertwined in the Spaniard." [11] Quitenians, like Limenians, correlated the two with happy results. When Philip III died, the entire city went into deep mourning and one Requiem Mass succeeded another. Shortly thereafter, when Philip IV ascended the throne of Spain, the choral music in the churches was supplemented by popular songs sung in the streets, just as the grand balls of the aristocracy found their prototypes in the gay dances of the plazas!

The observations made about 1800 by the great German scientist,

Alexander von Humboldt, "that there was a definite tendency towards the deep study of the sciences in Mexico and in Santa Fé de Bogotá; more zest for letters and for all that pleases an ardent and quick imagination in Quito and Lima" [11] was true of these places long before he visited them. There was also a very keen and meticulous sense regarding the prerogatives of good birth and good breeding.

Exterior

THE COMPAÑIA–QUITO

Interior

A bridge

QUITO

A street

Exterior of the Church of San Francisco, Quito.

Governor's Palace, Quito; house of Mariana at the rear.

Typical procession,

Two views of courtyard
nobles family; now the

Quito.

in the house of the Gra-
Carmelite Convent.

Mariana at the age of eight.

Cross Mariana de Jesús used for penance. Preserved in the Choir of the Carmelite Convent, which was once her room.

Door in the Granobles house.

Mariana de Jesús with her pupils. The original of this painting is in the Carmelite Convent.

CHAPTER I

Among the Spaniards of noble birth and personal distinction who, late in the sixteenth century, followed in the path toward the New World already hewn for them by the Conquistadores, was a certain Captain Jerónimo Zenel Paredes y Flores, by birth a Toledano. His mission was neither exploratory nor belligerent; he was sent by his father, Don Alonso, to collect a debt owed the latter for fine cloth which he had exported to Quito and for which he despaired of being paid. In order to undertake the journey, for such a purpose, it was necessary to obtain special permission from the authorities in Madrid. In the course of the formalities which took place before this was granted, questions and answers revealed that the captain was *cristiano viejo*, that is to say that his family had been Christians for a long time, without any admixture of Jewish or Moorish blood; that he was a *hidalgo*, that is to say, a man of noble birth; that he was a bachelor, about twenty years of age, of swarthy complexion, still without a beard, but with prospects of one; and that he bore on his right leg the scars of two wounds, apparently resulting from the bites of a serpent or some wild animal!

The document, which reveals these pertinent facts,[50] does not go on to tell us whether or not the young captain was successful in his mission. If he was, he must have entrusted the money due his father to some reliable envoy, for he himself did not return to Spain. Shortly after coming to Quito, he met a young girl by the name of Mariana Jaramillo de Granobles, herself a native of that city, but the daughter of Spaniards whose arrival there antedated that of the captain by only a few years. The two young people promptly fell in love, in due course of time were married and, in accordance with prevalent custom, went to live with the bride's parents, who were already settled in a commodious house.

This was located on a steep and narrow street (as indeed were most houses of its period) facing the Royal Hospital, a monumental and

truly magnificent building; and commanding, from its rear windows
and its garden, a beautiful view of the many hills surrounding the
city, which was built, like Rome, on a seemingly endless succession of
these. The house itself was, in every way, suited for the upbringing of
the eight children [51] who, in swift succession, were born to Don
Jerónimo and Doña Mariana. It was large enough to accommodate a
rapidly growing family and so arranged as to provide convenience, as
well as space. The six ground floor rooms which surrounded the central patio all led into each other, and a gallery afforded shelter during
the heavy rains which alternated with brilliant sunshine. But this gallery
was not so wide as to exclude light and air. To a very marked degree,
the interior of the house was unshadowed and correspondingly bright
and cheerful. Its upper stories, as well as its ground floor, were encir-
cled by galleries and these were supported by substantial stone pillars.
The wide staircases which led from one story to another were also
made of stone, while patio, galleries and all the rooms were paved with
it. This might have resulted in an effect of austerity and chilliness, had
it not been for the abundance of natural light, the many mirrors and
the lavish use of color and carving in everything made of wood: the
paneled doors, arched niches, columned beds, inlaid *bargueños*
(chests), monarchical chairs and tables and the gorgeous paintings
and plateresque figurines. Almost another hundred years were to pass
before sculptural art in Quito was to reach the magnificent heights it
eventually attained, but even during the early part of the seventeenth
century—the period with which we are immediately concerned—it had
been developed to a degree rare in the colonies of any nation except
Spain. Besides all this elegance and refinement of interior decoration,
there was the garden in which grew fragrant flowers and glowing fruits
at all seasons, for in Quito there is neither bitter cold nor merciless
heat, but warm sunny days and cool refreshing nights all year long.

In its physical aspects, therefore, the home of Don Jerónimo and
Doña Mariana offered every possible advantage to their growing family.
According to Rivera, they were *"personas principales,"* that is to say,
persons of consequence in what we call exclusive circles of society.
Both were of noble rank and thus entitled to family escutcheons. Theirs
was a patriarchal establishment, in which three generations lived har-
moniously together, so that the children were unacquainted with domestic strife. It was the scene of such sincere piety and such widespread
charity that it was known far and wide as the *Casa de Oración*—the
House of Prayer. As devotion to divine worship was the rule rather

than the exception in the city, the fact that any one private home should have been singled out for such a designation has special significance; actually, Don Jerónimo and Doña Mariana had become outstanding as being "*buenos cristianos, temeros de Dios y de sus consiencias*" and "*de mucho calidad y virtud.*" [52]

Devout though Don Jerónimo unquestionably was, he was also unquestionably arrogant. In fact, he went so far as to enter a complaint, before the Royal *Audiencia,* against a neighbor who had spoken to him in language "unbefitting a person who was addressing a *hidalgo*"; and without the slightest difficulty, he succeeded in having the offender fined! The smooth-faced boy, ruddy of complexion and sturdy of build, who had been sent a quarter of a century earlier to collect a debt, had become an impressive figure. His bearing was one of great dignity, his eyes at one and the same time keen and fiery. He was as slender and strong as the sword he always wore, his beard small and pointed like the sword's tip. Customarily, his dress was of velvet; but even if no breastplate and helmet were visible, they made their imminence felt. As one writer has graphically put it, he might easily have served as the model for almost any one in the group of grandees depicted by El Greco in the Burial of Count Orgaz.[53]

Doña Mariana was of gentler mold: deeply religious, infinitely charitable, devoted to her husband and her children, skilled in the management of her household and wise in aiding all those who looked to her for guidance. Of her appearance we are specifically told that her expression was benevolent, that she was tall, dark and graceful and that her manners were charming and collected; also, that she dressed "like the typical high-bred Creole." (It will be helpful for us to remember that, in Colonial Spain, a "Creole" was a person of pure Spanish blood who had been born in the Indies, whereas, in Spain itself, such a person was called an *Indiano.*) "Her skirt was of rustling silk, worn over hoops and voluminous petticoats and these billowed from a tiny waist. Her shawl was arranged in precise folds. At her throat she wore a diamond cross set in gold and fastened by a velvet ribbon. Her slim aristocratic hands, prematurely wrinkled, were loaded with jewels. When she went to the country, however, she was attired in an elaborate riding habit and her saddle was one distinguished by ornamental workmanship." [53]

This description is authenticated and supplemented by the pictures representing highborn ladies of the period and by the comments made by distinguished travelers who were received in good local society and who state that the dress of the ladies they met was "gay yet modest" and their walk "noble." "A Spanish woman," one such observer remarks, "whether her education had been finished or not, is in her nature a superior being. Her majestic forehead, her dark and thoughtful eyes assure you that she hath communed with herself. She can bear to be left in solitude; yet what a look is hers, if she is animated by mirth or love!"

It was in such a setting, with such parents, and with such spiritual, social and mental advantages as I have tried to describe that the elder sons and daughters of Don Jerónimo and Doña Mariana grew up. As they reached maturity, they all made suitable marriages, with the exception of one son, named for his father, who became a Franciscan friar, and one daughter, Inés, who died young. When, for the eighth time, Doña Mariana became pregnant, she was already a middle-aged woman and her general health had long given cause for concern. She narrowly escaped miscarriage and, as the time for her confinement approached, the anxiety of her family increased. Everything possible was done to ensure her comfort and well being. A large airy room on the ground floor was set aside for her accouchement and, from this, she could look through the gallery, across the spacious patio to the further side of the house and the hills beyond. During the day, this room was flooded with sunshine; and if she or any of those who were watching over her were fearful that, with the coming of night, the flickering flames of the candelabra would be inadequate for her needs, these fears were quickly dispelled. Never had the heavens been as clear or the stars as bright as they were when her travail began on the Eve of All Saints. The chamber where she lay was literally flooded with radiance. Not only did the stars seem more brilliant than they had ever been before but they seemed more numerous. The heavens were completely bespangled by them. Moreover, one brighter than all the others appeared to be shedding its rays directly over the hill top, above the walls beyond the patio and across the galleries which surrounded this, so that these beams reached into the room where the woman lay in childbed, illuminating it with supernal light.

"It is an omen of disaster, a fiery comet!" one of the waiting women cried in terror, shrinking away to a corner which she hoped the strange luminosity could not reach.

Another was wiser. She visualized not a portent of peril, but a

"Star of wonder, star of night, star with royal beauty bright," like the one which, centuries before, had shone above Bethlehem, guiding the shepherds to the place where the young Child was with His Mother.

She bent over Doña Mariana and saw that the moment of parturition had come. With the help of her strong and capable hands, Doña Mariana was safely delivered of a beautiful little girl.

CHAPTER II

Happily, none of the fears entertained for the safety of Doña Mariana's life were realized; however, she was unable to feed her baby herself, and the question of a wet-nurse became one of immediate and paramount importance. Doña Mariana's solution of this problem was original and significant—she chose not only one wet-nurse but two: a highborn Castilian lady, Catalina de Alcocer, and a humble Indian, Beatriz, whose surname, if she had one, is not recorded. This dual selection was not primarily the result of fear that one source of supply would be insufficient to nourish the baby adequately; rather, it was based on the theory that both races had something invaluable to offer, even to a newborn child, and that, quite aside from supplying actual sustenance, no one could come as close to this child as the nurse to whom it instinctively turned for the fulfillment of all its needs, and whose natural affection and solicitude for it, expressed in countless ways, would have a definite bearing on its development, mental and spiritual, as well as physical. Though all mothers do not act as wisely as Doña Mariana, she cannot have been alone in her realization of this, for the expression, "I drank that in with my mother's milk," meaning, "That is something I have known and practiced all my life," is a common one to this day, and its equivalent is used in many languages besides English, Spanish among them. The theory on which the saying is based was not only perceptive but sound.

The little girl whose birthnight had been illumined by the radiance of a star, and whose every need was anticipated with fostering care, was a beautiful baby who throve under the conditions so favorable for her well being. It was not the Quitenian custom, at that period, to baptize an infant within a few days of its advent into the world, unless it was obviously frail, but rather to wait until its mother was sufficiently recovered to attend a ceremony, which was usually an elaborate one. The baby in whom we are interested was born on October 31,

1618; it was not until November 22—St. Cecilia's Day—that the magnificent ceremony took place.

All the great parlors of the house were thrown open. The crimson carpets had been newly swept and the brass candelabra newly polished. The household servants moved about carrying great silver platters laden with the refreshments which had been prepared in advance for the entertainment of distinguished guests; and the aroma of vintage wines, already decanted, mingled with the scent of the roses and lilies brought in from the garden. Though everything had been prepared with thoroughness and efficiency, most of the staff was required to remain on duty at the house to make sure there was no last minute oversight or mishap, with one notable exception: Catalina, the Indian who had been longest in the service of the family, and who had never failed in faithfulness and devotion, was accorded the privilege, time honored under such circumstances, of carrying the baby to the church. Catalina was wearing her heaviest earrings and her many stranded scarlet necklace; her blouse was overlaid with multicolored embroidery in the form of flowers; her full bright skirt rustled like the one worn by her *dueña* (mistress), for today she, too, went clad in silk. Under her black braids, her broad face was wreathed in smiles. Her white teeth gleamed. This was the proudest moment of her life. But it was also a moment of supreme responsibility. As the baby, its long white dress foaming with lace, was placed in her strong copper-colored arms, her expression changed to one of gravity. She bent over her *amita*—her little soul—murmuring words of love and tightened her hold on her precious burden. Then she raised her head, watching for the signal to start toward the church.

The cortege was notable, befitting one which proceeded from a house "favored by fortune and heritage." It was composed of *personas principales, cristianos viejos* and *hijadalgos*, highly esteemed for their distinction as well as their virtue. They went clad in velvet and they made a lordly and splendid showing. They had a walk of two blocks before they could reach the *Sagrario*, the church chosen for the baptism, and they proceeded slowly, with measured tread, suitable for so great an occasion. The humbler passers-by halted their beasts of burden and stopped to watch this great sight, exchanging murmured words of admiration with their fellows. So there was a new heiress to the great house of Paredes y Flores! It was to be hoped that the heavens would shower blessings upon her!

The *Sagrario* was the sanctuary for the Sacrament, erected, according to Spanish custom, separate from the cathedral, but adjacent to it. The latter, as we have seen, was built with such "haste and zeal" that it lacked the usual amount of ornamentation. As if to make up for this lack, the *Sagrario* was embellished in every possible way with carving and color. It made a jewel-like setting for a baptism and, on the high altar, the fiery flames of the tall candles mingled their radiance with the soft light of midafternoon. The parish priest, Juan Demoin, clad in vestments of rich brocade, was waiting for the cortege in the vestibule, the chrism and the salt already prepared. His privilege was even greater than that of Catalina, who had so proudly brought the baby to him, and not only because he was about to pour baptismal water over a baby's head; this was a head "predestined for an aureole." [54]

The baby's maternal grandfather, Gabriel Melendez de Granobles, acted as her godfather. There was no godmother; at this time and place one godparent was considered sufficient; and, instead of having several names bestowed upon her, the baby was given only one; that of her mother. But as her most famous biographer, Morán de Butrón, has pointed out, this "comprises all the graces." [55] Partly to avoid the confusion of using exactly the same name to designate two different members of the immediate family, living in the same house, and partly because of the natural predilection all Spaniards have for the use of diminutives, the little girl was generally called Marianita.

She continued to thrive and she seemed to grow in grace, a gentle child, to whom all forms of devotion came naturally. She was only a prattler when she began to lisp the rosary; and having seen her mother kneel, with arms extended to form a cross, when Doña Mariana prayed beside her bed before retiring for the night, Marianita insisted on doing the same. She constructed little altars, arranged and re-arranged them, took them apart and began again, in the same way that most children build houses with their blocks. As frequently as possible, she visited the Chapel of Our Lady of the Angels, which was connected with the nearby Charity Hospital, and soon became sensitive to the beauty of its crimson and gold adornments. She appropriated a certain seat as her own and sat there contentedly. She enjoyed, rather than avoided, solitude, and often slipped away to her own room, remaining there quietly by herself, until someone came and sought her out. At other times, she found a hiding place in the shrubbery and, quite content, stayed there for hours. But she also enjoyed companionship and was greatly beloved by her playmates, of whom she had no lack. Her elder sister, Jerónima, had married before Marianita was born, and was the mother of three little girls, Juana, María and Sebastiana, all near Marianita's age. So were her sister Inés and her friend, Escolástica Sarmiento, the latter a frequent guest in the household. Marianita was a natural leader. Having been greatly impressed with the office of the *Tenebrae,* as she had observed this at the beautiful golden Church of the Compañia on Holy Thursday, she organized a procession which marched through the spacious corridors and galleries of her grandparents' house, carrying a cross on her shoulder. She also armed herself with a switch, as she had seen the penitents of Holy Week doing, and presented switches to all her young companions, who, apparently, accepted them without protest. Though she was not encouraged to carry her acts of imitation and contrition too far, neither was she rebuked nor prevented. Her elders understood that, in a childish way, she was trying to follow the example of those who were publicly portraying their horror of sin and their hope of leading holier lives.

Like most *Quiteños* of their rank, her parents and grandparents owned country estates as well as town houses and much of their time was spent at these delightful *estancias.* In location, they were superb, with magnificent unobstructed views of the snow-capped mountains which tower above the lesser hills encircling Quito. In extent, they were enormous. They were divided into tracts known as *caballerias,* from the fact that, supposedly, they could be covered with ease on horseback. Each of these tracts measured approximately thirty-three acres, and an *estancia* usually comprised fifteen or twenty of them. The manual labor was done by Indians, under the system known as the *Encomienda,* a direct result of the so-called *Edad Media* of Spain, which implied vassalage, but not slavery, and which, on the whole, was beneficent of intent if not always of action. On an *estancia* of this character, thirty or forty Indian families were required to cultivate the crops, which consisted of wheat, corn, barley and sometimes other grains, as well as all standard vegetables, and to care for the poultry—chickens, ducks and turkeys—and the animals—dogs, horses, cattle, sheep, donkeys and llamas. (The latter, like the donkeys, were then universally used as beasts of burden, as they are still sometimes used by Indians living in the high *sierras*—mountain ranges.) The spiritual needs of these workers were not neglected; they were made welcome at the chapel which always adjoined the great house and a resident priest, called the *doctrinero,* ministered to them. He taught the children their catechism, but other lessons were generally given them by the *dueño* and the *dueña* (the owners) themselves and a schoolroom was provided for this purpose. The great house formed three sides of a rectangle, the fourth side remaining open to give access to the court. It was usually, though not always, only one story in height; but no less than twenty rooms led into each other and provided all the space that a good-sized family would need, as well as plenty for the many guests who were received, as a matter of course, with true biblical hospitality.

Once, when they were on their way to Cayambe, where one of their properties was located, the small donkey Marianita was riding slipped on a stone while they were fording the Rio de las Ovejas,[56] and lost its precious burden. Doña Mariana was terrified. There was a strong current and it seemed inevitable that the child would be caught in it and swept down-stream before their faithful *mayordomo* (steward), Hernando Palomeros, could rescue her. But nothing of the sort happened; instead of being submerged by the rushing river, the child actually seemed to rise buoyantly and triumphantly above it. The donkey regained its footing, Marianita resumed her seat and they all went happily on their way.

As usual, the stay in Cayambe was a joyous one, but the return to Quito was saddened by the consciousness that Doña Mariana's health, delicate for some years already, was now definitely failing. She prepared for death not only calmly, but contentedly. Her husband, to whom she had been devotedly attached, had already died and her faith was such that she was confident of a reunion in heaven. Any anxiety that she might have felt because her death would leave her two youngest daughters orphans was assuaged by the knowledge that their elder sister, Jerónima, and Jerónima's husband, Cosme de Caso, would give them the same loving care as their parents; and her confident assurance of this was fully justified. Inés and Marianita became as near and dear to Jerónima and Cosme as their own daughters; and their little friend, Escolástica, continued to be a welcome guest in their household. All six learned their lessons together: to read and write, do fine needle-work, sing simple songs and play on the guitar and the clavichord. All six went frolicking together among the sheaves when the wheat was harvested at Saguanche, Don Cosme's family *estancia*. As one chronicler poetically puts it, "They might have been mistaken for crimson poppies in the golden fields." They learned to ride on gentle horses and donkeys. They had their pet puppies and kittens and lambs; and when at last overcome with drowsiness after their long hours of romping in the sun, they were not separated, but were sent to sleep in six little beds ranged close to each other.

These idyllic episodes and pastoral scenes are singularly charming and there seems to have been no effort made, as far as any of the children was concerned, to precipitate their spiritual development. As a matter of fact, no such need was indicated, for this came about as naturally as their healthful physical growth and their dawning realization of the beauties of music and the wonders of the printed page. By the time Marianita was seven years old, however, it was evident that she wanted and needed more expert guidance in matters of religion than her elder sister and her brother-in-law could give her. Wisely, Jerónima sought this out, and the mentor of her choice was Father Juan Camacho of the Company of Jesus.

She could hardly have made a more discerning selection. Father Camacho, an Andalusian by birth, was a man of great eloquence and learning, an outstanding theologian and jurist, a penetrating observer and—on the strength of his observations—a wise counselor. Almost instantly, he recognized Mariana's rare qualities and her actual need of spiritual fulfillment, in ways she had already begun to grasp, despite her tender years. Her precocity did not alarm him. He advised that she be permitted to make her First Holy Communion without delay, that thereafter she come to confession as frequently as she felt moved to do so, and that in matters of conscience she be allowed to follow her own convictions, even if these seemed to her family to verge on the extreme.

A portrait of her, painted when she was eight years old, still exists. It depicts a pink-cheeked child with a chubby face, a rosebud mouth, a full chin, straight dark brows above dark eyes, a high forehead and smooth brown hair, neatly parted in the middle and partially covered by a mantilla. The face is unusually grave for a little girl, but though the red lips are unsmiling, they do not suggest the firmness of purpose and action which we know was one of her predominant characteristics even at this early age; they are not narrow, they do not close in a straight unyielding line. Subsequent representations of her, both authentic and apocryphal, all present her with the same sweet mouth.

It was about the time this first portrait was painted that Marianita took a bold step: she ran away from home, with a definite project in mind, and, as usual, she had no difficulty in persuading her nieces, Juana, María and Sebastiana, her sister Inés, and her friend, Escolástica, to join her in her enterprise. She did not, like the Great St. Teresa at more or less the same age, start out to convert the heathen, with the hope that her quest would end in martyrdom; her aim was some desert place where she and the other children would live like hermits, while striving to revive the cult of the Virgin of Pichincha, which had once been a vital force, but which had lost its intensity since the volcano of the same name had ceased to be a menace to life and property. The little girls managed to leave the house unobserved, one day when Doña Jerónima was busy with visitors, and actually gained the open countryside without being stopped. As they started across an unenclosed field, however, they were suddenly confronted by a huge black bull of ferocious aspect; and while he was not actually charging in their direction, he was pawing the ground with his great hooves, jerking his powerful head this way and that and bellowing loudly—in short, plainly indicating in every way that he meant mischief.

The wayfarers took counsel together: was it their duty to brave the unforeseen danger thus presented and proceed with their mission? Or should they retreat and return to their home? With only a wide ditch separating them from the fierce animal, Marianita alone remained calm. She withdrew slightly from the others, prayed briefly and silently, and then informed her companions it was plainly not the Will of God that they should go and live as anchorites; the presence of the bull, blocking their way, was a sure sign of Divine Guidance. As she had always been singularly courageous, the others did not believe for a minute that fear had caused her to change her mind about their mission and they accepted her verdict without question. Nevertheless, they were all somewhat shamefaced when they tried to explain to their elders both their flight and the abandonment of their enterprise; all, that is, except Mariana. She gave an account of her actions without apology or embarrassment. She had believed she was meant to be a hermit; she now understood that this was not her destiny. Instead, she had other plans. That was all there was to it.

Cosme and Jerónima were keenly aware of their position in *loco parentes* as far as their little sister was concerned, and it is not strange that they were troubled by the wish she now expressed to follow a way of life which seemed to them more suited to a professed nun of mature years than to a child who had not yet reached adolescence. She insisted on wearing the plainest of wool dresses, without jewelry, even when her indulgent brother-in-law sought to distract her mind with silks and trinkets. She had determined views on the subject of both fasting and penance and put these into practice. She took a solemn vow of virginity, when it seemed impossible to her startled relatives that she could actually grasp the meaning of this; and, to cap the climax, she insisted that she was no longer to be known as Doña Mariana Paredes y Flores, but as Mariana de Jesús, because she belonged to the Company of Jesus!

In all this, Father Camacho upheld her, and Cosme decided, since there seemed to be no possible way of changing her bent, that a convent was the place for her, and that probably the sooner she entered one, the better it would be for all concerned. Two were considered eminently suitable: Santa Catalina, which was under the direction of the Dominicans, and Santa Clara, which was run by the Poor Clares or Second Order of St. Francis. Cosme gladly agreed to provide the usual dowry and to give the series of elaborate entertainments customarily held before a girl began her novitiate. Mariana firmly announced that she did not intend to enter a convent, that she would continue to live in the world, since she believed this to be the Will of God. Again, Father Camacho upheld her.

By "living in the world," she meant that she would reside in the home of her sister and brother-in-law, not, however, as a member of the family circle, but as a recluse. She asked that an upper chamber should be set apart for her, that it should be stripped of all elegancies and its equipment reduced to the barest necessities. In this upper chamber she proposed to remain, except when she left it for daily Mass at the Church of the Compañía and for the purpose of engaging in active works of charity. As a matter of fact, most of her charitable works could be performed at home, for the poor and ailing could come to her there. Of course, she could not see many of them in her upper chamber, but she was assuming that, for such a purpose, a room on the ground floor would be put at her disposal. When not attending to the needs of the unfortunate, her time, except for the few hours allotted to sleep and the equally brief periods devoted to music, reading and needlework, was to be spent in prayer, meditation and discipline. Her dowry was to be distributed among the worthy poor, with nothing being kept for her personally. Shelter she would accept from her sister and brother-in-law and a meagre portion of food—that was all. She had long since made private vows of poverty, chastity and obedience, which she considered as binding as if they had been taken before a priest and a Community upon entering a convent; she interpreted the vow of poverty quite as literally as she did the other two.

The pattern she had chosen was not only austere, it was sacrificial. From earliest childhood she had visualized herself as a *víctima*: that is, it was her soul's sincere desire not only to worship God, but to make her personal "Imitation of Christ" a literal one as far as suffering was concerned; nor was this solely for love of Him or with the feeling that she could best prove this love by sackcloth and scourging. The Deity of her faith was not a Loving Father; he was the Jehovah of Wrath, whose righteous anger must be continually appeased, lest sinful mankind should be visited with frightful forms of death and destruction. Fearless, as far as she herself was concerned, as to both life and death, she foresaw with dread the fate that she believed awaited her city and her country, as the result of widespread wrong-doing; and, convinced that she could be instrumental in helping to avert this, she surrendered herself to penitential discipline.

CHAPTER III

In order to approach an understanding and appreciation of Mariana de Jesús, it is necessary to achieve an understanding and appreciation of the way she thought and why, as well as to inform ourselves about external aspects of seventeenth century life in Quito.

We already have a general idea of what the town houses and the great *estancias* of the gentry were like and about the pattern of their being in these. We know that the architectural standard set by these private houses was high and that the residences of officials, and the churches and convents reached an even more marked degree of spaciousness, elegance, harmony and ornamentation. We know that schools and colleges not only existed but flourished, that sciences and classics were expertly taught in these by men of vast learning, and that the taste and talent for music and painting were developing along striking lines. We know that, ecclesiastically, Quito had the important status of a Bishopric and, civically, that of a Royal *Audiencia* and that social life, taking its tone from both, was characterized by piety, culture and urbanity.

Seen from the comfortable distance of time and space, the picture is certainly a pleasing one. As we observe it more closely, however, we find that the piety was not invariably proof against temptation, that the culture was corroded by inhumanity and that the urbanity was corrupted by vice. Among the lesser clergy, concubinage gradually became so general that it was often taken for granted; only the more thoughtful and devout recognized it as a menace to the power and integrity of the Church as a whole. The system of *Encomienda* resulted, far too often, in the oppression of unfortunate Indians. The *Presidencia* (Presidency), interpreted by such a man as Venegas del Cañaveral, had been debased when he turned his official residence into a commercial establishment where he and his wife derived their ill-gotten gains from the maltreatment of their employees; and it was still further debased when Morga established a bordello where he fleeced his guests in a more polished manner, but with as little scrupulosity as his predecessor had shown in working downtrodden weavers to death. As these and other deplorable conditions became more and more prevalent, their impact became more and more forcible. Those who still walked in the paths of rectitude began to blame themselves for what was happening and to feel that they should try to atone for the sins of others; and by atonement they did not mean merely that they should strive, harder than ever, to set shining examples of chastity, loving-kindness and honor; they believed that, unless they actually suffered in so doing, their efforts would be meaningless and ineffectual in the eyes of both God and man. Nor was it only persons of mature years who felt this way. Boys and girls, however sheltered their own lives, could not be kept in the dark as to the evils which surrounded them, and they reacted to these with the sensitivity of youth. Inevitably, in some cases, they found the *via crucis* too hard to follow and, after a brief experience of it, revolted and plunged into excesses of dissipation. In other cases, their very vitality and enthusiasm made it seem glorious to them and they kept seeking out new ways to prove their adherence to the rigid rules they had laid down for themselves.

The feeling in Quito was by no means a unique or isolated one. It was part of the spirit of the times, all over the world. Men and women were no longer required to die for their faith, as they had been in the first days of the Christian era. The medieval saints, with the exception of a few missionaries, were not martyrs, executed in a horrible way, like Peter and Paul, Cecilia and Agnes, for example. But they were inclined to feel that this was their loss and that, if they could not suffer martyrdom, they could at least practice mortification. We shrink now from the details of these penitential practices and prefer to think of St. Francis almost wholly as the gentle preacher to the birds and of St. Catherine as the adroit politician rather than of either one as fasting to the point of semi-starvation and scourging an emaciated body until the blood ran. In both these cases it is comparatively easy to do this, because so many other aspects of their lives can and should be stressed, as in the lives of various other saints, those of St. John of the Cross and St. Teresa of Avila, for instance. In many other cases— and that of Mariana de Jesús is among them—the penitential aspect is almost the only one that can be stressed. And, in any event, by failing to do so, we are failing to face facts, to recognize the essential difference between the modern viewpoint, that the body is the temple of the soul and as such must be safeguarded, and the viewpoint of

the Middle Ages and even of the Renaissance, that the more it was
subjected to torture, the less likely it would be to interfere with one
soul's salvation and the more likely to help save other souls.

As far as I know, St. Ignatius was the first to advise his followers
to pursue a different course; [57] and this was only in the case of missionaries, to whom bodily welfare was essential if they were to survive
the hardships of the travels designed to evangelize the heathen. For
those who remained safely sheltered in convents, discipline, and of
an heroic order, was still the rule. Insufficient sleep and insufficient
food were taken for granted; the biblical admonition that cleanliness
is next to godliness went unheeded if, indeed, it were remarked at
all; and apparently such physical ills as fainting fits, fevers and tuber-
culosis were never laid to wilful disregard of what we now consider the
most elementary precepts for healthful living, but were viewed as part
of a pattern of austerity and penitence which must be welcomed and
fostered.

This is the viewpoint we must try to understand. This is the pattern we must accept as belonging to the times. Unless and until we do,
we will never recognize the elements that went into the making of a
saint, as far as Mariana de Jesús is concerned, and that caused first
her fellow townspeople, then the local authorities of Church and State
and, eventually, the world to revere and hail her as such. It is not
enough, as I have said before, to know what sort of a house she lived
in and what kind of clothes she wore and how often she went to confession and Communion. We must know how she thought and
reasoned and why. Her thinking was clear. Her reasoning, guided by her
spiritual directors who were men of unimpeachable character and
great learning, was logical under the circumstances. Her unequivocal
purpose was that of atonement through suffering and sacrifice. When
she retired to her solitary sanctuary, she did so undisturbed by doubts
as to the wisdom of her consecrated cause.

CHAPTER IV

Mariana's views concerning the type of setting appropriate for seclusion and sacrifice were as definite as those about the way it should be inhabited.

She did not stipulate that she was to be restricted as to light, air or space. In these respects, her retreat bore less resemblance to a conventual cell, as we understand the term, than to the commodious apartments which many Spanish nuns of the same period were permitted to occupy, and which were sufficiently ample to provide for a bedroom with a connecting oratory, the latter often profusely decorated with paintings, statues and various other objets d'art. Such apartments were prevalent both in the Encarnación, the first convent of the Great St. Teresa of the Carmelite Order, and the Cistercian Convent of Santa Ana, also in Avila, as well as those located in many other places. The upper chamber of Mariana's selection was large as well as lofty and the windows, besides affording a pleasant vista (including a view of the Chapel of Our Lady of the Angels where she had spent so much time as a child), admitted an abundance of the warm sunshine and clear cool air, for both of which Quito is so justly famous. While there were no actual divisions into separate rooms, as in the Spanish convents mentioned above, a wooden screen, made in accordance with her directions, formed an effective partition between the section where she slept and dressed and to which she regularly carried pails of water, and the one where she spent the greater part of her time and received such visitors as were admitted.

It was not enough, however, to have this chamber stripped of the usual luxurious adornments of the time and place—draperies, rugs, tapestries, mirrors and so on—and its equipment reduced to the barest necessities—a straight-backed chair, a small table, a hard and narrow bed—it must likewise contain all the requisite implements for mortification and even harbor several gruesome representations of death itself and bodily corruption after death. Nevertheless, its austerity was somewhat mitigated by the presence of pleasant pictures: one of St. Ignatius, whom she now regarded as her special patron; one of the Trinity, to which she had such great devotion that, on the Feast of Pentecost she welcomed all would-be visitors without restriction; and an excellent copy of the painting of Our Lady of Loreto, which surmounted an altar at the Compañia, and which had been a favorite of hers since childhood. She retained all the instruments on which she had learned to play and continued to use them; music, she declared, was a means of raising the soul to God. Books were not excluded from her program, either. Indeed, as the years went on, she studied profoundly and became better and better acquainted with the lives of the saints whom she had especially admired, from the time she could read herself; and probably even before that, for all Doña Mariana's children listened to stories of holy lives at their mother's knee. Catherine of Siena and Teresa of Avila both provided examples which Mariana de Jesús strove to emulate, fully conscious that she had set her standards very high. She was also a great admirer of the Venerable María Vela, "The Strong Woman" of the Cistercian Convent of Santa Ana in Avila, who died—as did Santa Rosa de Lima—the year before Mariana was born and whose writings, according to Camacho, she read with avidity [58,59] and with the hope of imitating her. But there is much more resemblance between her life and that of Santa Rosa de Lima than between hers and María Vela's. The Castilian was a cloistered nun, whereas the two Spanish Colonials both continued to live in the world, even while retiring from it. As far as is known, María Vela engaged in no charitable works and did no teaching; her vocation was wholly one of prayer and penances, whereas the others sought to supplement these by active service. Mariana's design for living so closely resembled that of her fellow countrywoman,[60] whose Cause for Beatification had been introduced while the Quitenian was still living, that there can be no possible doubt there was conscious imitation and nothing could have been more natural or more praiseworthy.

Having established her daily regime to her satisfaction, Mariana next discarded the plain woollen dress which, for some time, she had insisted on wearing, not for something more ornate, but for a garment which very soon and very definitely was regarded as a habit, not only by Mariana personally, but by all those with whom she came in contact: her spiritual advisors, the members of her family, and the poor and sick to whom she ministered. Though modified enough to give it feminine form, it followed as closely as possible the model adopted

by the Jesuits; it was made of the same black material as theirs and it
was embroidered with their emblem. The veil, opaque like the dress,
was long enough to form a mantle over the shoulders; she wore no
other. According to tradition, she joined the Third Order of St.
Francis with the knowledge and approval of her confessor and was
duly invested with its cord and scapular. Considering her great devotion to the gentle friar of Assisi (whose image was always among those
in her retreat) and the fact that two of her nearest relatives—a brother
and a cousin—were members of the Franciscan Order, this would be
quite logical, even though there are, apparently, no documents to prove
it.[61] Moreover, it obviously was at her own expressed wish that the
habit of St. Francis formed her shroud; but she never wore this in her
lifetime, and her absorption by the Jesuits, in dress as in everything
else, seems complete. It was to the Compañia that she went daily, it
was the rule of St. Ignatius that she endeavored to follow, and she
herself declared, "I am all Jesuit," when she retired from the world.
There could hardly have been much opportunity for divided allegiance,
even if it took forms which were not contradictory.

Father Camacho was still her confessor and, in directing the distribu-
tion of her time, he ordered her to set apart four hours for sleeping,
and five for prayers to the Virgin. She was to wear haircloth under her
habit and take discipline twice a day. Gradually, less and less time
was given to sleep, more and more to prayer and more and more to
discipline. But at least an hour a day was set aside for weaving and
sewing and the money earned through this handiwork was given to
the needy. Moreover, a great deal of time was devoted to other charitable practices. The poor of the city came daily at noon to Don Cosme's
house and knocked on the outer door, knowing that they would not
be turned away. Mariana went out to them and made them stand in
line; then she chose among them the dirtiest and most ragged and did
what she could to improve their condition. Usually, her niece, Sebastiana, helped her with this part of her work. Afterward, Mariana
kissed the feet of those to whom she had administered and left them
briefly to go to her own room. When she returned, she carried a large
basket filled with bread.

Nobody knew exactly whence came this special bread which she
distributed daily. There was something mysterious about it, though all
Quito talked about the great loaf of white bread, which she had once
made—so it was said—from two scant ounces of dough, for her friends,
the Mirandas—gentlewomen in reduced circumstances to whom food

was regularly sent from the table of Don Cosme. And there was no mystery about that. But the bread which Mariana brought in her basket and divided among the miserable paupers, who had come knocking at her door, was regarded with reverent bewilderment. She never explained how she was always able to provide it and no one asked her. It sufficed to know that there would always be enough for everyone. In many cases, it warded off actual starvation; it was very generally known as the "bread of angels."

Mariana was also the benefactor of many who were not actually beggars, but who were unable to secure regular employment and who were often reduced to desperate straits in the periods when they were out of work. Their self-respect was still such that they were somewhat shamefaced about seeking relief, so they were accustomed to signal her at night by throwing pebbles at her window. She never failed to come to their rescue. Doña Jerónima knew that such an emergency was likely to occur at almost any time and left the keys to her larder with Mariana, who distributed whatever she found there. The results of this bounty were also tinged with mystery; no matter how many of the hungry she fed, there always seemed to be plenty of food left for the family.

Her charity was not, however, confined to those desperate men who knocked at her door and threw pebbles against her window. One of her special charges was a poor old priest who had lost his reason. While he was serving as a missionary among savages, a band of barbarians had put poison in the chalice he was using for the Celebration of Mass. Strangely enough, it did him no lasting bodily harm; physically, he recovered from the effects of the draught, but the shock of the outrage unhinged his reason. Until Mariana began caring for him, he recoiled from all human ministrations and, not unnaturally, regarded everyone who approached him with suspicion. If the chalice were not sacrosanct, where could he look for safety? Slowly and gently, she won his confidence. He waited and watched for her coming; and when he caught sight of the slender little figure clad in black, with its veil framing the pleasant rosy face which no amount of austerity deprived of its smile and its color, a glimmer of gratitude and understanding flickered in his dull sad eyes.

Among the noonday mendicants were unquestionably many of the maimed, the halt and the blind. But they had with them companions who could support and guide them and they went on their way again as soon as they were fed. And those who threw their pebbles under cover of darkness were, for the most part, young and vigorous, both able and eager to make their getaway before they were discovered. But there were many others who found their way to the asylum, now more truly than ever a House of Prayer—*Casa de Oración*—whose needs could not be met by bread alone. Many were ill; all were ignorant; the great majority were children—Indian children—Negro children.

Mariana's own education was elementary. She could read and write; she had been instructed in the catechism and familiarized with the life of Christ and saints; she could strum a guitar; she could weave and sew a fine seam. That was about all. Certainly, she had never had any training in caring for the sick or teaching the young. Yet she succeeded in establishing and maintaining what has been variously described as the first organized effort at Catholic Action, the first free clinic in Quito and "a seventeenth century kindergarten." All three descriptions are surprisingly accurate and they are not contradictory because, as a matter of fact, she founded and fostered all three.

"She gave the most tender care to everyone, even the most lowly Indians. She was their mother, their cook, their doctor and their nurse. She made their beds, she bathed their brows, she prepared their food and, if they were not able to feed themselves, she gave it to them. She prescribed such medicines as she knew how to use, and all who listened to her took heart. How could anyone continue to lack health who could draw on her strength? How could anyone weep when she smiled upon him? It may be said, with conviction, that through her all those who suffered found assuagement of pain."

This, in substance, is what Butrón, who obviously views her primarily from the clinical standpoint, says of what she did; and this in itself would be enough to rouse admiration and wonder, especially since she often felt very depressed and ill herself, though she created the illusion of joy and strength. But another chronicler, with a more comprehensive viewpoint, enlarges on this: "A woman unenlightened by learning, who had always lived a secluded life in the bosom of her family, lacking contacts with scholars, statesmen and persons otherwise experienced in the ways of the world, nevertheless undertook a campaign identical to the one proposed at the same time by the greatest authorities for the education of aborigines and the development of social welfare. Without the ostentation of publicity, without forming committees or making speeches, supported only by the will power which was founded on the love of God, she began the teaching of Indian children. She received no diploma for her philanthropic work, she was not decorated with any kind of a medal; but the consciousness of welldoing enraptured her; she was following the command of the Saviour, 'Love thy neighbor . . .' Under her supervision the little Indians learned to read, to write, to sing, to play the flute [62] and pray. They were encouraged to play games. Mariana bent over their books with them, her delicately chiseled profile clear and white against their copper-colored faces, and moved serenely among them, her slender black-clad figure silhouetted against their many-hued garments. Her whole heart, her whole soul went into her work. That is why the good she did is not limited to the narrow confines of her own era. She struck chords which have vibrated through the centuries and which can still be heard above the tumult of our own troublous times." [63]

Here is a picture on which we can look with pleasure: the little Indians, fed, clothed, tended, learning their letters, playing their flutes, singing their songs in the improvised schoolroom, (adjoining the improvised clinic) once the elegant and stately parlor of Mariana's grandparents, then romping in the spacious patio and straying unrebuked into the garden which was always bright with flowers. Here we can clearly visualize an aspect of Mariana's life which we have no trouble in reconciling with our own conception of saintliness; where there is no difference between the standards of the twentieth century and those of the seventeenth. Surely the chord which Mariana struck, and which has vibrated through time to our own troubled era, has echoed and emphasized the declaration made by Our Lord Himself when He said, "As ye have done it unto the least of these, ye have done it also unto Me."

CHAPTER V

O NCE THE pattern was established, it varied very little through the next few years.

Mariana went to Mass, practiced her penances, played her guitar, fed the poor, nursed the sick and taught the ignorant. She spent long hours reading the lives of saints and still longer hours kneeling in prayer; she communicated daily and confessed almost as often. Except that she slept less and less, ate less and less, prayed more and more and constantly strove for greater self-discipline, she did not disturb the rhythm of her days and nights. She saw no reason for doing so. This was what she had wanted and what she had achieved. She was not troubled by doubts as to the wisdom of her course. Though she sometimes experienced periods of aridity, in which the refreshment she expected from religious practices eluded her, these periods were neither prolonged nor overwhelming. She was not parched by them. Her faith might briefly cease to give her joy, but it remained a firm foundation and a vital force. In this respect, she was singularly blessed. It is rare, even among saints, that the cry, "O Lord, I believe! Help Thou mine unbelief!" does not rise from the anguished heart and escape the trembling lips.

The even tenor of her life and the comparable tranquility of her mind became increasingly effective in their results, not only on Mariana herself but on many others. She had pondered the motto of the Great St. Teresa and had taken it for her own:

> *"Let nothing disturb thee,*
> *Nothing affright thee.*
> *All things are passing,*
> *God never changeth.*
> *Patience gains all things.*
> *Who hath God wanteth nothing.*
> *Alone God sufficeth."*

"Though Mariana was not a learned woman, she managed, through meditation and communion with God, to acquire such profound knowledge of ecclesiastical questions that she often astonished professors and prelates by her words of wisdom. The great scholar, Alonso de Rojas, declared that in comparison to Mariana de Jesús he himself knew practically nothing of Christian principles; and though scholars learned a great deal from Mariana, it was, after all, the members of her own family who profited most by her wisdom. Happy were those starlit nights when, after the burden and heat of the day were passed, she took the household with her to heavenly heights of prayer and perfection." [58]

But it was not only in matters of religion that she proved wise beyond her years and her tangible and visible opportunities. Her opinions, intelligently, thoughtfully and prayerfully formed on all sorts of subjects, were eagerly sought both by her contemporaries and her elders and her advice, when followed, invariably proved to have been sound and wise. Quite naturally, when she decided to leave the worldly way of life, two of the nieces who had been her close companions from infancy and who were bound to her by ties of tenderness as well as relationship, clamored to follow her example. When their parents had failed in the attempt to convince them that, in their case, such a course would be premature, it was Mariana who succeeded in doing so; and in this instance, her gift of prophecy, which was later to be so noteworthy, was revealed, probably for the first time. Juana, she said, would find her vocation in matrimony, not in celibacy; on the other hand, Sebastiana, though she was now too young to do so, could in due time properly take vows of poverty, chastity and obedience, and she would die rather than break these. All this came to pass. Juana married Captain Juan de Guerrero de Salazar, who was later to play such an important role in establishing the Carmelite Convent and in promoting the Cause of Mariana's Beatification. The marriage was a singularly happy one and Juana was universally acclaimed as a model of all matronly virtues. Sebastiana, on the other hand, steadfastly resisted her parents' endeavors to persuade her that she should contract an admittedly advantageous alliance. The suitor who sought her hand was a man of wealth, as well as of culture and integrity, and, since the fortunes of Don Cosme and Doña Jerónima were by now greatly reduced, they could hardly be blamed for wishing to see another daughter suitably and honorably established. But Sebastiana, who was now nineteen years old, regarded her vows, though privately taken, as irrevocable, and prayed, provided only death would prevail against her parents, that she might die; and when preparations for the wedding were already underway, she was smitten with a sudden fever and died within a few days. [64]

Although she had so early dismissed the possibility of marriage for herself and had wholeheartedly supported Sebastiana in her resistance to it, Mariana rejoiced in Juana's conjugal happiness and recognized, as she had told this niece, that it was often in matrimony and not in celibacy that a true vocation could be found; in other words, her objective view of it was quite untinged with fanaticism on the subject of virginity, and she not only accepted wedlock unquestioningly as a sacrament, but very successfully insisted that the married women of her acquaintance should do the same, when they were inclined to take it lightly or view it with disillusionment. "Escolástica Sarmiento, the childhood friend of Mariana, had married Juan de Peralta, the *Escribano del Rey* [65] and failed to get on well with her husband. One day, at the Jesuit church, she confided her troubles to her friend, who suggested that they should take Communion together. Afterward, Mariana said, 'Go home now with an untroubled heart. I am confident that, henceforth, Our Creator will give you peace and happiness with your husband.' And so it came about, Doña Escolástica tells us, for, from then on, her husband showed her many delicate attentions and, recognizing the natural inflexibility of this man, she attributed the change to the miraculous intervention of the Servant of God.

"Mariana also transformed the Negro Juan de Rivera from a ferocious creature who tortured his wife, into a model husband. Juana de Sanguesa, the maltreated wife of de Rivera, took refuge at the Compañia in her flight from the wrath of this Negro and knelt down close to Mariana when Rivera pursued her with a dagger in hand. The charitable virgin rose and said quietly to this monster, 'Calm yourself. What manner of crime are you contemplating? Repent the great sin which you are about to commit!' Appeased, he fell back and left the church. Afterward, there was lasting peace between husband and wife up to the time of the Negro's death; and Juana attributed the blessing of this harmony to the intercession of Mariana de Jesús." [58]

While, as has been said, Mariana's prophecy in regard to her nieces, Juana and Sebastiana, was doubtless her first, the one regarding the establishment of the Carmelite Convent in her ancestral home has probably and understandably become the most famous. She made this several different times to several different persons and under several different circumstances. To Father Manosalvas, who succeeded Father Camacho as her confessor, she predicted that "the room where she lived would some day be the habitation of the brides of Christ"; and, in referring to this announcement later, in conversation with her friend

Petronila de San Bruno, " 'I wonder to whom will fall the happiness of becoming the slave of these virgins of the Saviour! What a joy to be chosen for the spouse of the King of Heaven and Earth! If I should live until then, I would be the first to seek the privilege of entering [this Carmelite Convent] for it is a great thing to be the daughter of my beloved and venerated St. Teresa!' Later, in the presence of her niece María de Paredes, the Indian servant Catalina, and María Arias, a Spanish friend, the young seer confirmed this announcement. She ordered that the door into the street should be locked and then said to these three, 'As to the supposition that this house will be a Carmelite Convent, you may be very sure that one will be founded here in time. Come with me and I will show you how it will be arranged'; and she indicated the position of the porter's lodge, the *torno*, the refectory, the kitchen. The choir, she told them, would be in her bedroom and the chapel facing the church at the time when the nuns came to live there. She felt such confidence in her prediction that she graciously charged members of her family, particularly Juan de Guerrero de Salazar, whom she thought would be the rightful heir to the house, to make a gift of it [to the Carmelites]." [58]

It is quite natural that this prophecy should be considered one of the most important made by Mariana, both because it was so detailed and because its fulfillment is visible and tangible even today. The privileged visitor to the Carmelite Convent in Quito—the one called the *Alto* to distinguish it from one of later foundation known as the *Bajo*—feels very close to Mariana in this spacious and charming house which was once her home, and is duly impressed with both the practicality and the harmony of the arrangements which have been made in strict conformity to her predictions. Some of her other predictions may, perhaps, be laid partly to intuition: the one concerning the date of Father Manosalvas' return to Quito from Riobamba, for instance, when he, as yet, had made no plans for this; the one in which she foretold the decline of the family fortunes; the one concerning her niece, Catalina de Guerrero de Salazar, whom she visualized as a bride of Christ and the foundress of the Carmelite Convent in Cuenca. And though the Canon Tomás Jijón y León, admittedly an impressive authority, gives her prediction regarding the foundation of the Congregación del Santo Cristo del Consuelo, in the Compañia, first rank among those she made, her close association with that church and all its activities put her in such a favorable position to know everything that was taking place, or likely to take place there, those who prefer to believe that she was observant, rather than clairvoyant, in this instance, are at liberty to do so. Other instances of clairvoyance, however, cannot be so easily explained away; those concerning several deaths, for example, described with great accuracy as to both date and surrounding circumstances. And, after all, why should we try to explain them away? The gift of prophecy, from the earliest biblical times, has been held in high esteem by the thoughtful and the learned, as well as the devout. The disbeliever in it is hardly more logical than the person who, because he cannot himself play the organ, finds it hard to understand how anyone else can do so.

There is nothing to suggest that Mariana herself felt her predictions were especially momentous. She made them with conviction, but with simplicity; they had their part in her pattern, but it was an incidental one and they did not alter it materially. The greatest changes which took place in her quiet and well-ordered life were embodied in the confessors who followed each other in more rapid succession than we would perhaps expect, each having a distinct and different effect upon her.

It is difficult, if not impossible, for the average modern woman, especially the English or North American woman, who is conscientious rather than devout in connection with her churchly duties, to visualize the importance of the role which a confessor long played in the life of his penitent throughout the Spanish Empire. He was not a dim figure, secluded on one side of a closed confessional, whom she was in duty bound to approach at least once a year from the other side, herself remaining almost unseen as she did so, and whom she seldom met on a less impersonal basis. The Spanish penitents did not stand in a long line of other persons, waiting more or less impatiently for their turn in the confessional, where they would all make their penitential disclosures as brief as possible, conscious that, if they did not, the time set apart for the purpose of hearing these would be over. The Spanish confessor was thoughtfully and prayerfully chosen in the beginning, with a view to mutual understanding and sympathy in worldly, as well as in spiritual, matters; and, once selected, he and he alone acted in the designated capacity and gave it his undivided attention. It would not have occurred to him to hurry his penitent through her confession; rather, he encouraged her to speak freely and fully to him. Neither would it have occurred to him to dismiss as trivial anything that seemed to her important, unless she were prone to scrupulosity and he felt she was attaching too much significance to sins so venial that they hardly could be classified as sins at all; in which case, she should not worry over them unduly. On the other hand, if her problems and her troubles were real to her, he tried to alleviate them. She consulted him about anything she chose and, to the best of his ability, he advised and admonished her. He was, in every sense of the word, her guide, her philosopher—and her friend. The element of friendship was extremely important. The penitent expected her confessor to be a man whom she could deeply respect for wisdom and sanctity, but she did not stand in awe of him on that account. The only awe she felt for him was based on his priestly office and not on the man as a human being. He was her liaison officer with the Almighty; but he was also the familiar figure in her home as well as in the church which she regularly attended. When she addressed him as Father, she did so with the same confident affection as when she spoke to the member of her own family whom she addressed in the same way.

All this, we should bear in mind when we speak of the distinct and different effects which Mariana's confessors had on her and in considering their several personalities.

We have already made the acquaintance of Camacho, the first of these in point of time and, by some, considered the foremost in other respects, also. Why he should have doubted his own fitness to foster the rare soul confided to his keeping, we do not know, but apparently he did. It seems unlikely that, otherwise, he would have entrusted it to anyone else, unless he were directed to do so, and that, too, seems unlikely. According to some authorities, the first change in confessors came because he was sent elsewhere in the province, for whatever reason; be this as it may, he was not permanently absent from Quito during Mariana's lifetime or estranged from her spiritually, for she and Sebastiana consulted him, when the latter revolted against her parents, and received his support; and Sebastiana's sudden death occurred only two months before her aunt's. However, he was succeeded as Mariana's confessor by Father Antonio Manosalvas, who was "young and humble of spirit when he began to direct her. He did not hesitate to admit that she surpassed him in the knowledge of the Divine Will. Often, he found no words with which to answer her and delayed his reply in order to consult others wiser than himself. He was of an experimental nature, disinclined to accept unquestioningly anything out of the ordinary. As a philosopher, he liked to investigate and make sure. He used the same system with Mariana that he did with others, and only when he was convinced there was no error did he accept her

Typical costumes of the period.

House of Mariana's family at Cayambe.

Statue of Mariana de Jesús in the Compañia, Quito.

Don Antonio de Morga (1559-1636). President of the Royal *Audiencia* of Quito (1615-1636). This portrait is in Osuna, fifty miles south of Seville, Spain.

Contemporary *Mater Dolorosa*, preserved in the Carmelite Convent.

Statue of Our Lady of Loreto, great beloved by Mariana.

Statue of St. Francis of Assisi, by Caspicara. In the Church of San Francisco, Quito.

Title page and illustration for Butrón's biography—The first written of Mariana de Jesús.

LA AZUZENA
DE QVITO,
QVE BROTO EL FLORIDO CAMPO
de la Igleſia en las Indias Occidencales,

LA VENERABLE UIRGEN MARIANA DE
JESVS, PAREDES, Y FLORES, admirable en Uirtu-
des, Profecias, y Milagros.

ESCRIBIOLA
EL P. IACINTO MORAN DE
Butron, de la Compañia de Ieſus.

OFRECELA D. MANVEL GVERRE-
ro de Salazàr Sobrino de la V. Virgen

A LA ESCLARECIDA
ſombra del Illuſtᴹᴼ· Señor Doſt.
D. Antonio de Leon, del Conſe-
jo de ſu Mag. Obiſpo que fuè de
Panamâ, y de Truxillo, y al pre-
ſente de Arequipa, y electo
de Quito.

Año de M.DCC.II.

QVITO

A. AZVZENA Đ QVITO. LA V.V. MARIANA DE-
ESVS, que por libertar à su Patria đ la peste, y terrem.º q̃ padecia
recio su Vida en sacrif.º Murió d 26. a.º d edad año 1645. llena d mer.s
J. ā Palom.ᵉ del.º et sculp. M.ᵈ

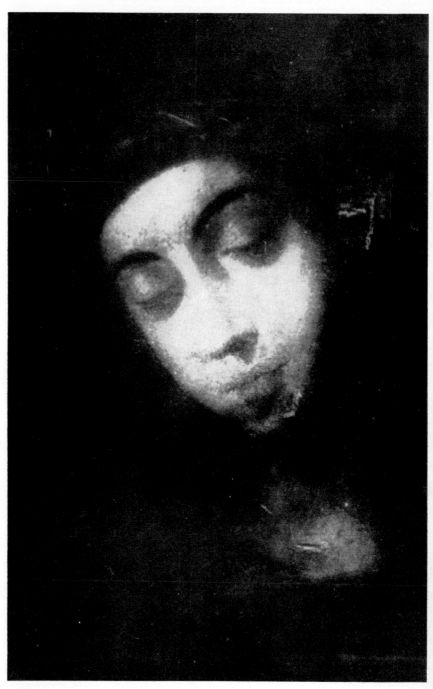

Portrait of Mariana de Jesús, painted by Hernándo de la Cruz after her death.

inspired decisions. He was a prudent man whose footsteps were firm. He did not like great heights or the dizziness of speed, but was deliberate about everything. Though he reduced the severities of his disciplines and the number of his fasts, he knew how to fulfill his ideals. He made a cult of humility; he waxed eloquent over the beauties of this virtue and his deeds revealed his devotion to it. Possibly, his philosophy was based on the principle that humility is truth. He left behind him a record of great prestige and his name was among the most outstanding in the colony." [53]

From this description, it would seem as if Manosalvas were wholly sincere, wholly conscientious, but possibly devoid of initiative and inspiration. If this surmise is correct, Mariana probably took his departure—for in this case, apparently, there is no doubt that there was a definite departure—with more resignation than she could have felt when Camacho was lost to her as a confessor. Father Luis Vasquez, "a man of science and of solid virtue," was next selected by his superiors to take charge of her. But "Mariana could not accommodate herself to her new confessor. She shed tears, she suffered affliction, she walked in darkness; her desolation was so great as to be almost inexpressible. But she still retained confidence in her Beloved; and, as she knelt in prayer, she heard a voice saying, 'Go to the Compañia, to the place where you always sit. Watch the door which leads into the Chapel of St. Francis Xavier and address yourself to the first religious who comes out of the cloister. Tell him that he is to be your spiritual adviser. Henceforth, he will direct you.' " [58]

Without hesitation she obeyed these instructions to the letter. Very early the next morning, she hastened to the Compañia and took her accustomed place there. Almost instantly, a lay brother, whom she recognized by sight as Hernándo de la Cruz, though she did not know him personally, came through the designated door. She went to the Sacristan, Brother Sebastian Delgado, and asked him to bring Hernándo de la Cruz to her.

The summons took the lay brother completely by surprise. He was too startled to comply instantly with this astonishing request; moreover, he could not properly have done so, for the rules under which he was governed forbade conversation with women, except by definite permission from a superior. But something moved him to seek this permission and it was granted. He returned to Mariana's side and listened, respectfully, but with increasing amazement, as she gave him the message she had been told to deliver. When he left her, he returned to

the sacristy and said, in a wondering voice, "Do you know, Brother
Sebastian, with whom I have talked? As surely as God is revealed in
His saints, this is no less a one than St. Catherine of Siena, a veritable
angel in the flesh!"

The next day, the Superior, through Father Lucas de la Cueva, gave
Hernándo de la Cruz the necessary permission. Since he was not a
full-fledged priest, he could not become Mariana's confessor; that duty
would devolve on the great scholar and orator, Alonso de Rojas.
Nevertheless, Brother Hernándo might act as her spiritual adviser
and devote two hours each day to her guidance and enlightenment.

This decision marked a great turning point in Mariana's life.

Hernándo de la Cruz was totally unlike any confessor she had ever
had, indeed, unlike any man she had ever known. He was not a Quitenian, but a Panamanian, the son of Don Fernando de la Vega and
Doña Leona de Rivera, who were both natives of Seville and both of
noble birth; and he had originally come to Quito solely for the purpose
of accompanying a beloved younger sister on her journey thither. She
wished to enter a convent of the Poor Clares and they had none in
Panama. Once his primary purpose was accomplished, he had had
every intention of returning home and no intention of becoming a
religious himself. He was young, rich, handsome, pleasure-loving and
gifted. His voice was as pleasing as his person, and he accompanied
himself as he played on various instruments. In his spare moments, he
wrote charming verses, but they were light in character; he did not
pretend to be a scholar. He also painted charming pictures, but though
he had spent some time at Lima dabbling in art, he did not take the
talent which enabled him to draw, any more seriously than he took
the ones which enabled him to play, sing and versify; it was a pastime
when nothing better offered, that was all. Actually, his favorite diversion was duelling, but he excelled in almost any physical exercise where
lightness, rapidity, resourcefulness and endurance were all primary
factors.

He saw his sister safely in her convent and set about his preparations for departure; but something in the fulfillment of her purpose
affected his own. In the course of their ocean voyage, they had come
closer to each other than ever before. Tender as their mutual affection
had always been, it was hitherto devoid of spiritual elements, as far as
he was concerned—or so he had thought. Now he began to wonder.
He had been greatly moved at the time of her investiture. Involun-
tarily, he found his thoughts wandering in directions they had never

taken before, and he could not dismiss them from his mind, though, at first, he tried to do so. Then suddenly he found himself involved in a duel—the sort of adventure in which he had always reveled. This time, though the outcome was not fatal or even disastrous, he was appalled at the thought that it might have been and resolved never to engage in another. He put off his departure for Panama, did more painting, wrote more verses,[66] sang more songs and began, for the first time, to study seriously; and still he found his existence incomplete. Then he decided that it was also futile and that he must put an end to such futility. Something impelled him to go to the Superior of the Jesuits and ask if, by any chance, he would be accepted as a postulant. The Superior was obliged to tell him that his education did not qualify him to become a priest. This was done regretfully, for the young man's personality was arresting and he was obviously very talented; but it was also obvious that he lacked learning and that he could not meet the high and rigid scholastic standards of the Jesuit Order. Of course, if he would care to become a lay brother. . . .

It may be questioned as to which of the two was the more surprised when he agreed to do so.

Such was the man to whose spiritual guidance Mariana was now entrusted. For the next seven or eight years, until the time of her death, they were together at least two hours every day. Outwardly, their lives were the same as before they had met; but appearances in this case, as in so many more, were misleading. Each gave the other something that had been lacking before. From the day of their meeting, their lives seemed to be perfect and complete. The harmony between them and the significance of this may unhesitatingly be compared to the harmony that existed between St. Francis and St. Clare. As far as earthly ties were concerned, they were all in all to each other. As far as spiritual blessings are concerned, the world has benefited throughout the centuries by those which they shared.

And so the years went on, in their established pattern, until the spring when Mariana was twenty-six years old.

CHAPTER VI

THE YEAR 1645 began with a series of catastrophes so crushing that Quito was overwhelmed by them.

First came a succession of earthquakes, overturning the spires of churches, leaving great fissures in the ground, shaking the Andean range and bringing death to more than two thousand persons. Next came an epidemic of measles and diphtheria to which two thousand Spaniards and ten thousand Indians succumbed; hardly a household in the entire city, which then had a population of fifty thousand, escaped bereavement. In the midst of the general mourning, the great volcano Pichincha, inactive for nearly eighty years, erupted for the first time since the coming of the Spaniards, venting its fiery lava on the surrounding countryside. Inevitably, such a succession of calamities was interpreted as signifying the Wrath of God. The feeling that it must be appeased grew stronger and stronger.

On the Fourth Sunday of Lent, which that year fell on the twenty-sixth day of March, Alonso de Rojas, the confessor of Mariana de Jesús, ascended the steps of the beautiful carved pulpit at the Compañia with a fixed purpose: he would not only declare that all the disasters which had visited Quito had been caused by sin and call upon the people to repent; he would offer himself as a propitiatory victim and ask that he might die to save others from the punishment they had brought on themselves.

He was a forceful and eloquent preacher, and he spoke with such fire and vehemence that even the most indifferent and hardened of the many who thronged the golden church that morning could not listen to him unmoved. One of them took immediate action: this was Mariana de Jesús who, as usual, was quietly seated at the foot of the pulpit, listening intently to the sermon.

She rose, gracefully and without haste, and, speaking in a clear firm voice, audible in all parts of the crowded church, announced that she would ask God to take her life in offering in place of the priest's, who could so ill be spared from the city, because of his great goodness and his noble example to others. Unworthy as it was, she hoped the Lord would accept it "in defense of her country, her compatriots and her kindred" and she besought Him "that she might be chastized for everything in the city which deserved chastisement." As soon as Mass was over, she rose again and walked with silent dignity down the aisle, where the people, too thunderstruck for speech, stood aside to let her pass. After leaving the church, she went straight to her home and never left it again, for she was instantly stricken with mortal illness. But, from that day forward, the earthquakes ceased, the plagues abated and the deadly volcano was again quiescent.

It is understandable that such disasters are bound to end, sooner or later, when they have run their course; if it will make us any happier to claim that their cessation in Quito, just at this time, was a mere coincidence, we are free to do so. It is also undeniable that Mariana had long been subject to intermittent illnesses and that, as she grew older—though she was now only twenty-six—these became more frequent and more severe. Nor should we attempt to deny it. Nothing is gained by falsifying facts, by pretending we do not know that, while some persons unquestionably require less nourishment and less sleep than others, insufficient food and insufficient rest almost invariably take their toll of the human body, even if it is subjected to no maltreatment, voluntary or involuntary. Mariana was afflicted by fevers, by terrible headaches, by digestive disorders; the frequent oral hemorrhages indicate that she, like St. Thérèse of Lisieux, was consumptive; the "severe pain in her side" to which there are numerous references was probably pleurisy. Although she insisted that she never suffered from hunger despite her rigorous fasts—and we have no right to doubt her word—she admitted to terrible thirst, which went unalleviated. She did not willfully injure her health. When advised by her confessors to modify her austerities, she heeded their instructions and numerous reliable physicians, to whose treatment she submitted obediently, attended her with great faithfulness. But no informed person needs to be told that modern and medieval doctors differ very greatly in their views and the way they put these into practice; indeed, we do not have to go back more than a century to find that bloodletting, either by the opening of veins or by the application of leeches, was a standard means of reducing fever, and that the amount of water permitted the feverish, for both bathing and drinking, was strictly limited.

In Mariana's day, primitive methods were, of course, far more prevalent.

It is quite logical to assume that the terrible emotional strain under which she had been living during the earthquakes and the plagues and the volcanic eruptions could have resulted in so much additional physical strain as to bring about a sudden collapse. Moreover, the very thought of having a confessor, whom she so greatly revered and with so much reason, sacrificed to atone for the gilded vices of such men as Morga, who had been President of the *Audiencia* most of her life, and of whose evildoing she must have been only too well aware, could well have precipitated this. If we feel it must be explained, without recourse to supernatural forces, it is easy enough to do so and quite proper to do so. We fail in fairness only when we deny the existence of such forces, because we ourselves are not sufficiently sensitive to be aware of them and to respond to them.

In Quito, there was no lack of awareness and of response to it. However we may feel, however we may reason, it is indisputable that the sacrificial action of Mariana had made a profound impression upon her fellow townsmen, and that their conduct during her last illness bore witness to the fact that they took it not only seriously but solemnly. On Palm Sunday, a fortnight after the stirring events at the Compañia, the plazas were crowded with people who had filled the churches where the Blessed Sacrament was exposed, or were on their way to fill them. Many went to visit Mariana, asking that she would intercede for them at the Throne of Grace, to which they were convinced she was very close. She received them cordially and cheerfully. Long before, she had prayed that her austerities might not show in her face, lest that might discourage others from following the hard way which she had chosen and which she believed to be the surest road to heaven. That prayer, like many of her others, had been answered. According to the description given by Butrón, her looks retained the freshness and charm that characterized the picture painted of her when she was a child: "a face rather full, but well proportioned, pleasant, gentle and kind. Complexion very fair, cheeks tinted faintly pink, eyes large and black under well-defined black brows; nose delicate and mouth small."

Everyone who came to see her was impressed with this extraordinary charm, this extraordinary freshness. It was hard for visitors to convince themselves that they were in the presence of a dying woman. And not only because of her appearance; her loving kindness was almost inexhaustible. It was not until very near the end that she said to her friend, Petronila de San Bruno, who belonged to the Order of the Poor Clares, "Sister, the moment has come when I need to speak to God and not of Him." From then on, she was silent most of the time. There were some who believed she had lost the power of speech, though otherwise she retained all her faculties. It would not be strange if Sister Petronila were not among those who held this opinion.

On Good Friday, her physician, Juan Martín de la Peña, decided that she should be bled to reduce her fever and, later in the day, as on previous occasions, the blood was reverently poured into a corner of the patio. There it moistened the ground in which a small nondescript plant, hitherto unobserved, stood dormant. Shortly thereafter, this put forth buds, identified as belonging to lilies, and, presently, it showed signs of more abundant bloom. Since then it has never failed to produce, in profusion, the beautiful lilies with which the name of Mariana has become universally associated.

As the day she herself had predicted for her death came closer, she asked for writing materials in order that she might set down instructions regarding her final wishes. After thanking her brother-in-law, Cosme de Caso, for his many benefactions, she requested that she be taken downstairs to the room of her niece Juana, as it was there that she wished to die. She directed that her sister and her niece should wrap her in her shroud and that they should permit no one else to touch her or to see her uncovered body after she was dead; and she further asked that she might be buried in the Compañía, at the foot of the altar dedicated to Our Lady of Loreto, to whom she had always felt such great devotion.

She had already received permission from the Director General of the Jesuits for such entombment, which she desired "for a variety of reasons." . . . "Because she was the daughter of the Compañía, which had nurtured her from her tenderest years; because she had learned the principles of virtue from its priests, who had always been her confessors; because with them and only with them she had discussed matters of major importance and because only Jesuits had attended her during her last illness and would do so at the time of her death; because she went to no church except the Compañía; and, finally, because she was 'all Jesuit.' " [67]

On Ascension Day, she managed to rise from her bed and go to the window which looked out on the Chapel of Our Lady of the Angels. She could only glimpse, from this distance, its glory of gold and crimson, which had so enraptured her during her childhood; but she could hear Mass as it was celebrated, and she listened to it, kneeling, again enraptured. The following morning, she listened to it again, in the same way. Then the faithful Indian, Catalina, assisted by others, carried her downstairs and a priest from the chapel came to administer the Last Rites. The news of her moribund condition had already spread through the city like wildfire, and many of its most distinguished figures had hastened to the house. Foremost among these was the Bishop, Pedro de Orvieto, who had been so largely responsible for the construction of the sanctuary which sheltered Our Lady of Quinche, one of the images most venerated by Spaniards and Indians alike, and who had been untiring in his efforts to restore the rights of the aborigines and raise the intellectual and moral standards of the lesser clergy. From the beginning, he had viewed Mariana's dedication to the ideal of sacrifice with admiration and sympathetic understanding; now that her life was drawing to an end, he felt impelled to pay her the tribute of his presence and she was deeply touched. Less warmly welcomed were the learned licentiate, Jerónimo Ortiz y Zapata, a Judge of the *Audiencia*, clad in the *garnacha* which identified his office, who came with his wife, Leonor Saavedra. State, as well as Church, sought to honor Mariana now and she was aware that this visit was a mark of respect, but she shrank from the presence of these dignitaries at her deathbed, as she did from that of "many other persons of consequence" who quickly assembled. Very different was her feeling toward her confessor, Alonso de Rojas, whose thunderous sermon had impelled her to offer herself as a propitiatory victim in his stead. It was fitting that he should be with her now; the spiritual tie between them was very close. Even closer, if possible, was the one which bound her to the lay brother, Hernándo de la Cruz; only death itself could break that. Indeed, it seemed to her that even death would not be strong enough to sever it instantly and completely. And she was right in this, as she had been in so many earlier prophecies.

She asked the blessing of Cosme de Caso, who had been her second father and whose paternal support sustained her until the last. Many members of her family had foregathered now, among them Juana, the niece who had been her childhood playmate, and Juana's husband, Juan de Guerrero de Salazar. So had others whom she held near and dear, even though they were not her kinsfolk: Catalina, who had carried her to church for her christening and never once, in the years since then, had failed in devotion; Sister Petronila de San Bruno, to whom she had confided her longing to stop conversing with men in order that she might then more freely converse with God.

There was no struggle, no agony at the end; all that was in the past, in life, not in death. She kissed the crucifix which was held out to her —the crossed feet, the pierced side, the crown of thorns; but when the Bishop tried to kiss her hand, she drew it gently away. Then she did not move again. As complete tranquility enfolded her, her lips were still parted in a smile and rosy color still suffused her face.

CHAPTER VII

J UANA DE CASO touched Hernándo de la Cruz lightly on the shoulder, but he did not appear to feel her hand. She spoke to him gently and he did not seem to hear her voice. He remained motionless before the little altar where he had fallen on his knees as soon as he realized that Mariana had died, and his face was transfigured. Gradually, it dawned on Juana and the others who were still in the room that he was oblivious of them and of everything around him; he was in a state of ecstasy. When, at last, he rose, his expression was still joyous, but it was no longer tinged with the supernal and he said in a clear firm voice, "We have a new advocate in heaven, for Mariana is already there."

Having made this announcement in such a way that it carried complete conviction and, consequently, great consolation, he began to give explicit directions. "Do not put on mourning and do not drape the house with black," he commanded the bereaved family. "This is a day of jubilee, it is Mariana's day of triumph. Therefore adorn the drawing rooms with tapestries, as you would on any other day of jubilee. Spread the bier on which the coffin is to stand with crimson and decorate it with the masses of flowers which all the convents will send, vying with each other to provide the most beautiful offerings. Line the coffin with crimson taffeta bordered with fringe and gold-studded bands and leave it open, so that the mortal remains of Mariana may be viewed with veneration by all." Having said this, he knelt again, this time not before the altar, but before Mariana, kissed her hands and her feet and, as he rose a second time, said in the same glad voice as before, "The Servant of God is already rejoicing in His Presence." [58]

His next announcement was apparently to the effect that, though he was now leaving the chamber, his absence would be brief. We do not know the exact order in which the next events took place; but it must have been very shortly after Mariana breathed her last that Hernándo de la Cruz painted the portrait, which was accepted as a true likeness by her family and which has been recognized as authentic ever since. Probably he was gone barely long enough to collect his canvas and brushes. The picture shows only her face, but a face so lovely that the loveliness of her whole person seems revealed in it. It has none of the gruesome and morbid attributes of the usual post-mortem portrait, much less the starkness and artificiality of a death mask. It shows the countenance of a gentle and sensitive woman, whose rare physical and spiritual beauty had been unimpaired by her transition into another world, and who was perfectly at peace when she left the one in which her dedicated life had been spent. It could have been painted only by an artist whose subject was supreme and whose understanding and devotion were as great as his skill.

When Hernándo de la Cruz left for the second time, it was to permit Mariana's sister and niece to proceed with her shrouding. Her wishes in regard to this were scrupulously observed. Jerónima and Juana allowed no one to help them as they prepared her body for burial, removing the penitential haircloth which she had worn to the day of her death, then clothing her again in the dress which was "all Jesuit" and which had so long been her chosen apparel, and further enfolding her in the habit of St. Francis—the same in which the image of her selection, which she always kept in her room, had been clad. Several Poor Clares had already arrived at the house, carrying garlands, branches of palm and sprays of snowy flowers; and as soon as they were admitted to the presence of the dead woman, they placed a crown on her head and a palm in her hands, as symbols of purity and victory. Then she was reverently taken to the stately drawing room, which was already adorned as Hernándo de la Cruz had directed with trappings of crimson, and the nuns scattered their sprays and garlands over the brilliant silks.

It was high time that everything should be in readiness. Again, the news about Mariana had spread like wildfire, and crowds filled the narrow street leading to the house of the Paredes y Flores and sought admittance there. Mariana had been regarded as a national heroine ever since the earthquakes, the plagues and the volcanic eruptions had ceased. Now the people believed that her death proved she had been acceptable to the God of Wrath as a victim and they were ready to acclaim her as a saint. Never in the history of Quito, even on the *dias de las estaciónes*,[68] had so many assembled with a single purpose: that of paying tribute to the "great Servant of God" whom they had known in the flesh. All sorts and conditions of men and women were in this throng: the leading figures of Church and State, the nobles, the gentry, the commons. All pressed forward, striving to come close to the bier, to kneel beside it, to kiss the dead girl's hands and feet, to touch her with rosaries and *algodones*; [69] most of all, they wanted to acquire something which they could preserve as a relic. Jerónima had foreseen this supreme desire and had tried to provide for it by making available bits of material from the clothing her sister had worn and strands of the cords she had used. But there were not anywhere near enough of these to go around.

All night long and all the next day the procession continued. It ceased, as far as the house was concerned, only because the time had come to transport the coffin to the church. It went adorned with ribbons [70] and preceded by guardsmen with unsheathed swords, for, by now, the people were ready to resort to desperate measures to obtain relics. Personages of note had requested the honor of joining members of the family as pallbearers. In the cortege walked the Bishop, Pedro de Orvieto, the members of the Royal *Audiencia* in a body, the two *Cabildos*, the regular and secular priests, the seminarians from the College of San Luís, great nobles, men and women of the people "without number" and also "countless persons from beyond the city limits whom the news of its loss had reached."

The Compañia had been decorated as for a great festival. Not a single black drapery was in evidence; instead, the hangings were all of crimson velvet and the most precious treasures belonging to the Congregation of Our Lady of Loreto had been put on display. Eighty seminarians from San Luís joined the leaders among the clergy to make a human barrier around the bier and protect it from demonstrations of devotion which, by now, had begun to assume excessive proportions. But it was soon evident that they could not defend it effectively, even after the coffin was closed, and so they decided that this should not be kept in the Compañia, but removed to the vault of San José for safekeeping, until a suitable tomb could be provided for it under the altar of Our Lady of Loreto. This was accordingly done. But a month after Mariana's death, a Solemn Requiem Mass was celebrated, at which her confessor, Alonso de Rojas, preached the funeral sermon.

He was a forceful and fiery orator, and his hearers, already keyed to a state of great emotional intensity, listened to his impassioned speech with increasing anguish and excitement. He took his text from a passage in Ecclesiasticus: *"Festina tempus, et memento finis, ut enarrent mirabilia tua."* ("Hasten the time, and remember the end, that they may declare thy wonderful work.") Then, dividing this into its three logical parts, he enlarged on each of these, applying its extraordinary significance to the life which had just come to such a spectacular end. Afterward, with mounting force, he thundered:

"Finally, she did not die of love or of mortification, but in answer to prayer. Listen and I will tell you how. I, an unworthy minister of the Gospel, was preaching in this place on the Fourth Sunday of Lent, a sermon based on the story of Joshua; and, distressed by the calamities which threatened our country . . . I besought God to accept my life as an offering for the salvation of my people. I asked that I might be punished for their sins and thus achieve their redemption. God did not hearken to my prayer, which lacked fervor, or accept the sacrifice of my life, which is worthless. But he did accept the same offer, ardently made at the same time and at the very foot of this pulpit, by Mariana de Jesús. This was the cause of her death. Do you ask for proof? It is not lacking. That very night she suffered the attack from which she died. Hers was a martyrdom not of mortification, but of powerful prayer. Our country should not only rejoice because this Servant of God has ennobled it with her patronage and today in heaven favors it with her prayers; it should also be moved to eternal thankfulness because it was through her sacrifice that the city was delivered from the fate inflicted on it by the God of Vengeance in punishment for its sins."

In this closing declamation, delivered with a vehemence which, in itself, carried conviction, lay the fundamentals of everything which the preacher had intended to drive home to all within sound of his voice. He had already presented Mariana to her people as their national heroine. When they surged out of the church, some with tears streaming down their faces, some sobbing audibly, some shouting loudly, some silent from their overpowering agitation, they had already accepted her as such.

CHAPTER VIII

Nothing could be more natural, considering the intensity of feeling about her, than that a movement designed to lead to the canonization of Mariana de Jesús should have begun almost as soon as she was laid in her tomb. Indeed, when her Cause was first introduced, this was done so promptly that every witness testifying in her behalf had known her in the flesh and their sworn statements as to her qualifications for sanctity are convincing and inspiring. True, the primary steps toward raising her to the altars were taken with equal promptness in the case of Santa Rosa de Lima; the witnesses in the Process had also all known her personally and their reports carried the same ring of authenticity. But it has been very rare in the history of the Church that this has happened; and in the case of Mariana, the second phenomenon—that of prompt beatification and canonization—did not occur; two hundred years elapsed after her death before she was beatified; three hundred years before she was canonized.

This was due, in the beginning, to such a succession of mishaps that if a writer of fiction introduced as many, and as melodramatic in character, into an adventure story, the critics with one voice would declare that he was twisting the long arm of coincidence out of joint and that his narrative was fantastic. The story of the disasters which beset those entrusted with presenting Mariana's Cause in Rome is undeniably fantastic. But it also happens to be true.

Only twenty-five years after the death of the Lily of Quito, as she was already very generally called, upon the petition of Captain Baltazar de Montesdeoca, the *Procurador* (Attorney) of the city, Alonzo de la Peña Montenegro, ordered that official inquiry regarding "the life, virtue, sanctity and miracles of the virgin Mariana de Jesús" be made at his expense. The Cause could hardly have had a more powerful sponsor; Alonzo de la Peña Montenegro, the author of a remarkable book entitled *El Itenarario para Parracos* has been described as "the most learned of all Colonial bishops" and had served with dis-

tinction as President of the *Audiencia* for four years, after accepting
appointment to this position with the understanding that it was only
a temporary one—for while it was not unusual that a man of outstanding ability should be asked to serve in both ecclesiastical and
civic capacities, the burden of holding two offices was so heavy that
he could not normally be expected to do this for long. While acting
as President, he had effectively suppressed the pirates who were ravag-
ing the seas in the vicinity of Guayaquil and his zeal, as well as his
brilliance, was such that it was very generally felt everything he undertook would be crowned with success.

Under his expert supervision, the Process continued for eight years;
but before arrangements could be made to send the relevant documents to Rome, the great Bishop died and his successor in the episco-
pal seat, Sanchez Andrade de Figueroa, was apparently less alert.
However, in 1690, he was approached by Juan de Guerrero de Salazar,
who requested official sanction for undertaking the mission. Again, it
would have been difficult to find anyone more suited for an important
task. Salazar was a thoroughly reliable man, who had married María de
Caso, a niece of Mariana and had known the latter well; therefore, he
naturally took a keen personal interest in the Cause and was duly com-
missioned to undertake the journey in question. But the *Vibora*, the
sailing vessel on which he embarked, was shipwrecked off the coast of
Cuba and all that Salazar was able to save—except his life!—was the
copy of the funeral sermon preached by Rojas which, though excellent
as far as it went, did not go far enough to satisfy the authorities in
Rome, when the poor man finally reached there.

As soon as this calamity became known in Quito, Juan's brother, José
de Guerrero de Salazar, and a devoted friend, Juan de la Cruz Zuñiga,
had a second copy of the first Process made at their expense, and
added to this certified lists of new graces and miracles, attributed to
Mariana, which had taken place in various parts of America. The two
friends next obtained special permission from the King of Spain, Carlos
VI, by means of a *Cedula Real* (Royal Decree), to raise money through
almsgiving for a second expedition. While José was perfecting the new
draft, he died in Cuzco, where he had gone to work on it.

A third attempt, financed in Quito, was now made to reach the
authorities in Rome and two reliable commissioners, Father José
Iguano Delgado and Father Jenaro Garofalo, started on their way; but
between Portobello and Cartagena their ship, *El Goberno*, was beset
by pirates and, this time, all lives as well as all documents were lost!

Some sixty years later—in 1757—after several other expeditions had failed, she was declared Venerable by Pope Benedict XIV. Nine years afterward her virtues were approved by Pope Clement XIII. (At that time, the title of Venerable was given when the cause was introduced.) She was eventually beatified in 1850 and was canonized in 1950.[71]

Despite these long and lamentable delays, the loving reverence with which Mariana was regarded by her own people did not diminish with time; rather, it continued to increase. Though no miracles, attributable to her, were officially recognized for almost another century, various phenomena were generally and enthusiastically acclaimed in Quito: the purple veil with which the crucifix in her room had been covered at the time of her death was removed by unseen hands every time it was replaced. Mysterious lights appeared in her empty chamber and mysterious music issued from it. Fragrant lilies blossomed in perennial profusion on the beautiful plant which, when first observed, had been only the dormant sprig of some insignificant shoot that had pushed its way through the ground in the corner of the patio where Catalina had been accustomed to pour Mariana's blood after she was leeched by her physician. Now the plant's florescence was one of snowy splendor. More and more it was associated, both symbolically and supernaturally, with Mariana.

But phenomena such as these, however convincing to the local laity, could not be accepted by the Rota as miracles, of which at least two must be authenticated before the Servant of God could be pronounced Blessed. Neither could the fulfillment of Mariana's prophecy regarding the house which had originally belonged to her grandparents and which had been her lifelong home, though this did, indeed, become a convent, no later than 1653, when the Carmelite Nuns took possession of it, locating the kitchen, the refectory and even the *torno* exactly where she had predicted. The absence of even a single communication, written in her own hand,[72] was undoubtedly a contributing cause to the deliberation with which the Rota proceeded; for personal letters, which so often reveal a great deal about the writer's characteristics, interests and ideals, are always given serious consideration and not infrequently have an important bearing on a Cause. However, there was actually no lack of miracles among which to choose, and Mariana's fame continued to grow; she was invoked by all sorts and conditions of men and under all sorts of circumstances. In 1894, the Archbishop of Quito, who was determined to prevent the entry into the capital of Alfaro, the presidential candidate, who was

an agnostic, actually coupled her name with that of the Almighty—
and to the exclusion of all the saints—in the impassioned pastoral
which he addressed to his flock: "The enemy is at our doors, but be
of good cheer! God is with us! The Lily of Quito, the Blessed Mariana
is with us! To arms, to arms, my people!" Several years later when,
despite archepiscopal opposition, Alfaro was firmly entrenched in the
presidential chair, he sought a truce with the Church by promising
that, if it would compromise with him, he himself would do everything
in his power to advance the Cause of the Canonization.

On the day when the long struggle ended triumphantly—July 9,
1950—Quito was brilliantly illuminated and every balcony in the city
hung with gorgeous tapestries. In the Compañia, the Papal Bull was
read aloud to a vast throng and, when the reading was finished, a great
shout arose, swelling in volume until it seemed to shake the very
walls. The 10th of July was declared a national holiday and a second
service, when the *Te Deum* was sung, took place at the Compañia,
which was attended by the President, Gallo Plaza, and all the leading
officials of the country. Never, in the history of Ecuador, had there
been such widespread rejoicing.

In Rome, the ceremony of Canonization began at half-past seven
in the morning, with an attendance of 45,000 and opened, as is usual
on such occasions, with a great procession. Though contemporary
accounts of this are not as detailed as we might wish, we do learn that
a magnificent banner, depicting on one side Mariana at prayer and,
on the other, Mariana teaching the children in her clinic, was an outstanding feature of this great processional; both scenes were based on
pictures made by Hernándo de la Cruz and it seems particularly fitting
that, in this way, he should share her day of glory. (At the end of the
Mass, the traditional offering of two huge candles was made to His
Holiness and each of these was painted with a picture of Mariana.)

When all the dignitaries, who had taken part in the procession, were
seated, silver trumpets heralded the imminent arrival of the Pope; he
was robed in glittering white and made his triumphant entry as the
Sistine Choir sang, *"Tu es Petris."* After the postulation and reply to
this, there was silent prayer and—reading between the lines of the
bare narrative which tells us no more than this—we are aware of the
hush that must have fallen on the vast assembly at St. Peter's, which
preceded the singing of *Veni Creator Spiritus* and the Pope's solemn
pronouncement:

"For the honor of the Holy and Undivided Trinity, for the exaltation of the Catholic Faith and the increase of the Christian Religion, by the authority of Our Lord Jesus Christ, the Holy Apostles, Peter and Paul, and our own, having deliberated carefully and invoked divine assistance frequently, and having sought the advice of our Venerable Brethren the Cardinals, Patriarchs, Archbishops and Bishops of the Holy Roman Catholic Church present in the City, We declare and define Blessed Mariana de Jesús de Paredes to be a Saint and We inscribe her in the Calendar of Saints, declaring that in each year the day of her birth, that is, the twenty-sixth of May,[73] her memory must be recollected by the Universal Church with the pious devotions proper to Virgin Saints. In the name of the Father and of the Son and of the Holy Ghost."

And now there is no longer a hush. Instead, a great cry goes up, greater even than the one which is shaking the walls of the Compañia in Quito: "Santa Mariana, *Santa Mariana*, SANTA MARIANA," and from the Dome of the Holy Angels, the trumpets sound again and the bells of St. Peter begin to ring and the bells of all the churches in Rome join in, until it seems as if the whole Eternal City were calling out, "Santa Mariana, *Santa Mariana*, SANTA MARIANA."

The Church in Ecuador was represented at the Canonization by the Apostolic Nuncio, the Archbishop of Quito, five Bishops, the Superior of the Jesuits in that country and several other important clerics. This group was supplemented by a special diplomatic delegation of thirty-five, headed by Don Enrici Arizaga Toral, Mayor of Cuenca and former Secretary of the Treasury, and by more than a thousand pilgrims, representing all sorts and conditions of men. These Ecuadorian delegations were received in Audience as soon as the ceremony of Canonization was over and arrived bearing gifts to the Holy Father, among these a reliquary in the form of an *Ostensarium*, having on it the Ecuadorian coat-of-arms and decorated with a silver lily and many precious stones. In accepting these gifts, the Holy Father, departing from the formal phraseology of the sermon in Latin at St. Peter's, addressed the pilgrims in their own language and referred to them as his sons.

"We are not dealing now with the foundress of a great religious order," he began, "such as Saint Emilia de Rodet, not with a personality prominent in history, such as Saint Anthony M. Claret; not an apostle of charity, like Saint Bartolomea Capitanio or Saint Vincent Gerosa; not a queen, like Joan of France; not a champion of the rights of the Church, like Saint Vicente M. Strambi; not a martyr of virginal purity, like St. Maria Goretti. But rather we are dealing with one who is, in a certain sense, like the final phrase of a symphony, which gathers up all the themes, taking from each one something characteristic, to put together the marvelous harmony of its spirit."

After this movingly expressive preamble, the Pope continued. "The story of Mariana de Jesús de Paredes is very brief. Sprung from a noble Spanish family, whose genealogical tree has roots both in Castile and in Andalusia, she was born in Quito in 1618. From the first moment, she had in her soul all the sweetness of that climate, all the brightness of that sky, all the grace of its palm trees and its flowers. Her piety was amazing, her soul precociously mature; at about the age of ten, she took vows of poverty, chastity and obedience. Clearly, the branch transplanted from the Iberian trunk was strong and the soil of the New World was generous. The example of the missionaries attracted her, enflamed her soul and filled her with the most lofty desires, which materialized in fervent prayers, extraordinary contemplation and other mystic abilities, together with such austerities that their mere enumeration would cause great amazement. A victim of her first love, she ended her days as a holocaust of charity in 1645, offering her life for her people. And when the earth stopped trembling and the plague vanished from the air, she breathed her last amid indescribable ecstasies, though still clad in her rough hair shirt. She was only 26 years old.

"She did not live in a cloister, because Providence wanted her to be out in the world; but she aspired to the same perfection as the most observant religious. She was not a great historic figure, but today she is the pride of a great nation which acclaims her as its 'national heroine.' She did not give her time exclusively to charity, but in the end she gave her life for her brethren. She loved the Church as much as the most zealous defender of its rights and she honored it with her virtues. Finally, she was not martyred by the fury of another, but she knew how to mortify herself with her own hands.

"In this Saint, may all men learn the immense power of Christian virtue, capable of bringing a spirit to maturity with more vigor than the sun of Quito, ripening the rich fruits of Ecuador. May the world learn of the energies hidden in prayer and sacrifice. May the epicureans of all time learn that the goal of the spirit is found at the end of the hidden road on which love seeks sorrow in order to overcome material bonds. May the worldly youth of today learn of that in their own circumstances which can make a soul enamored of the Lord. And

may all those who live today in the full light of devotion to the Most
Sacred Heart of Jesus admire the perfection of this innocent victim
who, in the dawn of the 17th century, already knew how to make
reparation the center of her spirituality.

"But it is evident that We will not be able to conclude these
words without addressing ourselves specially to the most noble representatives of Ecuador present here, including such a worthy portion
of the hierarchy, with hundreds of their faithful, led by an Extraordinary Delegation among whom are names whose merits are not unknown Us.

"Mariana de Jesús de Paredes is an example for all, but in a specific manner for you, beloved Ecuadorian sons. On many occasions,
the contingent alternatives of everyday politics can influence guiding
principles in such a way that values as fundamental as Christian education may be endangered. Do not permit it, but rather demand for
your future generations an education framed by the virtues which
made your Saint great. Offer to your sons the perfect model of your
'national heroine,' Saint Mariana de Jesús de Paredes.

"To her, beloved sons, we commend you, while, with a true effusion
of Our paternal affection, We bless you, begging you to bring, in
turn, Our blessing to your native lands and your homes as a pledge
of the love of the Vicar of Christ."

The Government of Ecuador was by no means alone in sending a
large and important delegation to the Canonization: Spain, Colombia,
Chile, Bolivia and Cuba were represented either by their Ambassadors
to the Vatican or by their Cardinals; in all, ten Cardinals and seventy
Archbishops and Bishops were present; and gradually, throughout the
world, Mariana has been accorded signal recognition. The distinguished
Jesuit, Ottavio Turchi, in his introduction to *The Travels of Mother
Frances Xavier Cabrini, Foundress of the Missionary Sisters of the
Sacred Heart of Jesus, As Related in Several of Her Letters,* tells us,
by way of emphasizing the value of these, "She [Mother Cabrini] lets
us hear the canticle of the Virgins in Paradise, and speaks with love
of the Lily consecrated to God with language drawn from the books
of Saint Ambrose upon Virgins. The names of Saint Agnes, Saint
Teresa, Saint Margaret Alacoque, Saint Rose, Blessed Mariana of Jesus,
the Lily of Quito, pass in her pages because they corresponded to the
virginal affection of her heart."

This, to be sure, is not going quite as far as Quito's Archbishop;
still, it does put Mariana in very exalted company; and that Mother

Cabrini was indeed very conscious of the Lily's high standing is evident from a letter she wrote in the course of a voyage from Panama to Santiago, in which she said, "While crossing the Equator, it is not becoming to wish for too many conveniences, because we are near and in a straight line with Quito, where Blessed Mariana lived in such austere penance, though this is rather to be admired than imitated. O dear saint, Lily of Quito, look upon these lands torn by a thousand rebellions and where immorality works such havoc! . . . . I rejoice to be able to give you a fresh description of these equatorial regions, of which I have heard hardly anything except that the heat is excessive and unbearable. It might be that the Lily of Quito, the Blessed Mariana, from her sepulchre in the Andes, or, rather, from Heaven where she sits happily at the side of her loving Jesus, sent us this fresh breeze to mitigate the heat of the voyage."

NOTES AND REFERENCES

1 Frances Parkinson Keyes, *Silver Seas and Golden Cities, A Joyous Journey Through Latin Lands* (New York: Horace Liveright, 1931). Quoted with the permission of Arthur Pell, Liveright Publishing Corporation, New York.
2 Dorothy Walworth, "He's Our One-Man Goodwill Mission," *Reader's Digest*, October, 1947 (condensed from *The Pan American: Magazine of The Americas*, October, 1947), Copyright 1947, Famous Features Syndicate, Inc., New York.
3 I have discovered only one in English. This was written by an Irish author, Michel O'Ferral, and published in London in 1850. To my great surprise, I have learned that one biography was published in Arabic. I am indebted for this information to Señor Don Carlos M. Larrea, former Ecuadorian Ambassador to the Holy See, who has one of the finest private libraries in Quito, and who keeps a complete bibliography of publications relating to Mariana de Jesús.
4 Charles Curtis, Vice President of the United States, 1929-1933.
5 María Wiesse, *Santa Rosa de Lima* (Lima: Librería Francesa y Casa Editorial E. Rosay, 1922).
6 José Antonio del Busto D, *El Arcabucero Gaspar de Flores, Padre de Santa Rosa* (Lima: *Revista Historica*, Vol. XXIII, 1960).
7 Francisco Lopez de Gomara, *Historia de las Indias*, as quoted in *The Conquest of Mexico and the Conquest of Peru* by William H. Prescott (New York: The Modern Library).
8 William H. Prescott, *The Conquest of Mexico and the Conquest of Peru* (New York: The Modern Library).
9 All quotes in this paragraph from Prescott, *The Conquest of Peru*.
10 Literally, a place consumed by fire or parched with heat. Colloquially, however, *quemado*—past participle of the verb *quemar*—can be used to define something that is close to what is desired or attained, but falls just short of it. Without doubt, this is the meaning Pizarro had in mind.
11 Salvador de Madariaga, *The Rise of the Spanish American Empire* (London: Hollis & Carter, 1947).
12 Germán Arciniegas, ed., *The Green Continent* (New York: Alfred A. Knopf, 1944).
13 Pizarro and his companions were eventually rescued by Almagro and they continued on their way, as follows: Isle of Gorgona; Tacumez; Puerto Pasado; Point of St. Elena—Guayaquil; Isle of Santa Clara; Tumbez; Cape Blanco; Payta; Sandy Plains of Lichura; Punta del Aguja to the site of the present

city of Truxillo. They then returned to Panama and Pizarro went to Spain. Pizarro's third expedition began in January, 1530. He went first to Panama, then to the Bay of St. Matthew, Puerto Viejo, Puna, Tumbez, San Miguel de Piura, Zaran, Caxas, Caxamalca (now called Caxamarca), Huanachuco, Pachacamac, Auxa, Alacay and Cuzco.

[14] It is sometimes puzzling for the average person, whose acquaintance with Latin American history is limited, to understand how Quito happened to be founded, as a Spanish city, a year before Lima, since it seems so much less accessible. The answer is that the route of the conquerors from San Miguel to Cuzco took them nowhere near the present Lima, and Benalcázar, Pizarro's lieutenant, was sent direct over the Inca Road to the second Indian capital, which was Quito. Lima was approached from Cuzco in an entirely different direction.

[15] All historical references that I have found speak of thirteen followers on the Isle of Gallo. Evidently, only one of the original thirteen—Nicolás de Ribera—was still with Pizarro when Lima was founded; but obviously historians regard the number thirteen as significant in connection with Pizarro.

[16] Like many of the missionaries who accompanied the Conquistadores, Friar Reginaldo and Father Cobo wrote in great detail about their activities.

[17] All quotations in this section, unless otherwise noted, are from "Lima, Past and Present," Raul Porras Barrenechea, in The Green Continent, ed. Germán Arciniegas (New York: Alfred A. Knopf, 1944).

[18] The Viceroys of Peru from 1544 to 1621 were as follows:

Blasco Núñez Vela, 1544-1546
Antonio de Mendoza, 1551-
Andrés Hurtado de Mendoza, second Marqués de Cañete, 1555-1558
Diego López de Zúñiga y de Velasco, Conde de Nieva, 1561-1564
Francisco de Toledo, 1569-1581
Martín Enríquez de Almansa, Marqués de Alcañices, 1581-1583
Fernando de Torres y Portugal, Conde de Villar—Don—Pardo, 1586-1590
García Hurtado de Mendoza, fourth Marqués de Cañete and son of the third Viceroy, 1590-1596
Luis de Velasco, Marqués de Salinas y Caballero, 1596-1604
Gaspar de Zúñiga y Acevedo, Conde de Monterrey, 1604-1605
Juan de Mendoza y Luna, Marqués de Montes Claros, 1606-1615
Francisco de Borja y Aragón, Prince de Esquilache, Conde de Mayalde, 1615-1621

[19] For a description of the Audiencia and its functions, see page 157 of The Prologue to THE LILY.

[20] It was the province of the Visitador to inspect the condition of the Courts of Justice and Finance throughout the land, with authority to correct abuses.

[21] Doubts have been raised as to the authenticity of the records in this respect, because they seem to be obviously incorrect in another. For instance, there are documents in San Germán, stating that María de Oliva, whom Gaspar did not marry until he was nearly fifty or past fifty (according to which date is accepted as that of his birth), was a "fellow citizen" of his in San Germán; and this despite the fact that her mother, Isabel de Herrera, declared under oath at Rosa's Cause for Beatification, that she herself was

a native of Tomaiquichua, a village high in the Andes (though she lived in Lima after her marriage) and that this was the birthplace of her daughter, María.

22 Toto Giurato, *Peru Milenario Historia y Gloria de Un Pueblo* (Lima: Editorial "Ecos," 1947).

23 Taking 1531 as the date of his birth, he was forty-six. By the more generally accepted birthdate of 1525, he was fifty-two.

24 *Tesoros Verdaderos de las Indias*, M. R. P. Maestro F. Juan Melendez of the Order of St. Dominic (Lima: 1681).

25 Father Cobo as quoted in *Vida de Santa Rosa de Santa María*, Ruben Vargas Ugarte (Lima: S. J. Talleres Graficos de la Tipografia Peruana, S.A.).

26 In the light of this certificate, the authenticity of which has never been questioned and which it would obviously be hard to question, it is hard to understand how any doubts can be entertained as to the birthplace of Isabel de Flores, Santa Rosa de Lima.

27 One such mine is described as producing enough silver to profit the owner two hundred *marcos* a *cajon*. A *marco* weighed slightly over seven ounces, a *cajon* six thousand pounds.

28 His surname is given in some early books as Grajales, but the majority designate him as Francisco Gonzalez.

29 This was until 1876, when it ceased to be even a hamlet worthy of mention. However, there are now many more than three Indian families in Quives and no family of European stock—only the wonderful French missionary priest, Father Dalle.

30 Leonardo Hansen, *Vida de Santa Rosa de Lima*, rev. by Zuavo Sevillo, Vol. I, Notes. César Miró, in his *Cielo y Tierra de Santa Rosa*, and several other authors give the legend in much the same form.

31   "O Jesus my Savior
                          How wondrous Your mien
                          Midst flowers and roses
                          And olive trees green!"

32 Mary Fabyan Windeatt, *Angel of the Andes* (Paterson, N.J.: St. Anthony Guild Press).

33 I have found no mention, in any biography, of the possibility that Rosa might have been familiar with the history of St. Frances of Rome, who insisted that she could see her guardian angel constantly at her side, and who is nearly always shown accompanied by it, in both paintings and statues. Therefore, in this case, there seems to be no chance that Rosa's imagination was influenced by her desire to follow a great example.

34 Trans. by Miss Capes in "St. Rose of Lima: Saint of the New World" in *Saints for Our Times*, Theodore Maynard (New York: Doubleday & Company, Inc.).

35 Theodore Maynard, *Saints for Our Times* (New York: Doubleday & Company, Inc.).

36 Rosa was asked by Dr. Castillo to tell him the color of the rainbow. "There is no color on earth in beauty to compare with it; it was full of many colors." "What figure and color had Grace?" Rosa answered, "Grace had a figure for distinguishing, but no color." Her closing words to Dr. Castillo

on this subject were as follows: "This is finished, and the journey is brief. Give me your hand . . . Well do you know that we have been good friends. For God's love, I pray you that, in the time left to me, you look for no favors of mine, for it is time I prepared to go to God. . . . I promise, when God has been served to take me into His glory, to ask Him to confirm you in Grace." (I have used, word for word, Malcolm Burke's rendition of this vision, as it seems to me the most beautiful of any I have found.)

[37] It is perhaps worth noting that in our own times Cardinal Mercier stood at the door of his cathedral and defied the German invaders to enter it. They never did. In like manner, Isabel of Castile defied a horde of rebels to storm the Alcázar in Segovia. That destruction did not take place either.

[38] Next to the degree of devotion Rosa felt for the Virgin of the Rosary in the Church of Santo Domingo, was certainly that which she felt for the interpretation in the Virgin of Atocha. María Wiesse describes it thus: "In the *santuario* of Santa Rosa is (still venerated) the image of *Nuestra Señora de* Atocha, better known as *La Virgen de Belén* (Virgin of Bethlehem). It is a canvas which represents Mary nursing her Son. The face of the Virgin is delicately outlined; Her cheek rests on the head of the Child—a vigorous baby—who seems to be looking fondly at someone. And, to look about Him, the Child has detached himself slightly from His Mother's breast. The scene is familiar, simple, human. The coloring is monochrome, but clear; it has lost none of its freshness through the ages."

[39] This house is now the Convent of Santa Rosa de las Monjas.

[40] As in the rendition of the visionary rainbow, I have quoted Malcolm Burke's version of these stories word for word.

[41] This simile, delicate and touching in its meaning, is hard to put into English words which will retain its symbolism. The Palm of Cades, or Cadi, grows luxuriantly in Peru and is valued above all others for the beauty of its leafage and for its produce, which is known as "vegetable ivory." Exquisite carvings have always been made from this. A palm in some countries, Peru among them, is not only a symbol of victory, but of supreme excellence of any kind, above all of virginity. In hailing the Blessed Mother as the Palm of Cades, Rosa was paying her the highest possible tribute.

[42]
> "Padre, my mother
> Will be alone.
> Please be her comforter
> When I am gone."

[43] Later, there was a third transfer. Rosa is now buried under an altar in the crypt of the Dominicans.

[44]
> "If the orange blossom is Lima's flower,
> Today, with greater good fortune,
> The Rose is Lima's flower."

The meaning, of course, is that, though up to now the orange blossom has been Lima's flower, from now on the Rose will be Lima's flower.

[45] Pál Kelemen, *Baroque and Rococo in Latin America* (New York, The Macmillan Company, 1951).

[46] Ernesto La Orden Miracle, *Elogio de Quito* (Spain: Ediciones Cultura Hispanica, 1950).

47 Julio Tobar Donoso, *La Iglesia, Modeladora de la Nacionalidad* (Quito: La Prensa Católica, 1953).

48 "After centuries of misrepresentation, the way Spain understood and organized the Indies is today recognized by all honest and well-informed persons as one of the most honourable in the history of mankind. There is a word which constantly recurs in the papers of those days—beginning with Hernán Cortés: the Spaniards wanted to ennoble the lands they had discovered. Where our moderns would say 'develop' or 'open up' they said 'ennoble.' They meant by it to raise the standards of material and moral living and to give the new lands a Christian order and polity. The word turns up constantly in documents and books; it is admirably defined by Solórzano Pereira: 'As the provinces of the Indies grew more and more populated and ennobled with the many cities and colonies of Spaniards founded and settled in them, and by bringing the many Indians who wandered afield to a political life . . .' That is what Hernán Cortes meant when as early as 1524 he wrote to the Emperor: 'Within five years (Mexico) will be the noblest and most populous city in the world.' Or again Don Francisco de Toledo to the King: 'And now when the land is so rich all that it produces can easily be consumed or exported, and men settle down and take root therein, and there are more and more buildings, and the cities grow nobler and nobler.' The work of the State and of the Church resolved itself therefore into one: to spread the faith was an indispensable preliminary to the spreading of the polity. And both the faith and the polity were understood as embracing Spaniards and natives as men different indeed in character, tendencies and aptitudes but equal before the law and the Cross."

The Rise of the Spanish American Empire, Salvador de Madariaga (London: Hollis & Carter, 1947).

49 Alfredo Pareja Diezcanseco, *Historia del Ecuador* (Quito: Editorial Casa de la Cultura Ecuatoriana, 1958).

50 This is the *probanza de noblessa* (proof of nobility) de Don José Bernardo de Paredes. The grandfather of Mariana asked permission from the Lieutenant of the *Corregidor* of Madrid, Dr. Leibana, on the nineteenth of December, 1588, to have his son undertake the journey in question.

51 These were María de Paredes, who married Jerónimo Ruiz de Ercilla; Jerónima de Paredes, who married Cosme de Caso; Jeronimó de Paredes, who became a Franciscan; Tomás de Paredes, who married Micaela Rodríguez; Petronila de Paredes, who married Francisco Rodríguez; Juan de Parades, who married Paula del Río; Mariana; and Inés Flores de Paredes, who died at an early age.

52 "Good Christians, God fearing and conscientious" and "of great quality and virtue." Cristóbal de Marino de Rivera and Isabel de Alvarado, quoted by Wilfrido Loor in *Santa Mariana de Jesús* (Quito: La Prensa Católica, 1954).

53 Germania Moncayo de Monge, *Mariana de Jesús Señora de Indias* (Quito: La Prensa Católica, 1950).

54 Though this description is not a literal translation of the one by Germania Moncayo de Monge, it would have not been possible for me to write it unless I had read hers and checked on various points with other authorities.

[55] Padre Jacinto Morán de Butrón, S.J., *Vida de Santa Mariana de Jesús* (Quito: Imprenta Municipal, 1955).

[56] El Rio de las Ovejas—The River of the Sheep—was later called the Rio Pisque and later still, the Rio Granobles y Pisque. All these names occur in books about Mariana, but Rio de las Ovejas is the earliest term and the river was thus called in her lifetime.

[57] "1) 'As to the hours to be spent in interior and exterior exercises, spend just half the time . . . devote the remaining half to study, the governing of your estates, and spiritual conversations, always managing to keep the spirit quiet and peaceful and ready to receive God. . . . It is a far greater virtue to be able to enjoy God at various occupations and places than at one alone.
"2) 'As for fasting and abstinence . . . do not weaken the body, for when it is feeble, the internal organs cannot function properly. . . . We should love and care for our body as long as it helps our soul. . . .
"3) 'As for scourging our body for Our Lord, it is better to leave it alone. . . . Instead of trying to achieve some benefit from drawing blood, look closer for God . . . in tears provoked by contemplation of our own or others' sins, or of the mysteries of Christ in this life or the other, or of the love of the Divine Persons. . . . Any one of these sacred gifts should be chosen in preference to corporeal acts. . . . With a sound mind in a sound body, everything becomes more sound.'"

This quotation is given as presented by Amarie Dennis, in her excellent book, *St. Francis Borgia*. She gives as her source, *Monumenta Ignatiana: Epistolae et Instructiones*, Vol. II, page 233.

[58] Enrique M. Villasis Teran, *Mariana de Jesús Azucena de Quito* (Quito: La Prensa Católica, 1946).

[59] Father Aurelio Espinosa, Polit, S.I., *Mariana de Jesús Hija de La Compañia de Jesús* (Quito: La Prensa Católica, 1956).

Vida de Santa Mariana de Jesús by Padre Jacinto Morán de Butrón, S.J. (The fact that all these reliable biographers, including Mariana's first one—Butrón— mention her enthusiasm for María Vela makes it seem certain that, somehow, the latter's works must have penetrated to Quito. How they could have remains a mystery, since, to the best of my knowledge and belief, no copy of her writings had left the Convent of Santa Ana until I was myself entrusted with one, which I have since translated and edited, only a few years ago. However, the statement that Butrón makes is especially convincing, for he affirms: "*Hablando de esto (amarguras y silencios místicos), dice el Venerable Padre Camacho estas palabras: 'Pidió à Nuestro Señor no la llevase por camino de regalos, sino de asperezas y trabajos, à imitación de Doña María Vela, a quien fue muy aficionada, y cuya vida leyó muy de ordinario para imitarla.'*"

[60] It should be remembered that Ecuador did not become an independent country until 1824. In Mariana's lifetime and long afterward it was still a part of Peru and Santa Fé.

[61] Some authorities claim there are no documents to prove this and Morán de Butrón, Mariana's earliest, and by many considered her best, biographer, quotes María de Paredes as saying that Mariana did not go personally to get the cordon, but received it "through the hands of a third person." Elsewhere in this same book, however, he states that Mariana herself went to the Church of St. Francis "to receive the cordon of the seraphic father."

Moreover, the rare volume entitled merely *Documentos Para La Historia de la Beata Mariana de Jesús, Azucena de Quito* contains the copy of a sworn statement signed by Fernando de Cozar, Provincial Minister of the Franciscan Order, and witnessed by his secretary, Juan Cazco, to the effect that she herself received the habit on November 18, 1640. This statement would seem to furnish conclusive proof not only that she belonged to the Third Order of St. Francis, but that she was personally invested in its habit.

[62] *Chirimia*, literally translated as flageolet, is a small end-blown flute, with four finger holes in front and two in the rear. It was, and still is, the primitive musical instrument most used and most beloved by the Indians of the *sierra*.

[63] This is the way it seemed to Germania Moncayo de Monge. As in the case of that author's description of Mariana's christening, I have adapted her account of the "seventeenth century kindergarten" in idiomatic and abbreviated form, rather than giving it a literal translation.

[64] Both Juana and Sebastiana are regarded with great veneration in Quito and several of Mariana's biographers, including Butrón, insist that they, too, are worthy of canonization.

[65] Literally, the Clerk of the King. However, the King's Commissioner would be a more effective translation, for, as a matter of fact, this functionary had a great responsibility and was entrusted with great power.

[66] Some of his verses, dedicated to Mariana, were accepted as evidence in the Process of Beatification. I quote two of these, herewith:

> "Es de Jesús Mariana
> Tan de su agrado que la amó temprana.
> Desde la tierna cuna,
> La miró en sus rayos Nueva Luna.
> Continuo relicario
> Jamás distante de él, pues fue Sagrario
> en cuyo trono porque sol moraba
> mortífero vapor no la manchaba."
>
> . . . .
>
> "Quién el candor no admira
> de Aquesta Luna y Sol
> que en ella gira?
> Oh poder, poder infinito
> que en el campo de Quito,
> Tal tesoro guardaba para el cielo!"

These lose much by literal translation—so much indeed that it seems inadvisable to present one, because expressions which are beautiful and appropriate in Spanish seem florid and exaggerated in English. Moreover, the mixed metaphor, which we are taught to shun, is freely and effectively used in Spanish. It would probably not occur to an Anglo-Saxon poet to begin by saying that his liege lady had been favored by Our Saviour from her earliest infancy; to continue by comparing her to the sun and the moon; to progress by announcing her as a tabernacle; and finally to give the city which was her birthplace the credit for preserving such a treasure for heaven! Yet that is exactly what Hernándo de la Cruz does, and in his words lie charm and rhythm and meaning.

[67] Wilfrido Loor, *Santa Mariana de Jesús* (Quito: La Prensa Católica, 1954).

[68] Literally, the days of the stations. The actual meaning is "even on Holy Thursday." That was the day when the faithful were accustomed to visit seven churches successively and to say the Stations of the Cross in each. The custom is still observed in some Spanish-American countries.

[69] Small pieces of cotton. It was believed that if the person or clothing of a saint could be touched with these, they would acquire supernal qualities.

[70] It was, and still is, customary in Latin American countries to place wide ribbons with long streamers across a coffin. The mourners who walk on either side, holding the ends of the streamers in their hands, correspond to honorary pallbearers.

[71] "The definitions of beatification and canonization, given in A *Catholic Dictionary*, edited by Donald Attwater and published by Macmillan, also serve to cast abundant light on the subject. 'Beatification,' we are here told, 'is the process by which enquiry is made into the sanctity of a deceased person and, upon proof thereof, permission accorded for his public veneration; this is usually limited to a particular country, diocese, or religious order and does not extend, without special permission, to the display of his image in church or to a Mass and Office in his honour. Beatification generally, but not necessarily, leads to canonization (q.v.) and both declarations can now be made only by the pope himself. But the initial enquiries are made by the local diocesan who reports to Rome and, if these are satisfactory, the cause or apostolic process is introduced and passes into the care of the Congregation of Sacred Rites, which subjects the life, writings and alleged miracles of the candidate to a most searching scrutiny; half a dozen or more stages are involved and so thorough is the enquiry that it usually lasts many years. The pope is the final judge and if he is favourable, the solemn beatification takes place in St. Peter's, when the brief is read, a picture of the *beatus* unveiled and venerated, and the new collect in his honour sung. He, or she, may henceforth be referred to as the Blessed so and so. The pope is not infallible in beatifying.'

"Canonization is defined as, 'A public and official declaration of the heroic virtue of a person and the inclusion of his or her name in the canon (roll or register) of the saints. Beatification (q.v.) having been accomplished, it must be proved that two miracles have been subsequently wrought at the intercession of the *beatus*; the tests and examinations are as rigourous as those which have gone before, and the miracles are discussed in three meetings of the Congregation of Rites; there are required two things to be proved: that the candidate was formally or equivalently beatified, and has worked two (or if equivalently beatified, three) miracles subsequent to beatification. The canonization is then carried out solemnly in St. Peter's by the pope in person, whereat the bull of canonization is read and a Mass sung in honour of the saint. Canonization involves that the saint not only may but must receive public honour; a day is appointed for his feast and a liturgical office composed therefore; his relics are publicly venerated, churches and altars dedicated in his honour, statues or pictures displayed in churches, and prayers made to him publicly. This judgment of the Church is infallible and irreformable. Owing to the amount of careful work involved and the sumptuous scale of the final ceremony, canonization is an exceedingly costly process. This is probably the chief reason why so large a proportion of canonizations are of priests and religious, many of whom were public characters and whose cause is supported by the resources of a diocese, nation or religious order. It must not be supposed that a person was not a saint because he had not been canonized (i.e., declared or certified as such): some of our greatest saints were never formally canonized; but at least since the 12th century public veneration without the permission of the Holy See has been unlawful. The first solemn canonization was of St. Ulrich of Augsburg by Pope John XV in 933.'"

The Third Mystic of Avila: The Self Revelation of María Vela, a Sixteenth Century Spanish Nun, trans. and with a foreword by Frances Parkinson Keyes (New York: Farrar, Straus & Cudahy, Inc.).

72 The words of two songs which she frequently sang, the authorship of which has very generally been attributed to her, have been preserved. I present them, herewith, in the original Spanish:

> "Cristo Jesús de mi vida,
> hermosísimo Cordero,
> con vestiduras nupciales
> sales enamorando al cielo."
>
>   .   .   .   .
>
> "El gran monarca Jesús
> del Padre Eterno heredero
> teniendo la cruz por cama
> hacer quiere testamento,
>   porque la corona y clavos
> le tiene ya casi muerto,
> Estando enfermo de amor
> por sanar al hombre enfermo.
>   Enfermedades de amor
> nos le han puesto en tal extremo
> y es tan agudo al achaque
> que no se le halla remedio."

As in the case of the verses by Hernándo de la Cruz, these lose so much by literal translation that it seems best not to offer one and for much the same reasons: in one and the same verse Mariana refers to Our Saviour as "The most Beautiful Lamb" and as a beloved bridegroom ascending enraptured to heaven, clad in nuptial garments. In the very next verse, the reference is not to a lamb or a bridegroom, but to a great ruler, heir to the Eternal Father, reduced through love to the last extremities of suffering. I can only reiterate that, in the original, none of these expressions seems exaggerated, illogical or fantastic, and it might be worth the captious critic's while to re-read certain passages in the Canticles.

73 As Mariana's actual birthday was unquestionably the 31st of October, this reference must be to the date of her death, that is, her spiritual birth in the Kingdom of Heaven.

BIBLIOGRAPHY

THE ROSE

Spanish and French

Anguló, P. Domingo, O.P., *Santa Rosa de Santa María*, Prologue by Carlos Alberto Romero. Lima: Sanmarti, 1917.

Bermudez, Sr. Dr. D. José Manuel, *Vida de la Gloriosa Virgen Dominicana Santa Rosa*. Lima: Librería de Benito Gil, 1869.

Compendio Histórico de la Vida de Santa Rosa de Lima con un apendice de la Gloria Póstuma de la Misma Santa, based on the writings of P. Leonardo Hansen and brought to light by R.P. Presentado Fr. León Elvira. Valladolid: Imprenta de Aparvelo, 1828.

de Loaysa, P. Fr. Pedro, O.P., Confesor de la misma, *Vida de Santa Rosa de Lima*. Lima: Sanmarti y Cia., S.A., 1937.

del Busto D., José Antonio, *El Arcabucero Gaspar de Flores, Padre de Santa Rosa*. Lima: Revista Historica, Vol. XXIII, 1960.

García y Sanz, Presbítero Pedro, *El Pastor La Patrona y El Apostol de Lima: Panegíricos de Santo Toribio de Mogrovejo, de Santa Rosa de Santa María y de San Francisco Solano*. Lima: Imprenta y Librería de San Pedro, 1893.

Giurato, Toto, *Peru Milenario: Historia y Gloria de Un Pueblo*. Lima: Editorial "Ecos," 1947.

Hansen, P. Fray Leonardo, *Vida Admirable de Sta. Rosa de Lima*. Trans. from the Latin by P. Fray Jacinto Parra, rev. by Zuavo Pontificio Sevilla. El Santísimo Rosario—Vergara, 1929.

Homenaje de la Rosa del Peru a Santa Rosa de Lima. Arequipa, 1917.

Marmontel, M., *Les Incas, ou la Destruction de L'Empire du Pérou*, 2 Vol. Paris: Lacombe, Libraire, 1777.

Melendez, M.R.P. Maestro F. Juan, *Tesoros Verdaderos de las Indias*. Lima: The Order of St. Dominic, 1681.

Miró, César, *Cielo y Tierra de Santa Rosa*. Buenos Aires: Editorial Schapire, 1945.

Osende, P. Victorino, O.P., *Vida de Santa Rosa de Lima*. Lima: Tip. de El Smo. Rosario, 1927.

Press clippings from Peruvian papers, covering a fourteen year period. Supplied by Dr. Albert A. Giesecke.

Proaño, Juan Felix, Dean of the Cathedral of Riobamba, trans., *Vida Auténtica de Santa Rosa de Lima*. Lima: Imp. de El Bien Social, 1897.

Recuerdo de las Fiestas del Tercer Centenario de la Muerte de Santa Rosa de Lima, pub. by la Comisión de Señoras encargadas de las Fiestas del Centenario. Lima: Artistica, 1917.

Roca y Boloña, Father José Antonio, *Sermón Panegírico en honor de Santa Rosa de Santa María*. Lima: Imprenta y Librería de Benito Gil, 1886. Preached in the Cathedral of Lima, August 30, 1864.

Rua, R.P. Fr. Angel Menéndez, *Reseña Histórica del Santuario de Santa Rosa de Lima*. Lima: Sanmarti y Cia., S.A. 1939.

Ugarte, Ruben Vargas, S.J., *Historia del Santo Cristo de Los Milagros*. Lima: Sanmarti, 1957.

———— *Vida de Santa Rosa de Santa María*. Lima: Talleres Gráficos de la Tipografía Peruana, S.A., 1951.

Vida Edificante de la Gloriosa Santa Rosa de Lima. Lima: Carlos Prince, Impresor y Editor-Librero, 1886.

Weisse, María, *Santa Rosa de Lima*. Lima: Librería Francesa y Casa Editorial E. Rosay, 1922.

Zuñiga, Alberto Gonzalez, *La Rosita Limeña*. Lima: Editorial P.T.C.M., 1948.

English

Arciniegas, Germán, ed., *The Green Continent: A Comprehensive View of Latin America*. New York: Alfred A. Knopf, 1944.

Burke, Malcolm K., trans., unpublished manuscript based on the testimony for Rosa's beatification.

Clifton, Violet, *Vision of Peru: Kings, Conquerors, Saints*. London: Duckworth.

Dargan, Ena, *The Road to Cuzco*. London: Andrew Melrose, Ltd. Preface by Salvador de Madariaga.

de Madariaga, Salvador, *The Fall of the Spanish American Empire*. London: Hollis & Carter, 1947.

———— *The Rise of the Spanish American Empire*. London: Hollis & Carter, 1947.

Isherwood, Christopher, *The Condor and the Cows*. New York: Random House, Inc.

Keyes, Frances Parkinson, *Silver Seas and Golden Cities, A Joyous Journey Through Latin Lands*. New York: Horace Liveright, 1931.

Kropp, Miriam, *Cuzco: Window on Peru*. New York and London: The Studio Publications, Inc., in association with Thomas Y. Crowell Company.

Maynard, Sara, *Rose of America*. London: Sheed & Ward, 1944.

Maynard, Theodore, *Saints for Our Times*. Garden City, New York: Image Books, Doubleday & Company, Inc.

Prescott, William H., *The Conquest of Mexico and the Conquest of Peru*. New York: The Modern Library.

Squier, E. George, M.A., F.S.A., *Peru: Incidents of Travel and Exploration in the Land of the Incas*. New York: Harper & Brothers, 1877.

Windeatt, Mary Fabyan, *Angel of the Andes*. Paterson, New Jersey: St. Anthony Guild Press.

—— *Lad of Lima*. Sheed & Ward, 1942.

THE LILY

Spanish and Italian

Arias, Augusto, *Mariana de Jesús*. Quito: Talleres Gráficos del Ministerio de Educación, 1944.

Boletin de la Academia Nacional de Historia, Vol. XXIX, Num. 73. Quito: Romero, 1949.

Cantos y Himnos en Honor de Santa Mariana de Jesús. Quito: Editorial Artes Graficas, 1951.

Diezcanseco, Alfredo Pareja, *Historia del Ecuador*, 2 Vol. Quito: Editorial Casa de la Cultura Ecuatoriana, 1958.

Documentos Para la Historia de la Beata Mariana de Jesús Azucena de Quito. Quito: Imprenta del Clero, 1902.

Donoso, Julio Tobar, *La Iglesia, Modeladora de la Nacionalidad*. Quito: La Prensa Católica, 1953. With a Prologue by Father Aurelio Espinosa Pólit, S.I.

Homenaje Oficial a la Azucena de Quito. Quito: La Prensa Católica, 1948.

Jouanen, R.P. José, S.J., *La Iglesia de la Compañia de Jesús de Quito*. Quito: La Prensa Católica.

Loor, Wilfrido, *Santa Mariana de Jesús*. Quito: La Prensa Católica, 1954.

Los Procesos de Beatificacion de la Azucena de Quito. Quito: Tipografía Salesiana, 1896.

Miracle, Ernesto La Orden, *Elogio de Quito*. Bilbao: Ediciones Cultura Hispanica, 1950. With a Prologue by the Marqués de Lozoya.

Monge, Germania Moncayo de, *Mariana de Jesús Señora de Indias*. Quito: La Prensa Católica, 1950.

Morán de Butrón, Father Jacinto, S.I., *Vida de Santa Mariana de Jesús*. Quito: Imprenta Municipal, 1955.

Papàsogli. Giorgio, *Vita di S. Maria Anna di Gesù*. Rome: Tipografia Pontificia Università Gregoriana, 1950.

Pólit, Father Aurelio Espinosa, S.I., *Santa Mariana de Jesús Hija de la Compañia de Jesús*. Quito: La Prensa Católica, 1956.

Pólit, Dr. D. Manuel María, Canónigo Honorario de la Iglesia Metropolitana y Superior de las Carmelitas de Quito, *La Familia de Santa Teresa en América y La Primera Carmelita Americana*. Friburgo de Brisgovia (Alemania) 1905. B. Herder Librero-Editor Pontificio Viena, Estrasburgo, Munich y San Luis (América Sept.).

Terán, Enrique M. Villasís, *Mariana de Jesús Azucena de Quito*. Quito: La Prensa Católica, 1946.

English

Archives, Jesuit Seminary, Quito.

de Madariaga, Salvador, *Bolívar*. London: Hollis & Carter, 1952.

——— *The Fall of the Spanish American Empire*. London: Hollis & Carter, 1947.

——— *The Rise of the Spanish American Empire*. London: Hollis & Carter, 1947.

Dennis, Amarie, *St. Francis Borgia*.

Keleman, Pál, *Baroque and Rococo in Latin America*. New York: The Macmillan Company, 1951.

Keyes, Frances Parkinson, *Silver Seas and Golden Cities, A Joyous Journey Through Latin Lands*. New York: Horace Liveright, 1931.

——— trans., *The Third Mystic of Avila: The Self Revelation of María Vela, a Sixteenth Century Nun*. New York: Farrar, Straus & Cudahy, Inc.

Prescott, William H., *The Conquest of Mexico and the Conquest of Peru*. New York: The Modern Library.

The Travels of Mother Frances Xavier Cabrini, Foundress of the Missionary Sisters of the Sacred Heart of Jesus, as related in several of her letters. Published by Giovanni Serpentelli, Streatham Hall, Exeter, on behalf of the Most Rev. Mother General of the Missionary Sisters of the Sacred Heart, Rome.

Ybarra, T. R., *Bolívar, The Passionate Warrior*. New York: Ives Washburn, 1929.

INDEX

FRANCES PARKINSON KEYES, *whose books have been best-sellers almost every year since 1936 and are published simultaneously in England and the United States and in as many as twelve foreign languages, was born at the University of Virginia, where her father, John Henry Wheeler, a Bostonian transplanted to the South, was head of the Greek department. Her mother was Louise Fuller Johnson, a New Yorker who had earlier moved to Newbury, Vermont. After Dr. Wheeler's death, Frances and her mother spent their summers in Newbury, Vermont, and their winters in Boston, a city which was to become the scene of* Joy Street *(Messner, 1950), a best-seller of 1950-51. As a girl, she studied in Geneva and Berlin, as well as Boston, and with a governess. She speaks four languages and even today spends much time in travel. She was married at eighteen to Henry Wilder Keyes, whose home, Pine Grove Farm, near Haverhill, New Hampshire, was just across the river from Newbury, Vermont. In 1917 he became governor of New Hampshire. In 1919 he was elected to the United States Senate and served three terms, during which Mrs. Keyes divided her time between her family of three sons and the beginning of a literary career, initiated with articles in the Atlantic Monthly and a novel,* The Old Gray Homestead *(Houghton Mifflin, 1919). Her interest in her husband's Washington career led her to depict Washington political life in a series of letters to American women which became a Good Housekeeping running feature entitled* The Letters from a Senator's Wife *and was later published in book form by Appleton in 1924. In 1923 she began a novel set in Washington which appeared in 1930 as* Queen Anne's Lace *(Liveright, 1930). From 1923 to 1935 she was an associate editor of Good Housekeeping and from 1937 to 1939 editor of the National Historical Magazine. Mrs. Keyes has spent much time in France, which led to the biography of St. Thérèse,* Written in Heaven *(Messner, 1937) and the life of St. Bernadette of Lourdes,* The Sublime Shepherdess *(Messner, 1940), and a more personal record,* Along a Little Way *(Messner, 1940). In 1940 she visited Mexico to write* The Grace of Guadalupe *(Messner, 1941). Mrs. Keyes holds degrees of Litt.D. from Bates College and George Washington University, and in 1951 received the degree of Doctor of Humane Letters from the University of New Hampshire "as a distinguished author, ambassador of good will, and interpreter of American life." In 1946 she received the Siena Medal awarded annually to "The outstanding*

Catholic woman in the United States"; in 1950 the Silver Medal of French Recognition for her aid in reconstructing the Abbaye of the Benedictines at Lisieux; and in 1959 she was decorated with the Order Of Isabella the Catholic in recognition of her work in Spain. She still retains her ownership of the Oxbow, her ancestral homestead at Newbury, Vermont, and her legal residence is still at Pine Grove Farm, the Keyes' family home at North Haverhill, New Hampshire; but in the winter she uses the historic Beauregard House, in New Orleans, which she has restored, as her writing center. Among her books besides those previously mentioned are: The Career of David Noble *(Frederick Stokes, 1921),* Silver Seas and Golden Cities *(Liveright, 1931),* Lady Blanche Farm *(Liveright, 1931),* Senator Marlowe's Daughter *(Messner, 1933),* The Safe Bridge *(Messner, 1934),* The Happy Wanderer *(Messner, 1935),* Honor Bright *(Messner, 1936),* Capital Kaleidoscope *(1937),* Parts Unknown *(Messner, 1938),* The Great Tradition *(Messner, 1939),* Fielding's Folly *(Messner, 1940),* All that Glitters *(Messner, 1941),* Crescent Carnival *(Messner, 1942),* Also the Hills *(Messner, 1942),* The River Road *(Messner, 1945),* Once on Esplanade *(Dodd, Mead, 1947),* Came a Cavalier *(Messner, 1947),* Dinner at Antoine's *(Messner, 1948),* Therese: Saint of a Little Way *(Messner, 1950),* All This Is Louisiana *(Harper Bros., 1950),* The Cost of a Best Seller *(Messner, 1950),* Steamboat Gothic *(Messner, 1952),* Bernadette of Lourdes *(Messner, 1953),* The Royal Box *(Messner, 1954),* The Frances Parkinson Keyes Cookbook *(Doubleday, 1955),* St. Anne: Grandmother of Our Saviour *(Messner, 1955),* Blue Camellia *(Messner, 1957),* The Land of Stones and Saints *(Doubleday, 1957),* Victorine *(Messner, 1958),* Station Wagon in Spain *(Farrar, Straus & Cudahy, 1959),* Frances Parkinson Keyes' Christmas Gift *(Hawthorn, 1959),* Mother Cabrini: Missionary to the World *(Vision Books, 1959),* The Third Mystic of Avila *(Farrar, Straus & Cudahy, 1960),* Roses in December *(Doubleday & Co., 1960),* The Chess Players *(Farrar, Straus & Cudahy, 1960).*

THE ROSE AND THE LILY *(Hawthorn, 1961) was completely manufactured by American Book-Stratford Press, Inc., New York City. The body type is Electra, designed for the Linotype by W. A. Dwiggins, one of America's best known typographers and designers.*

A HAWTHORN BOOK